SELECTED ESSAYS

Also by HENRY DE MONTHERLANT
and uniform with this edition:
THE BACHELORS translated by Terence Kilmartin

SELECTED ≡ESSAYS≡

by

HENRY DE MONTHERLANT

*Edited and with an Introduction by
Peter Quennell*

*Translated from the French by
John Weightman*

THE MACMILLAN COMPANY
New York
1961

© Henry de Montherlant 1920, 1924, 1932,
1935, 1938, 1953, 1955, 1957

English Translation © 1960 by
George Weidenfeld and Nicolson Ltd

Printed in Great Britain

CONTENTS

Introduction by Peter Quennell	7
An Easter Service at school during wartime (in 1916)	19
Hold fast to all things, while keeping each in its proper place	24
Mademoiselle de Plémeur	27
The Death of Peregrinos	39
A Jew-Boy goes to War	55
Explicit Mysterium	87
Foreword to *Service Inutile*	111
The Samurai's Umbrella	138
The 7th March 1936	143
A good thing to live in 1938	155
The September Equinox	163
The 1940 Armistice (in Marseilles)	208
The Family, the Fatherland, etc.	210
Work	213
The Assumption of the King of Kings	221
Saint-Simon	230
The Goddess Cypris	242
Coming back from the Bibliothèque Nationale	262
Extracts from the Notebooks of Henry de Montherlant—1930–1944	267

INTRODUCTION

ON 8TH OCTOBER, 1911, a paper published in southern France, entitled *Le Torero*, found room under the heading *Nos Jeunes* for the following brief announcement:

> *A Burgos dans une becerrada privée un jeune aficionado de 16 ans, de Paris, Monsieur Henry de M... a expédié supérieurement son adversaire, ce qui lui a valu une ovation.*

The young aficionado mentioned by the journalist was the future author of *Les Bestiaires*; and this was not his first experience of French and Spanish bullrings. Three years earlier, during a visit to Bayonne, he had discovered the delights of tauromachy; and on that occasion the thirteen-year-old Henry de Montherlant had written in prophetic terms to a school friend of his own age: '*Je ferai certainement plus tard quelque chose là-dessus, c'est une des choses les plus magnifiques et enivrantes qui soient.*' Montherlant was already trying his hand at literature—since he was nine he had been filling his notebooks with tales, embryo novels and small dramatic pieces; but what he saw and felt in the bullring seems to have quickened and confirmed his gifts. Once he had registered his allegiance to the Sign of the Bull, he had begun his progress towards literary manhood.

There was nothing, however, in his immediate ancestry to explain this sudden predilection. His parents, both members of the French provincial *noblesse*, were neither of them natives of the south; and, despite their ancestral link with the provinces, Paris had now become their home. In Paris Henry de Montherlant was born on 21st April 1896—an only child; for, after his birth, his mother, a delicate, nervous, emotional woman, remained a life-long invalid; and her son was brought up in a somewhat circumscribed and overshadowed household, which consisted of his father, always tormented by financial difficulties, his mother, who, though active in mind, rarely left her bed or chaise longue, a maternal grandmother '*de caractère sombre et anxieux*', and an uncle and grand-uncle, '*célibataires très "originaux"*', who were afterwards to provide the writer with valuable hints for one of his most important novels.[1] From the slightly claustrophic life that he led at home, Montherlant presently escaped into the more stimulating world of school friendships. Those friendships, like many associations of the same type, had both an intellectual and a sentimental basis; and it is clear that they exercised a lasting effect upon the development of the future novelist's mind. No less influential, by way of contrast, was his relationship with his possessive, devoted mother. During his adolescence, Montherlant tells us, '*j'étais, comme il convenait à mon âge, plongé dans les "amitiés particulières", c'est-a-dire dans des amitiés sentimentalo-sensuelles avec des camarades de collège plus jeunes que moi. Tantôt ma mère les foudroyait, me menaçait . . . tantôt elle en venait à s'y complaire, m'en parlait avec gentillesse, à la fois parce que . . . c'etait la meilleure façon de capter et garder ma confiance, et parce que cette atmosphère "carte du Tendre" était au fond ce qu'elle aimait le plus au monde*'.[2] The reader will note that in Montherlant's novels and dramas a conflict is frequently described between two opposing forms of love—between 'the comedy of the passions', to use Byron's phrase, in which feminine guile and feminine possessiveness often play an ugly part, and the honest, uncomplicated masculine affection that depends on sympathy and genuine understanding and involves neither sentimental deceit nor any loss of self-respect.

Montherlant's school days, nevertheless, came to a sudden and disastrous end. Early in 1912 he was expelled from the Collège de Sainte-Croix at Neuilly, as a result of the sentimental crisis from which he would derive the subject-matter of a particularly moving play, *La Ville dont le Prince est un enfant*. His mother then made some ill-fated attempts to thrust him into social life; but her son preferred sport to society—besides bullfighting, his favourite sports included

[1] *Montherlant* par Henry Perruchot. Gallimard. 1959.
[2] *Sur ma mère*, quoted by Pierre Sipriot in *Montherlant par lui-même*.

INTRODUCTION

football and cross-country running—and the austere companionship of suburban playing fields to light conversation in Parisian drawing-rooms. During the year 1914, his father died, followed by Madame de Montherlant a year later. She had implored him, so long as she lived, to avoid the risks of active service; but, once she had disappeared, he joined a fighting regiment, where he refused to accept commissioned rank and was seriously wounded by a bursting shell. He had applied to return to the front line when the German armies in the west collapsed.

Meanwhile, as early as 1916, he had embarked on the composition of *La Relève du matin,* a series of closely connected essays inspired by his attachment to his ungrateful school, and all that it symbolized in terms of human faith and comradeship, of which the section named '*Pâques de guerre au collège*' is translated among the present extracts. Having been refused by eleven publishers, Montherlant's first book was finally issued in 1920 at the author's own expense. Almost overnight, it established his reputation; and, in 1922, *Le Songe,* his first novel, a story of warfare on the western front, earned him even wider fame. *Le Songe* was succeeded in 1924 by *Les Olympiques* and *Chant funèbre pour les morts de Verdun,* the former a book dedicated to the praise of sport, and the moral and social qualities that sport encourages: the latter, written with the intention of strengthening and prolonging through literature '*la fraternité de la guerre qui a tant compté pour lui*'.[1] Both are governed by the idea of brotherhood: they are conspicuously idealistic and romantic works.

Especially interesting, however, is *Le Songe,* since it establishes an emotional pattern that was repeatedly to reappear. Alban de Bricoule, a difficult, moody, aristocratic young man, who seems to incorporate some suggestions of a self-portrait, has been debarred by a recent illness from service in the front lines, but grows weary of civilian life and sets out towards the battlefields. It is neither military distinction he seeks, nor the opportunity of selling his life dear: '*Je rejette la couronne d'épines! Je rejette le besoin de la gloire! Il est nécessaire que je me repose dans l'action.*' At the same time, he is drawn to the front by his affection for a school friend—Stanislas

[1] *Montherlant* par Henri Perruchot.

Prinet, an orphan and only son, '*de naissance un isolé*,' a being as awkward and immature as Alban is adventurous and determined. Alban's relationship with Prinet, which culminates in a tragic estrangement and Prinet's death, gives the narrative its true centre. But Alban is also platonically involved with the Amazonian virgin Dominique; and, although Dominique's athletic prowess does something to redeem her sex—she is immoderately proud of her classic strength and grace, and stands naked admiring her splendid muscles—her passion for Alban at length betrays her into a conventionally feminine pose. She offers her love and is harshly rejected: the kind of passion that Dominique offers cannot satisfy Alban's most deeply rooted needs. He turns back again to a life of repose in action: '*et dans son coeur il fait jour*.'

To say that the ghost of Prinet comes between Alban and Dominique might be to over-simplify the author's plan; but there is no doubt that both Dominique and Prinet—the one emotionally exacting, despite her purity and her real integrity: the other, a disinterested comrade, neither the tyrant nor the slave—represent types of human affection that re-emerge in many later books. *Le Songe* is certainly a brilliant first novel; yet it has some of the obvious defects of its qualities. The tone is eloquent; but the writer's eloquence occasionally degenerates into declamation. It includes admirable descriptive passages; but we are often aware of a touch of literary artifice—they seem to have been imposed on the text rather than to arise from the inward development of the theme. And, although *Les Bestiaires,* his second novel, published in 1926, marks an important literary step forward, the love story of Alban and Soledad remains throughout a trifle unconvincing. For Soledad exemplifies a principle—that of the Eternal Feminine, personified in a very young girl, selfish and perverse and destructive, bent upon the hero's ruin; whereas Jesus, the boy from the slums of Seville, who acts as Alban's assistant in his agonizing conflict with '*le Mauvais Ange*'—the bull whom he had been incited to engage by Soledad's deceptive feminine attractions—typifies courage and the spirit of masculine brotherhood, which makes no emotional demands and leaves behind no bitter taste. Having killed the bull, Alban enters

INTRODUCTION

a church to offer up a grateful prayer: '... *Il remercie Dieu d'avoir permis qu'il ait vécu cette journée grande auprès de quelqu'un pour qui il a de la sympathie*'. But the true strength of *Les Bestiaires* lies not in its attempts at characterization so much as in its sheer descriptive force. Never have the strange atmosphere of the bullring and the almost devotional passion that pits man against beast been conveyed with more imaginative energy.

By the time *Les Bestiaires* reached the public, Henry de Montherlant had bidden good-bye to France. His grandmother, with whom he had been living, died in 1925; and he thereupon pulled up his roots and plunged into a lengthy course of foreign travel. During this period, he wrote two books, based on the experience of a solitary traveller, *Aux Fontaines du Désir* and *La Petite Infante de Castille*, to which he has given the general title *Les Voyageurs Traqués*,[1] as well as *Les Bestiaires*, written during a visit to Spain in 1925, and *La Rose de Sable*, his third novel, begun in 1928. It was a critical period of the author's life—as unhappy, he tells us, as the year that had followed his reverse at school; and he extricated himself at last from a mood of restless self-abandonment by setting to work on a major novel inspired by his vision of North Africa, with particular reference to the colonial problem and the plight of the Arab people under French government. The complete text of *La Rose de Sable* has not yet been issued—the novelist was unwilling to add to his country's difficulties by publishing his own adverse impressions; but a single episode, *L'Histoire d'amour de 'La Rose de Sable,'* has been printed as a separate story, and has taken its place in the Montherlant canon among his most attractive works. Tenderness is not a quality he often displays—the typical Montherlant hero, Alban, Guiscart, Costals, is an adventurer, endowed with prodigious strength of will, who triumphs over the hesitations and servile irresolution of his fellow human beings; but here his protagonist is a weak and sensitive young man, the victim of a passion that defies control, a passion that strengthens its grasp at the very moment when physical appetite declines. Auligny clings

[1] The third volume in this group, *Un Voyageur solitaire est un diable* did not appear until 1946, and then only in a limited edition.

to his little Arab mistress not only because she has aroused his senses, but because she has awakened his capacity for loving, and the love she has stirred presently extends to include her whole downtrodden race. His affection for Ram becomes a moral touchstone by which he establishes an entire new world of values. For once Montherlant sides with the weak, with a foolish hero who is also innocent in spirit.

Soon after completing *La Rose de Sable,* the novelist returned to France, where at first it proved extremely difficult to take up literary and social life again; '*être patriote, et être Français, en 1932*' (he confided to his notebooks), '*c'est vivre crucifié. La France est en pleine décomposition*'—hence his decision that the full text of his North-African novel for the time being must remain unpublished. But, having eventually settled down, he wrote his fascinating novel *Les Célibataires,* in which Léon de Coantré is treated, at least in the closing chapters, with something of the same indulgence as he had already accorded to Lieutenant Auligny; and, when the Académie Française awarded him its Grand Prix de Littérature, he sent ten thousand francs to General Giraud, then commander-in-chief in Morocco, requesting that it should be distributed both to the victorious French troops and to the defeated Moroccan rebels, '*puisque, après tout, des deux côtés, on fait son devoir également*'. Montherlant displayed a similar impartiality in his attitude towards current political problems, contributing to Right Wing as well as to communist papers, and surrendering his whole-hearted allegiance neither to the Right nor to the Left. '*Cette position strictement apolitique*' (we learn) '*est admise par tous les partis.*' It has, nevertheless, created some confusion, and during and immediately after the Second World War exposed the writer to some unjust attacks. But such an attitude, whatever the risks it involved, was an essential feature of his scheme of life and work. He remains uncommitted —*Montherlant,* '*homme libre*', to quote the title of a recent critical study; and since the Second World War he has deliberately refrained from any form of public controversy. '. . . *A partir de la dernière guerre*' (he remarks in a personal letter) '*je ne me suis plus jamais exprimé sur mon pays ni sur l'actualité en mon nom propre.*

C'est pourquoi je me suis dévoué particulièrement au théâtre où l'auteur s'efface derrière des personnages.'

Montherlant's dramatic achievement cannot be discussed at any length here. Yet, although his plays form a subject apart, and naturally the novelist and the dramatist employ entirely different methods, they reflect the same creative character and deal with much the same preoccupations. '... *Je suis chez moi partout où il y a de la gravité*', declares Ferrante in *La Reine Morte*, the play that, in 1942, first revealed Montherlant's dramatic talents to the general public. Some of his dramas, such as *Celles qu'on prend dans ses bras*, might possibly be described as comedies, whereas *La Reine Morte*, *Malatesta* and *Port-Royal* have the scope of classical tragedies. But they are never comedies in the more frivolous meaning of the word; and, whether the scene of a play be mediaeval Portugal, Renaissance Italy, a seventeenth-century convent or modern Paris, the protagonists are always inspired by some profound and serious passion, and move across the stage in an aura of strong poetic feeling. '*Nos passions sont les anges du Seigneur*,' exclaims the heroine whom Ferrante condemns to death.

In addition to his dramas, of which the latest *Le Cardinal d'Espagne*, was published early in 1960, the mass of work that Montherlant has produced up to the present day may be divided into two main sections. There are his novels, *Les Célibataires*, issued in 1934, and the tetralogy of books, under the inclusive title of *Les Jeunes Filles*, consisting of *Les Jeunes Filles*, *Pitié pour Les Femmes*, *Le Démon du Bien* and *Les Lépreuses*, which began to appear in 1936. Secondly there is a very large group of essays, discursions and philosophical writings, reinforced by a volume of *Carnets* into which he has transcribed the contents of his private notebooks. The extracts here translated by Mr John Weightman belong to the second category, and have been selected not only for their own sake but with the purpose of supplying an introduction to their many-sided author's point of view. Or rather, to his varying points of view; for Montherlant's genius is nothing if not protean, and like Keats he would seem to have decided that 'the only means of strengthening one's intellect is ... to let the mind be a thoroughfare for all thoughts, not a select party'. '*C'est une conception de professeur*' (he declared in 1923) '*que voir le oui et le non dans deux camps opposés . . . Une âme saine, ayant ce fond de simplicité qui caractérise et permet les choses grandes, sera toujours assez flexible, assez abondante et assez vigoureuse pour fondre joyeusement dans une unité supérieure la plupart de ces prétendues antinomies. . . .*' Yet certain ideas and images have continued to haunt him at every period of his literary life, just as certain human virtues excite his respect in varying characters and situations. Among terms that describe the affections, '*les mots . . . qu'on retrouve le plus souvent dans mes livres*' (he observes) '*sont* sympathie, camaraderie, *et* gentillesse'; and the characters he depicts with the greatest sympathy are human beings of a fairly simple type, recommended by their unpretending, unselfconscious *gentillesse*, such as Prinet in *Le Songe* and, in *Les Jeunes Filles*, the hero's youthful son.

Pretension, whether emotional or intellectual, has always been among his chief targets; and, noting his regard for the life of action and for the simple virtues of courage, endurance, loyalty, an English critic once ventured to draw a comparison between Henry de Montherlant and Rudyard Kipling. Few comparisons could have been more deceptive: in Kipling's restricted view of humanity, sexual appetite plays a minor role; whereas for Montherlant phys-, ical pleasure is the justification and the crown of life, no less enduring than the joy of artistic creation to which at times it bears a strange resemblance. The heart may delude; the senses never deceive—that is Montherlant's often repeated axiom: '*Tout ce qui est du coeur est inquiétude et tourment, et tout ce qui est des sens est paix.*' Through sensuality combined with tenderness we escape the perils of romantic love: '*La sensualité*' (he tells us) '*alliée a la tendresse ne fait pas chez moi de l'amour. C'est une de mes grandes forces, d'échapper à l'amour en connaisant, mêlées, la sensualité et la tendresse.* Thus Montherlant is both an anti-Romantic and, to some extent, an anti-feminist writer; and *Les Jeunes Filles*, which includes some striking diatribes against the romantic pretensions of the opposite sex, relates how a famous novelist, beleaguered by possessive women, resists every attempt to extort his love and betray him into emotional servitude, when all that he is willing to concede are tenderness and the warmth of physical desire. Costals, too, aims at a clarification of existence, like Montherlant concentrating his energies upon '*les deux grandes affaires essentielles—l'amour et la création artistique*'; and, although Costals and Montherlant should not be confused, the student of his notebooks will admit that they share a number of decisive traits. 'Unum necessarium—*Il est pour moi d'aimer et de créer*', wrote Montherlant in 1934; and earlier: '*Faire passer sans cesse toute sa vie dans un tamis. Secouer sans cesse, et ne garder que ce qui reste . . .*' What remains are a man's quintessential interests, which at any price he must learn to distinguish and preserve.

Lastly, both Costals and Montherlant may be described as born adventurers. '*J'ai été un aventurier*' (Montherlant has said). '*Non pas un aventurier littéraire . . . mais le vrai aventurier celui qui se cache de l'être.*' Daring, of course, is the adventurer's watchword—'*tenter la vie: peu importe ce qui en sort.*' In *Le Songe* and *Les Bestiaires*, the hero throws down his personal challenge to life; and it is the charm of bullring or battlefield that they provide him with the dangerous conditions he needs, in which, as in the experience of physical love, he can at length realize his true character. Montherlant has been called a 'Man of the Renaissance'; and certainly he shows little likeness to the average twentieth-century artist—a lapsed Catholic who cannot forget his faith: an aristocrat who has ridiculed the nobility without losing his sense of inherited privilege: a solitary who had never ceased to prize the companionship of his fellow human beings, and who has now and then hoped to found an order in which the virtues he chiefly admires might somehow reach their full expression. As a personality, if not as an artist, he is difficult to fit into the pattern of present-day life: and, although in some respects he may recall the Renaissance—its bold eclecticism and vigorous love of pleasure—he also suggests the aristocratic head of one of those military-religious organizations which flourished during the Middle Ages, where asceticism and sensuality, devotion and unorthodox practices, frequently existed side by side, the Knights Templar, for example, with their voluptuous hidden rites and secret idol Baphomet. He is a natural heretic who would no doubt have aroused the suspicions of any moderately vigilant Grand Inquisitor.

For his success in the role of artist, however, none of these attributes can be held directly responsible. An artist's ideas, like his personality, will always deserve examination; but, as Mallarmé said, provoked by an amateur poet's complaint that he had been endeavouring to write a sonnet and found it impossible to finish the poem, although his ideas were exciting and plentiful enough, 'poems, my dear Degas, are made not with ideas but with *words*.' Montherlant is the possessor of original ideas; more important, he is an accomplished master of language, the medium that not only enshrines ideas but gives them a value they could not otherwise claim. Montherlant's ideas may be interesting; not until they have been incorporated into a coherent and self-contained work of art do they become deeply moving; and even then they are most moving when they operate beneath the surface. *Les Jeunes Filles* is an attack on Woman, inspired apparently by the writer's own attempts to contract an alliance with a conventional young girl in 1924 and 1934. But the qualities that give these books their strength are primarily artistic qualities—the acuteness of the novelist's observation, his blending of observation with literary imagination, his humour (of which I have written elsewhere), the passages of poetic insight that soften the effect of harshly satirical outbursts. The novelist is not a dispassionate spectator, as in a Flaubertian novel of the later nineteenth century. At moments, he appears to identify himself with his irritated, restless hero; or again he may deliver a broadside in which he seems to be addressing us in *propria persona*. But then he restores the balance by some stroke of sympathy or understanding, through which a character he has previously ridiculed acquires a wholly new aspect. Pity prevails over indignation; the satirist becomes a poetic analyst.

Consider, for instance, his treatment of the vulgar and foolish Madame Dandillot, Costals's prospective mother-in-law, against whom both hero and novelist have already joined to do their worst. But now Solange has been deserted by Costals; and Madame Dandillot awakes in the night with a sudden unbearable pang of apprehension, and hurries precipitately towards her daughter's room. There Solange, too, is lying awake:

'*Elle glissa la main sous le bras de sa fille . . . passa l'autre main sur le front de Solange, comme pour y ramasser et en expulser les mauvais génies. . . . Cet être—visage et corps—qui était pour elle la chose la plus chère au monde, c'était le même être qui faisait bâiller Costals, d'ennui; le même être que des milliers d'hommes et de femmes croisaient ou bousculait dans la rue avec indifférence; le même être pour lequel d'autres hommes se fussent damnés de désir: tout et rien, souverain et désarmé. Solange avait l'habitude . . . de dormir toujours, même en été, la bouche couverte. Mme Dandillot reconnut à sa moiteur l'endroit du drap qui venait de reposer sur la bouche de sa fille et y enfouit son visage un avec petit gémissement. . . . Elle atteignait en cette minute a ce qu'il y avait de vraiment fort en elle, et à ce qu'il y avait de valable.*'

Here one thinks of a particularly poignant episode in *L'histoire d'amour de 'La Rose de Sable'*, where Auligny, transported by love and compassion, looks down upon his sleeping mistress. Montherlant's poetic gifts are all the more conspicuous because he holds them on so tight a rein. Except in *La Songe*, and to a lesser extent in *Les Bestiaires*, he is never rhetorical or declamatory. His prose style is vigorous and masculine, composed of many different elements, for which he is indebted to seventeenth-century literature—the classic period of French prose—but also to the current spoken language, with its graphic idiom and colloquial turns of phrase. In translation, some of his nuances are bound to escape the English reader; for both his style and the character that engendered it have a peculiarly French cast; and a multitude of French critics, elsewhere divided, agree that Henry de Montherlant is their country's greatest living writer, a master of language and a splendidly adventurous and independent spirit. '*Ce qui me plait chez Montherlant*' (wrote André Gide in 1927) '*c'est un accent d'indéniable authenticité . . .*' Montherlant's cult of 'authenticity' is reflected in every book he publishes, together with the passion for independence that derives from much the same source. His personages are constantly at work striving to distinguish between the essential and inessential: even Costals, that ruthless amorist, is cruel in the cause of honesty—

among his shifting affections and inclinations, which at a certain juncture propel him towards Solange, he seeks always to reach the moment of truth, an unmistakable assurance of what he genuinely thinks and feels. To realize himself, the writer must stand alone: he is responsible to no exterior judge. He should write as if he had already died: '*A s'être mis dans les conditions où on sera quand on sera mort . . . on y prend la mesure du plus ou moins de faculté qu'a son oeuvre à se défendre toute seule.*' He must be oblivious to critics past and future: '*L'écrivain*' (Montherlant announced in a public discourse) '*donne son oeuvre comme le pommier sa pomme, sans se soucier si elle sera ramassée et, si elle l'est, de quelle façon le cuisinier l'accomodera.*' His talent takes its shape according to the laws of its own organic growth; and, in so far as its development is sane and harmonious, it will command the reader's interest. Such were the rules with which Henry de Montherlant began his literary career in 1920; he continues to follow them in 1960. Plato remarked of the citizens of ancient Akragas that they appeared to build their temples as if for eternity, but enjoyed themselves at their banquets as though each banquet were to be their last. Similarly, Montherlant has paid innumerable tributes to the pleasures of the passing moment—'*Je ne puis me soutenir qu'avec un plaisir vif par journee: faute de cela, je languis et m'étiole*'—but plans his literary work with an eye on the future, regardless of contemporary critical modes. The resulting edifice is at once solid and homogeneous, despite the variety it often displays in detail. No French playwright or novelist now alive has made a more substantial contribution to modern European literature.

PETER QUENNELL

AN EASTER SERVICE AT SCHOOL DURING WARTIME (IN 1916)

MY MIND GOES BACK to an evening service, that Easter, at my old school.

In the congregation were parents, pupils, not a few priests who Moses-like, had raised their hands in battle against their brothers and not a few 'classicists' and 'scientists', whom you had only to look at to see that they would be killed, so serious was the approach to life expressed on their countenances. However, it was only those standing in the choir who caught the eye; they formed a little group, set apart from the rest of the congregation and marked down for slaughter. *Ave, morituri te salutant.* Petals of light fell in showers.

The soldiers stood there side by side, facing their fellow-men and God. Since they had been at the front, their features had hardened and the hollows between them had become ashen, as happens with the faces of people listening to some sublime piece of music; their eyes had grown bigger, like the eyes of people journeying through a forest. They were just men, whom the advancing shadows were already forcing back on to the frontier between life and death; they already enjoyed supernatural freedom, since the power of disappointing had been taken from them and they had been given absolution for the past and the future; petrified like statues, they were as pure and remote as the horizon and the stars. All of them had left school with the intention of taking part in life. Came the day when the voice of a child of ten had cried from each pair of lips: 'I didn't do anything wrong!' For a fleeting moment, there had been tears on the whitish-blue rings of fatigue under each pair of eyes. Tears, touching tears. Now, everything was in order again.

Everything was in order. *It is best that each of us should follow his course; mine leads towards death, yours towards life,* said Socrates, after he had been condemned. Everything was in order. Everything was welcomed and accepted.

'We'll see it through. We'll not shirk or try clever dodges. We are the ones who are always put in the front line. Never mind, we'll see it through, even if it means taking the rap for other people.' That is what they were implying, those young fellows who had come to the service wearing their helmets, their spurs and their revolver-cases because they were quite pleased, even so, to produce a slight sensation. But the Angel who sees into hearts shivered behind his wings as he recorded their unspoken words for inscription on invisible columns.

There was no one present who, in that hour, did not discover a new reason to justify his endeavours and a ratification of the best within himself. The soldiers, finding themselves surrounded by schoolchildren and by gestures and passions that had been their own, repeated now in the same places and with the same care, were obscurely conscious of being unimportant and easily replaceable, a passing ripple on the surface of life, while at the same time children around them were proclaiming why it was necessary to fight. The unfit and those whose call-up had been deferred lifted their heads again. 'Couldest thou not watch one hour with me?' The questioning voices of the fighting men were stilled. The stay-at-homes were able to meet the gaze of the men from the firing-line, and they were saying: 'We will suffer and repay. But speak up and tell us what we have to do. We cannot hurt ourselves any more. We cannot go on hurting ourselves.' To each mother they were saying: 'I grant you the right to know what I am doing with my life.' On all sides, there was the same bursting of the bounds of self; all present were suffused with a single emotion like that which unites choirboys when they cluster about their hymn-book and sing, roundmouthed. We believed that evil had ceased to exist, that irony had ceased to exist, that no one present could ever again be cold, remote, distant or hostile. The throbbing in our breasts regulated the heart-beats of the whole of France. Each spirit had been melted down and recast in the mould of honour.

AN EASTER SERVICE AT SCHOOL DURING WARTIME (IN 1916)

The fighting-men especially—for soldiers always harbour a degree of unvoiced bitterness—were warmed by it all. The prayers of their peers shielded them like a coat of armour; also, each one of them was enhanced by the fact that some of his fellow-soldiers were living with him through the same experience at the same time. In the regions of death they had thrice denied their old school, thinking it naïvely stupid and out of touch with things as they are; but now they gazed around with a look of recognition and then, lowering their eyes, let themselves relax once more in their spiritual home. They had often waited in vain for letters, had often been the first to write, had often felt those nearest and dearest to them disappearing below the horizon like a distant shore—and now, suddenly, they were again conscious of being supported by those they loved. They had been thrust on desperately towards the future—but the present moment now drained all colour from the future, because it seemed to them that everything had been achieved. When the monstrance was raised on high, many a one who had never before done more than bow his head, got down on to his knees; many a one who had always been too self-conscious to take part in the singing joined in the chorus of the *Magnificat*, with his eyes on his dearest friend to make sure that his friend sang exactly like himself. It was as if a flag had been hoisted; or perhaps only the overflow of an excess of emotion, a powerful inner surge which borrows words and sounds to express itself and so unburden the heart.

Before the congregation dispersed, the Father Superior of the College came forward in front of the altar. He, too, knew the strain and stress in the firing-line, what painful protests underlay acceptance, how often departures were untempered by farewells. . . .

He began to speak. And when he explained the meaning of the Easter Feast and affirmed that all the bodies of the dead would rise again, as St Augustine says, 'because they were beautiful', and would be reborn in the form in which those present had seen them but a little while before in those very gardens and courtyards and cloisters when they were still able to hold their youth in their arms, at the far end of the chapel, women began to throb and weep.

They throbbed and wept and died and lived again. They saw again in memory smiles and freckles and little gestures copied from their own, and which would live for all eternity (they saw all this, for their only hope lay in recollection). They did not notice that, as the speaker continued, his body gradually disappeared until nothing was visible of him except his forehead and the flashes which issued from his mouth: everyone was looking towards those who had triumphed over death and who seemed to be burning as on a funeral pyre. They, too, felt that what was being said justified many moments of weakness in their lives. Their faith was no longer that wan instinct which comes into play under shell-fire, that blind need to cling to any mysterious protection; it was a certainty attested by a swelling of the heart, and everyone, acknowledging the risk of being duped, surrendered himself to the Better Life, drunk with assent.

The priest finished speaking. Everyone knelt down, heavy with love. Like a drifting dream, the school floated away on waves of hope. A weary schoolboy noisily moved a bench.

The congregation filed out of the chapel but only a few people went into the school itself. Everyone felt the same need to keep the miracle alive a little longer, to achieve mutual interchange in words. In the entrance hall, lit by daylight from above, there was a tremulous, touching moment, a moment of suspense and uncertainty, during which people were vaguely waiting for each other to make the first move, looking at each other speculatively, questioningly. Then, in one great impulse, all those present came together and intermingled.

Everyone spoke to everyone else, although for the most part they did not know each other. Those who were leaving that evening for the front, wrapped in noble severity, scanned the faces of their juniors to see whether the good effect of the experience had not already worn off. But what they mainly deduced from the indifference expressed by those faces was that they themselves were well and truly 'old boys', and strangers to the younger people. . . . And for them, that was the first moment of the day to be marked by fathomless melancholy.

AN EASTER SERVICE AT SCHOOL DURING WARTIME (IN 1916)

They were approached by boys of their own age who were staying behind, and whose eyes, like no other eyes in the world, begged them not to die. They held out their bare hands as a pledge of mutual fidelity. Each hand felt the warmth of the other hand like a little flame.

Mothers in mourning peered closely at the big boys so like their own, asked them about life at the front and silently compared them with *him*. The crowd was dispersing but they remained hesitantly behind, as if fascinated by a notice that seemed almost to smile from the wall. When, just before going through the door, they paused under the framed list of old boys who had died in battle, to read once more the name they knew only too well to be there, a name which would never again be involved in the affairs of this world, it seemed to them that the list of the dead and the adjoining notice about those awarded the *Croix de Guerre* were one and the same list, bathed in the same unsullied bliss. For one brief instant, the like of which would perhaps never occur again, they felt their sons' death to have been worth while since it had made possible an experience such as this.

La Relève du Matin 1920
(Written in 1918)

HOLD FAST TO ALL THINGS, WHILE KEEPING EACH IN ITS PROPER PLACE

THE ETHICS OF SPORT do not require the elimination of all sensitivity, delicacy or spontaneity of feeling, or all compassion. They require that these things should take second place and should, if necessary, be held in check; it is disastrous if they invade the whole personality, but it is also a misfortune if they are totally lacking. I admire organization in a man's life as I admire the economy of the stars in the heavens. The main difficulty is not renunciation, and let no one jeer when I say that renunciation would be no trouble at all. The main difficulty is to know which principle should predominate and then to sustain it, while holding fast to all things, and keeping each in its proper place. The virtuous man is not he who renounces the flesh, but he who keeps the flesh in its proper place, uses it as far as he needs, and stops at the right point. Such a man, without being incommoded by the flesh, enjoys a valuable experience of which the other remains ignorant, and his solidarity with life is, as everyone must agree, more complete. I could also quote the case of a hot-tempered fellow I know who does not worry unduly about keeping his temper in check, because he knows he has enough will-power to refrain from acting in anger. (He will say to his son: 'I'll deal with you when I've calmed down.') Consequently, his anger is a source of pleasure and has no ill effects; he gains both ways. And I could also quote the answer given by a religious man to people who were trying to interest him in 'the Catholic novel': 'Educate girls so that they have the strength of character to read anything and there will be no need for Catholic novels.' To be too mistrustful is to worry, and worry is a confession of weakness. A rider who is in control of his horse can let it have its head.

I remember a football field where in clear weather we could always hear the angelus ringing towards the end of our matches. At ground level, there was a fine, head-on rough-and-tumble, narrowly circumscribed and marked by total concentration on reality, while from high above came a faint melody which touched secret springs of feeling and awoke a sense of the mystery of the world. I should like the angelus to ring out over all sports grounds, not because of the precise message uttered by the bells but because of the suggestion of gentleness they convey. And they do so with discretion so that they are heard only by ears which want to hear—like a woman sitting a little way back in a circle of conversationalists and saying nothing herself and not unduly eager to please, but smiling so as not to be forgotten.

No, we should renounce nothing. The old doctrine of the union of opposites, formulated by Heraclitus, Hippocrates and, indeed, by all the Fathers of Greek thought, has not ceased to bear fruit. The good life always depends on a balancing of contrary forces, such as the Ancients symbolized in Mercury's wand, which consists of two hostile serpents rocking together in love and between them supporting the winged branch. The reason for this is simple; nature sets us the example. Nature, within herself, makes night alternate with day, heat with cold, rain with drought, calm with tempests; and, within bodies, fasting and food, activity and sleep; but no one argues from this that nature is incoherent or that her variety leads to confusion. Like her, I refuse to make a choice, I wish to enter ever more completely into the universal law of alternating rhythms and the divine interplay of compensation; to put it in the language of my times, I wish to be effective in all directions. It is a pedantic conception to see the yea and the nay in opposite camps, and wearing different coloured jerseys, like football teams. A healthy soul, with that basic simplicity which both distinguishes and makes possible great things, will always be flexible, copious and vigorous enough to reconcile, in a higher and joyous unity, most of those so-called contradictions which give pause to the many spineless creatures we see around us. Happiness, suffering, innocence, impurity, wisdom, madness—they are all mine and I want them all, since everything suits me, if nothing suits me completely. And let me live all the lives, the diversities and the contradictions in the world, intensely and yet with detachment; so be it, since it is within my power. Have everything within one's power, in order to lead the fullest life. Do everything in order to experience everything, experience everything in order to understand everything, understand everything in order to express everything; how great will be our reward when we look at ourselves and see ourselves as a mirror of creation and think of God as made in the image of man!

Les Olympiques, 1924
(Written in 1923)

MADEMOISELLE DE PLÉMEUR
Champion of the 'Three hundred metres'

UNLIKE MOST ATHLETES and most spectators (it is curious to see how cruelly and unfairly female athletes are made fun of by the very people who extravagantly over-estimate the social role of women), I maintain that sports as practised by women—running, jumping and throwing the javelin—can provide the keenest enjoyment, both athletic and aesthetic. No doubt it is more difficult for a woman than for a man to be a satisfactory, average athlete, but at almost any female athletic meeting, you will find a handful of women who show themselves to be perfectly accomplished and whose performances, from the technical point of view, are no less interesting than those of the men. This is true for France and, still more so, for other countries.

The new contribution made by women to athletics is not technical, but aesthetic and moral.

Aesthetic. We see women as they could be if the duplicity, viciousness and bad taste of the male did not force them into disastrous courses of action: the distortion of the body by corsets, tight shoes[1] and high heels and of the figure by clothes; not to mention make-up. Morphologically, the only difference between men and women is in the chest and the pelvis, which are both more pronounced in the female for utilitarian reasons: gestation and

---

[1] The male tries to make the female 'doll-like' or even frankly ridiculous, to maintain his advantage over her. The female connives in this through stupidity. Do women realize, for instance, that their superstitious belief in the prettiness of small feet is only a survival of the masculine idea: 'With small feet, she will be handicapped and will be easier to keep under control'? The Chinese admit that this is their intention in crippling their women's feet. The Phoenicians put their girls' feet in fetters so that they should not be 'loose', in any sense

suckling. If the female pelvis is too broad, it is ugly; it makes the silhouette clumsy, by appearing top-heavy above the shortened and rather bandy legs. The breasts, even when prominent, are beautiful, if they remain firm. The muscles, in a woman as in a man, are always beautiful provided they are not too pronounced; there is no beauty, nor even gracefulness, where there is no suggestion of inner strength, the 'discrete strength' that Aristotle asked for (just as the soul can have no valid feeling if it is without strength). Even a young child cannot be beautiful unless he displays a certain latent vigour; stature has nothing to do with the matter.

All that was enunciated in the Greek canon of the Golden Age, which is perfect both for men and women. To depart from it ever so slightly is to fall into error.

Up to the age of twenty-three, I was disconcerted by the paradox that nature makes us burn with desire for bodies which are ugly, and which we know to be ugly. The female bodies depicted by the painters and sculptors of the day, the bodies I had seen undressed, although they belonged to 'pretty women', and even professional models, were horrible, yet opinion was unanimous in proclaiming that the rolls of fat, drooping dugs and bulging behinds of these saddle-backed, blown-out, shapeless creatures, were the most sublime, and indeed the only, expression of Beauty with a capital B. Never having come across, in real life, any female bodies resembling Greek statuary or the women in certain old masterpieces, I concluded that they were idealized inventions. But in 1919, I saw young girls practising on sports grounds, and others who had been trained according to George Hébert's 'natural method', and I read Hébert's indispensable book, *L'Education physique féminine*. What a revelation! It was as if I had discovered another sex. I suddenly realized that the female body could be beautiful, if it were exercised. For six years or more,[1] I was literally unable to take an interest in any women other than athletes. I could hold my head high and approve of the feeling which drew me to them, whereas until then I had been ashamed of being attracted in spite of myself

[1] This introduction to *Mademoiselle de Plémeur* was written in 1938; the rest of the story dates back to 1923.

by bodies that satisfied neither my reason nor my taste. At last I had found women with whom I could be on an equal footing.

As for the moral effect of female athletics, I don't know whether it has been important for many men, but it certainly was for me. It was in Sports clubs that I was able to experience the strange and charming feeling of pure comradeship between men and women—all of them lightly clad. There were two quite distinct categories: the body and the flesh. The body of a woman member of the club was merely an object of beauty and of athletic prowess. If she aroused other feelings in me, they were kept on a short lead and released only outside the club; and even then I considered them as being a due that had to be paid to nature. I approved of them, of course, but on their own level; and I accepted the rule that the flesh must take second place, when this rule was formulated by athletics, whereas it seemed ridiculous to me when it was put forward by religious and moral codes. Sometimes, the flesh even seemed a corrupting influence! The story of the young man and the girl in *Le Songe* is based on this conception.

Later, I adopted a different philosophy of life: I came to believe that nothing mattered. But even now, if I happen to meet women athletes, the mewings and crowings of the male suddenly seem very vulgar; I may add that I have observed this reaction, which was characteristic of Peyrony[1] in 1920, in a number of young Frenchmen in 1938. And I remain convinced that my conduct with regard to girl athletes between 1919 and 1925 stood rather high in the scale of refinement. There was some affectation in it, but only a little and that little was of good quality.

However, it was a relationship that was always to some extent *sui generis*. On the sports field women arouse no more emotion than do men or boys, but the emotion is different. The sounds of their lax Ionian harp, or erratic Phrygian flute, which upset the severe Laconian functioning of male athletics, can be heard in the story of Mademoiselle de Plémeur.

... It was one July, during an Atlantic crossing. I can still see her leaning against the rail beside me, erect, serious, smiling towards

[1] A character in Montherlant's early writings.

the horizon, with her smile gleaming from the highest point of her person as a peal of bells rings out from the highest point in the sky. Her arms were naked under their transparent blue covering and in the sun they had the muted light of the sun during a time of eclipse, and when the shadow of a sail fell across them they took on the appearance of tawny sand glimpsed through a liquid dream. I moved to one side a little to get a better view of her and the wind brought me the wholesome scent of her hair.

Without turning her head, she said: 'I saw your name written on the waters.'

I have found, among female athletes, a number of girls who represent the last, extreme flowering of those aristocratic Breton families in which an independent, rebellious spirit has been perpetuated throughout the centuries. They were girls who had gone in for athletics as their brothers engaged in Left-Wing politics. They threw all the rich qualities, all the better humours of their ancient blood into what was, for them, a misdemeanour.

When I first got to know Mlle. de Plémeur, she was the pride of her club: champion of the three hundred metres and, in her day, unbeatable in France over that distance. She was, moreover, very much the artistic type in athletics—uneven, capricious, easily discouraged and easily elated, and so outlandish in behaviour that, but for her ability, she would have been expelled from the club as being 'impossible'.

She was twenty-four, which, for a girl, is late autumn. Her long and shapely limbs passed more or less unnoticed, perhaps because she lacked the piquancy that Frenchmen prefer above everything else; also, perhaps, because she was always impossibly dressed. Her face was not worth looking at (but how insignificant a face is compared to a body!). As an athlete in action, she was transfigured, and escaped into a form of human perfection.

Her brother was in the camel corps in Africa, after getting himself involved in some unsavoury affair; old M de Plémeur had come to the police-station and sobbed, while the inspector left his titled catch to cool off on the bench where they usually put the pimps; and the policemen had kept looking round and sniggering: 'Just think of it. A Viscount!' She, we understood, through a sudden whim or intolerable boredom, had left her noble father who, hidden away in his filthy ancestral home at Morlaix, was drowning in drink the anguish of gradually having to admit that he would soon be a pauper. She detested 'society' and lived in a little boarding-house, steering back—so it was said—to her ancestral home, all those who feather their nests with the plumes of decadent aristocrats. And sometimes, when physical exercise was no longer giving her face the sublime expression of a virgin-maenad, I thought I could discern there the sadness I notice every day, and always with the same pity, on faces I pass in the streets: 'Perhaps I shall never get married.'

Am I mistaken? But athletics, like religion, can sometimes be a substitute activity. I have known young men and women look upon the mastery of their bodies as a means of recovering self-confidence, of compensating for some weakness or failure in their everyday lives. A fresh idol and a fresh illusion.

One day, to everybody's surprise, Mlle de Plémeur was soundly beaten in the three hundred metres through proving unable to put on a final 'spurt'. She accepted defeat in that sporting spirit which is so praiseworthy when it occurs in a female temperament. But, without saying good-bye to anyone, she stopped coming to the sports ground, gave no sign of life and it was only by chance that we learned, after an interval, that she had gone back to Morlaix.

Three months later, there was a ring at my door. It was Mlle de Plémeur, dripping with rain, who had come all the way out to Neuilly. In the sitting-room, as soon as she had taken her hat off and shaken her head like a little girl to loosen and fluff out her Breton hair, which would suffer no parting, she declared without any preamble:

'I gave it all up. I'm getting too old, aren't I? I could see the fat coming back and my muscles getting stiffer. And then, a month ago . . . You know, the last spurt of flame just before the fire goes out . . . I can feel in my body that I've got my old form back; it's unbelievable. No good trying to understand. Form is still half a mystery to us; it comes and goes, like a snake or a will o' the wisp. Now that I've lost my sprint I've been practising longer distances on my own. And I'm sure—do you hear?—absolutely certain I can break the women's record for the thousand metres, which is three minutes sixteen seconds. Only I must make the attempt straight away; I may lose my form from one day to the next. That's why I've come here. All the officials are away at the club. So I thought of you. Tomorrow, if possible, you must come and time me . . . I'll only come back to the club and take up the good old life again where I left off if I can do it with you to testify that I've broken the record . . . You must . . .'

There was no need to beg. She had convinced me. No doubt there wasn't much point in her desire to break the record, because even if she succeeded, her performance would not be officially recognized, not having been properly checked. But what did that matter? I would be making her happy and doing no one any harm. When people have only desires of this kind, should we not make haste to grant them without fuss the trifle that will satisfy? It is so soon too late.

However, rather mischievously, I let her run on, as pressing, over-eloquent and absorbed in her subject as Emma Bovary must have been when she was begging cash from M. Guillaumin. Sitting opposite her, I realized with curiosity that in three months I had forgotten many of her facial expressions, whereas I remembered tiny particularities of her body, as if she had belonged to me. From childhood, I have always attached more importance to bodies than to faces, and a sweet little face on a teratological body—the typical Parisian product—has never given me the same emotion as indifferent features above a beautifully shaped figure.

'You will put an end to love-making!' groan the opponents of female athletics, who consider that for a young woman to show a bare leg anywhere except behind the footlights is to endanger the future of the race. '*Let woman retain her mystery!*' Whichever way I twist this egregious injunction, I cannot get it to mean anything other than: 'Hide three-quarters of a woman's body from view if we want her to appear beautiful. For the love of the fair sex, leave the coverings in place and don't look too closely.' This strange defence amounts to an insult; what are we to think of women who approve of such honeyed caddishness! How can one fail to be struck by the lack of self-confidence betrayed by their age-old frenzy for disguise! It makes one think of the poet's fine phrase: 'Is there any better mark of a legitimate and authentic power than that it should not be exercised behind a veil?' (Valéry) In Mlle de Plémeur's case, I realized with sadness that she had done herself harm, socially, through not taking advantage of her 'mystery'. Her very straightforwardness and accessibility had classed her, once and for all, as an eternal comrade, and no one, apparently, had ever expected her to be anything more. To a certain extent, she was paying for her healthiness by not being happy.

We decided to go to the club ground next morning at eight. Mlle de Plémeur took her leave. After getting half-way through the door, she came back into the entrance hall:

'G. (this was the director of the club) has written to tell me that Serrurier (one of the other women athletes) has resigned suddenly because one of the younger girls gave her a horribly mocking look once when she made a clumsy mistake during practice. He says that, from now on, to prevent the young girls making fun of the older ones, he has put them in separate groups and is training them at different times. To think that we've had to come to that! It's a battlefield, isn't it?'

'No, just a chicken-run, with the hens pecking each other slowly to death.'

'You can guess, can't you, why G. wrote to tell me?'

'No...'

'Why, don't you understand? He's implying: "If you went off for the same reason as Serrurier, you have nothing to fear; you can come back now, the old ones are in a separate pen."'

'No,' I said, taking pity on her, 'that isn't the way I understand his letter at all.'

She gave a wry, forced little smile, a pathetic little twist that hardly moved her lips:

'Well, we'll see where I stand tomorrow morning."

I much prefer, to the official grounds of famous clubs where the fine ladies along the touch-line burst out laughing if you sprawl on the turf with the ball, those patchy suburban sports fields, where you play on a litter of old tins, to an audience of thirty shivering citizens, between factories which, with their tall chimneys, are like huge steamships that have come to rest in port. And I like the Paris suburbs, with their splendid, infinitely evocative place names —*La Plaine, Le Point du Jour* . . . In a book I wrote when I was twenty, *La Relève du matin,* I referred to the 'delicious working-class suburbs'. When, next morning, I walked on to the misty, sodden and deserted field overlooked by the fortifications, my heart was that of a man who is going to act as second at a duel. Mlle de Plémeur came towards me impatiently, as if I were late; I held out my watch, which said five to; she took this as a personal affront. When I saw how far her three months in Brittany had brought her down from that lofty plane of dignity and reason to which athletics had once raised her, I sensed what a collapse was in store for her if her attempt failed.

She began her preparations, running on the spot in little bursts and nervously rolling the lower hem of her shorts; she unwound the bandages from her feet which were already black with cinder dust from the track, and I saw again her rather thick ankles, which were of the kind that I both approve of mentally and find very much to my taste. The skin on the front of her legs bore no trace of the scratches that had often been left on them, in her active periods, by the track shoes of some (well-intentioned?) opponent she had been closely following during a race. I particularly recall the moment when she sat down on the grass and the masseur massaged her legs (downy calves and smooth thighs). And while the sensitive hands climbed tremblingly like flames, higher and higher, until they went under the wide openings of her shorts, I watched her face with intense, stealthy attention, to discover some imperceptible sign which might enlighten me about the fundamental meaning of the moment. But her upright posture, the lift of her head, which was like a bird of prey's, her gaze which remained fixed in the distance, her pinched lips in her blanched face and the suggestion of rigidity which petrified her whole being, expressed only the choking tenseness of anxiety. And I was so uncomfortable myself that I called out: 'Come on!' to speed up the start.

She had been walking; now she was running. It was as if a spoken sentence had ended in song. Like a singer, a dancer or an evoker of harmonies, she had become a link between the sublime and ourselves. Oh, woman, instrument of the ineffable, we humbly salute you for your great virtues! Why did I mention your mistakes, your shortcomings, your pettiness? You are now wholly justified.

She covered the first lap in three seconds more than the French record time. This was good going, and I called it out to her as she went past. Then her features stiffened: Joan of Arc, leading her men into battle, must have had that grave, sealed countenance; Joan of Arc, or perhaps Mlle de Plémeur's ancestor, the regicide member of the *Convention*, when he cast his vote in favour of Capet's death? On she ran, the light-footed maiden, and her lithe leg movements, so marvellously delicate and piercing that I imagined them leaving on the cinder track a pointed trace like the marks of goats' feet, were replaced by a more vigorous stride which brought even her neck muscles into play. Even so, when she came round again she had lost two seconds more. I thought that the wiser course was to call out: 'Equal time!'

She began on the third of the four laps.

If I close my eyes, it all comes to life again, the early morning with its faint, pricking drizzle, the loneliness, the silence and the girl, no longer in the first flush of youth, running in the bleak open air. There were only the two of us, she and I; and her whole achievement was a waste. She was running with a beauty there was no one to witness to accomplish an aim no one was interested in; she was running, perhaps for the last time, and surpassing herself, perhaps for the last time; she was running in a state of sacred horror, as if fiercely pursued by age and sad time. Two centuries ago, wearing a hair shirt and crazed by the Cross, Mlle de Plémeur would have trudged with bleeding feet along the roads. On that suburban running-track, I saw re-enacted the eternal effort of all those who once believed that, to hear the Oracle, they had only to make the offering of a moment's noble madness.

She passed me again, with her head on one side, and her face already expressing fatigue, suffering, a deeper self that I had not known before, a further reason why she should be loved. How many young women athletes have I seen display, for the benefit of the curious and while their mothers were looking on, the final secret released by a contorted face, that spasm of pain that formerly only the husband had the right to wallow in, since he was its creator and its master! She had lost three more seconds, making a total of eight. The situation was irretrievable. I shouted: 'You've lost four seconds.'

How long did the harsh sentence take to travel from her mind to her body? I could take a stone and mark the exact spot on the track where her strength flagged and jibbed. From then on, it was only a question of will-power, character and anger; it was no longer the body which ran but the soul—a naked soul, a breath of life, which followed the track as a will o' the wisp follows the course of a river.

For my part, pressing her emotion against my own, I would have liked to rush to meet her, to catch her by her beautiful, darling wrists and say to her: 'Poor little thing, my poor little old thing, stop all this at once! What are we doing here? It's true that I'm younger than you are, but don't you see that I'm your father now talking to you and that you are my wandering child? I have said, I have even proclaimed, that only victory could inspire me with love, and yet I love you more in your hour of distress than I did in all your triumphs, and I am going back on my word and I shall do so again, thirty, forty, fifty times because it pleases me to do so and I can do anything I wish. But, I beg of you, don't be unhappy to so little purpose. Don't waste your aptitude for suffering; you should keep it in your most secret heart for the man who is perhaps waiting for you and who will unleash it with equivocal pride.' What happens to all those words that come to our lips but are never uttered, and yet are always the kindest words? If an angel records them somewhere and a day comes when they are made known, how completely exonerated we shall be when we awake!

The reader will excuse me if I don't go into the details of the finish. When she appeared in the straight, I was as worked up as she was. By a brave effort, she had managed not to lose any more time; nevertheless she was still eight seconds over the record. Should I tell her? Should I kill her last hope and bar her from the possibility of greatness? Ought I not to assure her that she had been successful?

She threw herself on to the tape with a contorted corpse's mouth, snapping and sucking at the air as if she were dying and trying to bite at life.

The record was three minutes sixteen seconds. I stopped the watch, and read off the time:

'Twenty-four.'

When I looked up, she was walking off to the dressing-rooms. I followed her and pushed on ahead a little so as to see not her but the clear, comforting space in front; her legs had been white with talcum powder but the cinder dust from the track had stuck to the sweat and blackened them up to the knees; her face was pale, but a rather disquieting band of sharp pink ran across her forehead and round her temples, near the roots of her hair. We covered some thirty yards or more in this order. Suddenly I heard a noise, understood what it meant and swung round. She had collapsed; her chest and face were in the mud and she was shaking with sobs.

I looked at her for a moment, then turning my back towards her, I walked up and down as we do when we are waiting for someone who happens to be late. For the first time, I felt really in love with her, more in love than I could have been, had she been sobbing because of me. However, the illusion lasted only a moment.

Soon she got on to her feet again and, using the flat of her hand, squashed her tears on to the rings under her eyes, which were as blue and shimmering as aponeuroses. We went on towards the dressing-rooms without uttering a word.

When she was dressed again, she began to make jokes, laughing that grating sort of female laugh which is only bearable if we feel the urge to stop it with a kiss. She asked me for a cigarette. She had never been in the habit of smoking, because she had always been in training. This gave me a glimpse of her internal collapse and of the sad depths above which there was now nothing left to hold her.

When we parted, she thanked me for having proved, by refusing either to deceive her or pity her, that I did not despise her.

She was never seen at the club again. Athletics were Mlle de Plémeur's only support, her backbone, her nunnery. What can have become of her, since, into the bargain, she hadn't a penny? The young men of my generation only marry their mistresses. Has Mlle de Plémeur at last 'understood'?

Les Olympiques, 1924
(Written in 1923)

THE DEATH OF PEREGRINOS

FROM THE very first lines of the biography of Peregrinos by Lucian of Samosata, we are struck by the fact that the philosopher was a kind of specialist of psychological variety; he had, we are told, 'assumed a thousand different forms and played an infinite number of parts,' and liked to be called Proteus. Proteus! What a wealth of meaning in the name!

Peregrinos's last metamorphosis was 'to change himself into fire'. He put into practice, literally, the axiom of the Stoics: 'All that which is fire will return to the fire,' for the philosopher-poet was made of fire before he burned himself to death. His overwhelming love of fame and his desire to lead an extraordinary life actually prompted him to commit suicide during the Olympic Games, on a funeral pyre that he had reared with his own hands (AD 165). This is the death of which we propose to give an account.

In his early youth, Peregrinos was taken in adultery. He was only too pleased to escape with a horse-radish stuck between his buttocks; this, apparently, was the penalty for adultery in second century Athens. A little later, he was caught *flagrante delicto* with an Armenian boy. 'You'll have to pay for this!' said the child's parents, but they were respectable people and agreed to keep quiet for three thousand drachmas. The course of sexual satisfaction never did run smooth! Think of Sophocles having his cloak stolen from him by an urchin he was squeezing up to on the city walls at Athens: the story has fortunately been retrieved for us, thanks to the efforts of the Association of Ex-Service Writers.[1] But are there

[1] Ch. XIII of *Atheneus*, translated by Thierry Sandre, President of the Association of Ex-Service Writers.

still people of Pierre Louÿs's generation who think that love was an easy matter in the Ancient World?

Peregrinos's third exploit was the strangling of his Dad. 'He did not wish him to go on living beyond the age of sixty,' writes Lucian. This was carrying to excess the belief that there is a gap between the generations. The most favourable supposition is that our hero could not bear to see the good old man decline into his second childhood, a state in which he could no longer be properly respected. Still, he had allowed him to reach the age of sixty: he had given him a good run for his money.

And now, Proteus wandered from country to country. To be a haunted traveller was, for a time, his whim.

When the curiosity stimulated by these wanderings had been slaked, what could he invent to give himself a fresh lease of life, and to revive his curiosity? It was about the time when Marcus Aurelius was organizing a 'Kindness Week', on fifty-two occasions in the year, and withdrawing troops from the frontiers; in short, doing everything necessary to show that he loved peace, that is, ruining his country, a process which, as is well-known, took him only fifteen years to accomplish. Peregrinos realized that, if he did not wish to be considered an old fogey, it was imperative that he should appear 'kind and good'. He immediately went the whole hog and was converted.

Peregrinos 'frequenting some of the Christian doctors . . . soon showed them that they were mere children compared to him'. He expounded their books and wrote others himself. He was a great success. But he was arrested as a Christian and put into prison. What a stroke of luck for a lover of publicity! Perhaps he had engineered it himself. As it happened 'this event gave him great authority and earned him the reputation of having accomplished miracles'. A multitude of pathetic creatures, slaves, old men, women, orphans and failures of all kinds, in short, the usual followers of the 'crucified sophist', brought him food, collected around his prison and attended him through the watches of the night. Certain towns in Asia dispatched representatives of the whole Christian community to console him, help him and defend his cause.

In all other matters, the 'practical joker' side of Peregrinos would not appear shocking. One can even admit that it is a good thing for a hidden current of humour to run beneath our serious pre-occupations in order to sap the strength of those always crassly healthy assertions required by life in society: the absolute is the language of the innocent. And, at the same time, when there are so many reasons to wish humanity ill, it is a sign of good nature to be satisfied with pulling its leg. But there are sacred things, for which men live and die and which cannot be trifled with. However, the scandal was caused less by Peregrinos himself than by the Christian leaders. They had been taken in and, in their turn, were leading astray the 'credulous, simple men' who had placed their trust in them. There is something horrible in the spectacle of these dim-wits lost in admiration of an invert and a phoney who sniggers to himself while they are celebrating 'a victory of grace' and wonders: 'What new trick can I think up now?'

When, after a short lapse of time, the shockingness of this 'conversion' became apparent, the Christians tried to find excuses for the particular doctor who had been mainly concerned with bringing it about, Proteus himself having only been concerned to see that it was properly staged. It was argued that the doctor had not yielded to any false pride in conversion nor tried, through more or less conscious snobbishness, to launch Christianity in the fashionable world of which Proteus was, at the time, one of the chief ornaments; on the contrary, the *naïveté* of his conduct was said to be a proof of his great-heartedness and of his slight acquantance with human duplicity. Nevertheless, the consequences remained. The wicked man triumphed; the good had been taken in; a few pious souls, who had not lost their clear-sightedness, seeing their doctor's mistake, wondered if, on the spiritual level where they could not follow him, he was not guilty of others just as bad, and they were dismayed; the pagans, who knew what sort of character Peregrinos was, had a good laugh and conceived a still greater contempt for a religion the leading lights of which were such jackasses; Jesus Christ wept because, in addition to being crucified, He had had to be made ridiculous. For my part, I see the harm that was done, and I cannot see any excuse for it. If the doctor in question was a dreamer, unskilled in dealing with men, why did he get himself involved in the matter? There should be no pardon for dupes.

However, after a little while, Peregrinos was released by the governor of Syria, a man 'devoted to letters and philosophy, who, having decided that he deserved no punishment, set him free'. You can feel the governor's benevolence, the exquisite product of his disdain. He was like Pilate wanting to set Jesus free.

Once he had been released, Peregrinos returned to Parium, his native town. The populace, incensed at his father's murder, wanted to drag him before a court of law. It was then that Peregrinos had an inspiration worthy of a philosopher; he announced that he was returning to make public distribution of the dead man's possessions. He was carried in triumph. 'And if anyone, at that moment, had taken upon himself to mention the old man's demise, he would have been promptly stoned to death.' How is it that La Fontaine never dealt with this splendid subject?

Later, Peregrinos had the idea of asking the Emperor to restore to him the inheritance he had abandoned to his fellow-citizens. The Emperor returned the answer that a gift is a gift.

Since he could expect no further benefit from his conversion, Peregrinos decided that the time had come to squeeze the last possible effect out of it; he was *deconverted*. Once again, for a week or so, his name was in all the newspapers.

Peregrinos had experienced the love of boys and the love of women, the sweetness of 'belief' and the bracing pride of disbelief, freedom and imprisonment, triumph and failure; he had seen the most varied landscapes. Already a practising philosopher, he felt the time was ripe to become a professional. This meant shaving his head, just as our stupid young men, a few years ago, put on horn-rimmed spectacles to show that they were thinkers.

The fashionable notion, the 'United States of Europe' of the day, was that things in themselves are of no consequence. To give clear proof of this, Peregrinos, for instance, had himself beaten on the behind with a stick. We should not smile at such peculiarities, which we would treat with complete respect had they been performed in a monastery, for the love of some God instead of for an idea.

He went to Rome and created a scandal. He did not respect the rules of the game. He adopted the principle that no truth should be left unsaid, which is the greatest crime against society. The governor of Rome had him banished from the town. Life becomes impossible if frankness is tolerated.

Peregrinos experienced the bitter pleasure of knowing himself to be hated, a pleasure all aristocrats find so sweet that we may be sure it cheered the last days of the condemned at the time of the Terror. The urge to blame Peregrinos caused lots of people to have feelings and attitudes which were quite unexpected even for themselves. For instance, being annoyed with the Emperor, he gave free rein to his invective, and people who did not care a fig for the Emperor suddenly veiled their faces. False indignation is perhaps the most disgusting form of hypocrisy.

His life continued. He travelled and excited admiration and contempt, sometimes in turn, sometimes simultaneously. How can we pass judgement on him? Aulus Gellius calls him 'a man serious in behaviour (oh! oh!), steadfast in soul, and noble and instructive in conversation'. Ammian Marcellinus refers to him with some signs of affection. Lucian, his chief witness, despises him. But Lucian is a very limited creature; some of his reactions are so stupid as to bring a cry of astonishment from the reader;[1] and his mockery may be as much the result of obtuseness as of good sense. For instance, he blames Proteus for having accused Herod Atticus of pampering the Greeks because Herod had water piped to Olympia, where the spectators at the Games were parched with thirst. It would be just as logical to praise Proteus for having reminded a decadent population of the *ancient virtues*. Be that as it may, it is certain that Proteus never achieved that unanimous approbation

---

[1] For instance, in disapproving of Peregrinos's death, he asks: 'Would you wish your children to follow this example?'

which some apparently satisfied souls still long anxiously for in secret. 'He fell into contempt; he no longer enjoyed any consideration and for a long time had seemed an unexciting, uninteresting figure. In the end, unable to invent anything new or anything capable of arousing in his spectators that admiration which alone could satisfy the ardent thirst for glory with which he had always been consumed, he conceived the mad plan of throwing himself on to a blazing pyre and, at the last Games, announced to all the Greeks that he would burn himself to death at the next Games.'

It should be noted in passing that the ease with which people killed themselves in those days casts some doubt on the happy atmosphere attributed to them later by certain anxious souls, or rather anxious bodies, since the longing for a return to antiquity is a product of the flesh rather than of the mind. There is also a further proof of the wretchedness of the period. People must have been sorely tried to accept Jesus Christ.

When the day appointed by Peregrinos arrived, Olympia was full of wildly excited people. Some were weeping and crying: 'Stay alive for the sake of the Greeks!' Others, on the contrary, were shouting: 'Get on with it! The time has come!' They were all consumed with the same curiosity as Peter, following at a distance when the soldiers were leading Jesus away, 'to see how the matter would end'. Peregrinos (did he hesitate when it came to the point? Lucian suggests that he did) announced that he would carry out his promise during the following night.

Peregrinos's decision to sacrifice himself had been taken freely. If he had changed his mind, no one could have forced him to go through with it, without committing a crime. But we may be sure that if, during that night, his flesh had proved weak and he taken refuge in flight, a mob—not a howling, but what is much worse, a laughing mob—would have chased him back like an escaped animal. The populace considered that Peregrinos, by promising his death as a spectacle, had given them the right to demand it as such. 'A gift is a gift,' as the Emperor had replied in circumstances we have already related. Under the amused gaze of the police, a group of idle, and implicitly murderous, lookers-on surrounded the old man's tent.

The details of his end have no spiritual importance. But it was a curious sight. Lucian, that arm-chair sadist, went to the trouble of getting up in the middle of the night. The performance was not to be missed. A friend came to fetch him—we almost expect to read 'by car', so closely does his state of mind seem to have resembled that of the women who, on coming out of the theatre, drove with their gigolos to the villa where the police were shooting at the besieged bandits, Bonnot and Garnier.

Peregrinos, of course, waited till the moon was up, as if nature herself ought not to miss any detail of his exploit. Followed by his disciples, all carrying torches, he approached the pyre, which was now surrounded by an immense concourse of people. Each disciple used his torch to kindle the blaze. Peregrinos sprinkled a few grains of incense, recommended himself to his Genii, threw himself into the flames and disappeared.

The farce now being over—and farce is the word he uses—Lucian went back to bed, half amused and half cursing at the idea of having got up to see the *roasting* of a *stupid old man,* whose *poisonous stench was nauseating.* When Jesus expired, the centurion cried out that a just man had been crucified. But centurions were nobodies, without the advantages of a middle-class conscience.

On his way home, Lucian told passers-by as a joke that when Proteus disappeared, the earth had trembled and groaned, a vulture had risen from the centre of the flames, etc. . . . Half an hour later, a venerable old man had already heard the news and was swearing on oath that he had seen the vulture with his own eyes. What was more, he had just met Proteus himself clad in a white robe and crowned with olive. The earth had shaken! The dead had risen! At this point, our rationalists must suppress a smile. They are delighted to catch a miracle in the very act of coming into being.

II

When Hercules burned himself to death, it was in the attempt to shake off Nessus's poisoned shirt. The Christian who embraces martyrdom is using it as a means to salvation; like the Phoenix he will rise again, enhanced, from his ashes. The Brahmin has a devout love of death. Peregrinos was impelled by none of these reasons. This is a point that should be firmly grasped, since it is very important.

He was not fleeing from anything; he knew that life could still be very pleasant. His biographer tells us that, shortly before his death, he was sailing on the Aegean Sea in the company of 'a rather handsome boy, who was acting as his Alcibiades'. Naturally, there was no question of his seeking salvation; his Christianity had never been more than opportunism. As for the love of death, not a bit of it! On five different occasions we see him shunning death. Once, to escape from the populace, he abandoned his possessions to them. Once, when he was on the point of being stoned to death, he took refuge at the altar of Zeus. Once, when a storm arose at sea, he began to snivel. Once again, *eleven days* before he threw himself on to the pyre, he had an attack of fever and asked his doctor to supply him with remedies. Lastly, he seems to have hesitated on the brink of sacrifice. Lucian says that when the crowd shouted: 'Go on! What are you waiting for?' he 'went pale, trembled and fell silent'. It is clear, then, that the only purpose of his voluntary death was to perpetuate his memory, a result which his life, as he well knew, was not sufficient to achieve. Had he not explained this himself, it would still be obvious from the reply he gave his doctor on the occasion just referred to. When the doctor argued against supplying him with medicine, saying that, since death was knocking at the door, he should just let himself die, without bothering to build a funeral pyre, he replied that he was not going to accept an end which did not redound to his honour.

'I am sixty,' he reflected. 'I have achieved notoriety, but not fame. Now it is too late.

'The injustice lies not so much in my being inadequately appreciated—a good part of my life has been a failure, and I know it—as in the fact that so many of my inferiors are appreciated. Things for which I am reproached are forgiven them, or even admired in them. Everything I do (and yet, God knows, I have been active in the most different directions), is turned against me. And with what subtlety! Maliciousness is truly female.

'They have called my riches confusion, my pride fatuity, my sublimity bombast, my virtue hardness, my eloquence rhetoric, my profundity hermeticism, my staunchness stupidity, my frankness impudence; and when they do not know what fault to find with my behaviour, they say I am striking an attitude. What weapons have I to answer them with? Soldiers armed with slings are lucky, because they have their slings to retort with. I have no means of answering. I am imprisoned in other people's opinion of me, which is more paralysing than being encased in iron fetters. And according to that opinion, nothing I do is to be taken seriously.

'In fact, they are a lot of bastards. (Apart from those that admire me, of course. But even they are always mistaken in their admiration and are therefore just as irritating as the rest.)

'This being so, I spurn the baubles that men delight in. I am incorruptible! etc. I have a conscience! etc. I have turned down the *Légion d'honneur* a dozen times. What I mean is I have refused to entertain even the possibility of accepting it. As a matter of fact, they have never offered it to me because I have been had up once or twice on a serious charge.'

In these bitter reflections, Romanticism (which was already an old doctrine, its inception dating back to Adam and Eve) proved extremely useful to the philosopher. It allowed him to wrap himself nobly in solitude and contumely, whether real or imaginary, exaggerate them to his heart's content until, in the end, they appeared as congenial as success. The doctrine according to which our greatest troubles can be made to yield satisfaction (unfortunately it is powerless to help us against the minor ones, which consequently become the worst) deserves to be classed among the most glorious achievements of mankind. But at times when his excitement flagged, Peregrinos found himself deeper than ever in melancholy.

Then, suddenly, one day he had a brain-wave. It wasn't too late after all! If your life has been a failure, you can still make a success of your death. About your intelligence or your virtue, argument may go on for ever, but no one can withhold applause if you die for an idea. Only a little gesture is needed, and you are everlastingly in the right. Everything at once becomes perfectly easy. I remember a young soldier who was trying to get himself transferred from the auxiliary to the active forces in 1916, writing: 'I don't mind where they put me or how useless I am, provided I run a risk.' How many lives were given too generously and in vain during the war, because of the belief that death brings honour quicker than any talent, and because of the passionate desire to be thought well of which was current at the time! But life refuses to admit that death should be an excuse for not living, so that by now public opinion has reached the almost impious point of considering the *Saint-Cyriens* who went into battle wearing white gloves as being just so many idiots.

Peregrinos loved his life and yet he sacrificed it, because he loved himself even more than his life. He sacrificed his remaining years of pleasant living in order to win the praise of stupid humanity, praise, moreover, that he himself would never hear. I must say, I find this astonishing.

Can we say that such a passion, raising him above the failure of his life, lifts him to the level of greatness? Or is it ridiculous, especially in someone who professes detachment with regard to outward things? Should we envy him for still being so freshly resilient at his age, or pity him for being taken in by such an illusion?

For years I wooed fame. I despised the people who confer fame, but not fame itself. I realized the inconsistency and accepted it, because the men I most admired had accepted it too. But one night I had a dream. A pig with ass's ears and a snout dribbling with stupidity was placing a crown on my head. I snatched it violently away, thinking it was a mockery. Not at all; it was a laurel crown, the genuine badge of fame. From then on, I rejected both the gift and the giver.

Since I despise the fame that men award to talent, how could I fail to despise their esteem for character? Greatness which depends on men is not greatness. The thought that I am tensing my will merely to impress men takes the point out of the effort. I can no longer key myself up with the hope of an exemplary death. Why should I undergo stress and strain simply to please men? The idea is repellent and would incite me rather to cowardice.

Peregrinos, being encumbered by his personality, was revived by the thought of his death. When he announced that he would throw himself on to the pyre in four years' time, it was with the intention of living on his death during those four years and getting the benefit of it. And, I am sure, not only an enhancement of his reputation, but also an improvement in his soul. Sudden death is a blessing; but so is death long foreseen. It gives you time to reflect on important matters.

Being a highly imaginative man, he extracted from his decision a poetry as heady as wine. He changed his name from Proteus to Phoenix, in reference to the bird which throws itself into the fire when it grows old. 'He spread among the people ancient prophecies according to which he should be regarded as the tutelary spirit of night. He was clearly asking for altars to be raised to him and he hoped that a golden statue would be erected in his memory.' Already he was encouraging his disciples to build a temple on the site of his funeral pyre. Perhaps he foresaw the time when the inhabitants of Parium would set up statues which would act as oracles and perform wonders. He celebrated his own mysteries. He idolized both himself and his aberration. I feel the contagion passing to me. Let us all rave together. The soul cannot be put into a straitjacket. No poet will ever bring himself to reject religions completely. If his reason rejects them, his poetry will take them back again. How can he brand them as anathema when, in the most mysterious part of his being, he himself cherishes the dream of being worshipped? It is true that in this case the god is the only one who need not be a believer. For my part, to judge from the feelings inspired in me by the people who applaud me after a lecture, once I am changed into a Minotaur, my only urge is to devour my worshippers. The supply of adoring potential is thus promptly exhausted.

The old man was bothered by the thought of heroism. He had forgotten what the thirst for greatness that he now rediscovered within himself was like. When the music is loud and we are close to the orchestra, we want to build a palace or rape some weird creature or die for some cause or other. Once he had got himself worked up by the music he had unleashed within, he became intoxicated with the great dream of his death. But if later, in a quiet moment, he happened to drink a strawberry sherbet or something similar, he would weaken: 'Is it worth it? What a bore to have to kill oneself!' Which of us would not say the same? Often, too, he would sigh, with obvious weariness: 'Being judged! Always being judged!' Lucian says that he hoped to get away with a burn or two, and that he proposed to yield as soon as the crowd begged him to spare himself. May be. But these are eminently intentions that Lucian himself would have had. We are flabbergasted when we see the motives that people attribute to us and the weird, and always derogatory, interpretations they find for our behaviour. Between the public and us, *everything*, admiration as well as hatred, is based on misunderstanding.

On the eve of his death, according to Lucian, our hero 'who walked in the night', pronounced his own funeral oration. This would justify my use of the term Romanticism, if the sheer conception and arrangement of such an end did not suffice. There is no denying that dear old Peregrinos squeezed a lot of enjoyment out of his ashes! Charles V, who got a little thrill out of his funeral, Chateaubriand who started preparing fine phrases about his demise ten years before it occurred, Hugo who looked forward with delight to a pauper's hearse, Barrès who gave a heart-rending performance over his six feet of earth, all belong to the same group, and the leader of the band is a dead woman, that ravishing creature in stone on a column in the Musée de Céramique who is plucking a lyre above her tomb. Why should we give them a sour look? Death is not very funny. If there are people who are magnificently preposterous enough to put up a slight defence by means of a resonant phrase or a hint of *bravado*, then we should hail their effort as a victory by mankind.

'That's all very well,' it will be answered, 'but you still haven't made your Peregrinos out to be anything other than repellent and ridiculous.' Here we have the great complaint: he is not *likeable*. People do not want a man to have ability or even to be a character; they want him to be likeable. This is the trend of the age: be likeable, which means, be accommodating, fit in with shady little schemes, be a success. This is what public opinion wants, because it is dominated by women and women want only one thing—that men should appeal to them. This being so, everything which is above the ordinary or out of the ordinary is disapproved of, since it is the commonplace which appeals, because with it our judges feel at home: that is why geniuses are usually admired for their least original features, in which the crowd can recognize itself, and *in spite of* their originality. A young man who proposes to get married, a man who wants to be a member of Parliament, or an old man who wants to be Pope all follow the same policy: they draw in their horns and try to appear insignificant. Every outstanding man is an insult to society, and society will crush him, if he does not ask forgiveness for being what he is, and forgiveness will be granted only if he bows and scrapes. 'In France anything in the least like strong meat appears outrageous,' says Stendhal. And Goethe: 'Polite society, which is loath to tolerate any eminent man in its vicinity . . .' And Tolstoy: 'Sextus the Fifth's crutch must be the pilgrim's staff of every outstanding man.' On this point, there is unanimity.

As for what is simply out of the ordinary, it appears *ridiculous*, particularly in France, a petty-*bourgeois* country, which loves smallness and pettiness. Dante, Michel-Angelo, Shakespeare, Byron and Wagner were at first considered ridiculous in France, because they were 'peculiar', that is not petty-*bourgeois*. We call the seventeenth century *le grand siècle* because it emasculated everything it touched, classical antiquity as well as the Moorish epic. The conviction that an ideal translation is one in which anything powerful is systematically weakened and anything unusual reduced to ordinariness is only now beginning to die out. There is in each one of us, as there was behind Chateaubriand, a Fontanes,[1] whose function it is to bring

[1] Louis de Fontanes, 1757–1821, a friend of Chateaubriand and a member of the Académie Française.

into line anything exceptional in our feelings or behaviour. I asked someone what his or her reaction was to the death of Peregrinos and the only answer I got was: 'In very bad taste.' But all contact with mediocrities (even on grounds of art, observation, etc.) is a mistake: you are never quite the same after it. To engage in discussion with them is even worse. So I said to this person that I agreed at least about Peregrinos's bad taste in so far as his liking for the young Armenian was concerned. In Marseilles, little Armenian boys have a monopoly of the business of selling newspapers in the streets. Their enormous beaks and sallow complexions, their unsightly get-up and, above all, the moustaches and hairy-leggedness which disfigure them even in early childhood, explain the massacres by the Turks. I wanted to end so serious a digression by a pirouette that was also *in bad taste*. Grind your teeth, dear respectable friends.

Peregrinos gave his mortal life to posterity in order that posterity might confer immortal life upon him. Posterity took Peregrinos's life and has given nothing in return. That old fogey Lucian, and after him Voltaire and Renan and even the biographical dictionaries which provide us not only with the life-stories of prominent men but also the opinions it is thought fitting to entertain about them (which is shameful, the only function of a dictionary being to give us information), have merely supplied variations on the theme of 'the stupid old man'.

This is a dreary piece of confidence trickery. Naturally no protest is possible. There was only a propitiatory sacrifice to fate, and fate did not accept it. But even so! Anything that mediocrity does is approved of with revolting indulgence: 'He is so nice!' And there is not a soul, not a single soul, to admire Peregrinos's perfect burnt-offering! Death does not grant everyone a crown and how many hearses deserve the respectful salute we give them? There are men who remain little men even in death and it is they, we may be sure, who have tried to wrest from Peregrinos the second crown that death conferred upon him; the first had been the gift of hate.

His death has been called a farce, as if someone who sacrificed his life, for whatever cause, could ever be termed a mere joker. He is said to have shed tears when his ship was in danger of sinking and this has been held against him, as comic evidence of his lack of courage, whereas it would be more logical to suppose that if he were fond of life he would need all the more courage to give it up. People have even gone so far as to falsify the account of his death, which he wished to be an exemplary act, and have written that he 'uttered piercing cries'[1] as he died, a piece of base slander, totally unsupported by evidence. 'Laugh at all the crazy fellows you find admiring him' is Lucian's final word. Well, I shall count as one of the crazy fellows; normally, it is a good sign when people laugh at you. Besides we need have no fear in honouring Peregrinos's act; nowadays his kind of example will not prove contagious. And if the story is not a mere fable, if Peregrinos really existed, if he rushed to his death to achieve fame by force, and if the world has refused him fame and has rescued him from oblivion only to put him into the category of the grotesque, then this is a rather solemn moment; Iam giving him some faint shadow of the reward he though he was obtaining by the sacrifice of his life, but which has been refused him for eighteen hundred years. My denial weakens the verdict of eighteen hundred years! My feeble strength cleaves through time and reaches back to where a contemporary of Marcus Aurelius languishes in his limbo. I touch him in his centuries-old despair and raise him up again, justified.

We have seen that Peregrinos hesitated on the point of accomplishing his act. It is my belief that when he found himself faced with the crowd which included not only disciples and people who were genuinely moved, but also a great many Lucians, glowing with evil delight—both the sort who 'know not what they do' and the sort who know very well what they are doing—he realized that it had done him no good to give himself away, piece by piece, in speech and writing, no good at all to give himself away

---

[1] Descubes, *Dictionnaire biographique*, 1889. Lucian, the only writer who witnessed his death, merely says: 'As he said these words (O my Genii, etc.) he threw himself into the flames and disappeared.'

completely, body and soul, since, in that final hour, he was still insulted. He must have understood that the posthumous unanimity he was aiming at was even now beyond his grasp and that his death was a waste of effort. I imagine him on the verge of the fire, experiencing a second's astonishment, yes, naïve astonishment, such as only *ridiculous* individuals are capable of, on realizing that his enemies had not been disarmed in the slightest by all he had done, and then an uprush of horror, not so much at them as at himself, because, in the last resort, he had been vanquished. But this time it was too late, really too late. And so, shouting 'I abandon myself to my Genii', which is the cry of all those who throw themselves into the bosom of nature, or to the beasts or to God, in short, to anything other than man, he went through the fiery gates into the majesty of the void. This brings him still nearer to us because we, who can neither have faith nor do without greatness, muse on the implications of a voluntary death in the service of some cause that we do not believe in. True greatness is greatness that has no point, and will gain us no reward, either in this world or the next; a genuine fraud in which there is no deceit.

Neuilly 1921—Cadiz 1926
Aux Fontaines du désir, 1924

A JEW-BOY GOES TO WAR

WE WERE ENGAGED in rifle practice that morning in the spring of 1918 about a mile and a half behind the front, when we heard the elastic thudding of Ack-Ack fire, like the noise of huge goddesses at play in the sky and whacking a ball with their tambourines. We looked up. The plane, with ominous deliberation, was moving to and fro above as if it were travelling along an avenue in which every tree was the puff of a bursting shell. A few men slipped into the shade of a little wood near by, to prevent the group being spotted. The others stayed out in the open to watch.

'She's off!'

Having completed its mission, the plane put on speed in the direction of the German lines and the smoke wisps from the shells, which followed but could not catch up with it, provided it with a silver wake. The men came out from under their leafy screen and gazed after the glistening bumble-bee as it dwindled from sight. Suddenly, there was a whistling noise. Each man fell to the ground where he stood, swallowing up his shadow. The explosion rang out behind us. When I got up again, a javelin's throw away black smoke was rising amongst the trees.

For a minute or two, all was confusion. Since we were not defending any position, my instinct was to run as hard as I could away from the little wood which was no doubt going to be the target. But in the middle of the motionless, hesitant group, an individual will asserted itself. The lieutenant began to give orders as he made for the wood:

'Follow me. There are trenches here.'

What stupidity! I thought. He's leading us straight into the trap. He should have said: 'Scatter as quick as you can, wherever you like, but not in the wood.' However, while thinking this, I followed the others, partly through gregariousness but mainly through fear of embarrassment. 'I'd look fine if I were the only one to run like a hare! And yet, I'm not responsible to this officer. I don't belong to his platoon. I was just seconded here for rifle practice.' That is how bad reasons can defeat reason. When I reflect that I might have been killed that day through gregariousness and fear of embarrassment, neither of them characteristics with which I am over-supplied, I ask myself: 'How many other people did they kill?'

In the wood, we found several little trenches, each a few paces long—the so-called anti-artillery trenches, about two feet deep. We got into them.

'Spread out!'

Each man took up his position and stood waiting. But the lieutenant stayed out in the open. 'He would be like that!' I growled. 'He gets his men killed but he behaves like a hero.' And again I felt how tragic it was that we should have gone docilely, stupidly, to our appointment with death and should be settling in and waiting for the end. At the same time, I felt the greatness of this insipid-looking young man's act of will-power in quelling the soldiers' natural impulse, in forcing them to take the most difficult course, and in holding them to it.

The whistling approached again, getting louder and louder. My whole being contracted as I pressed against the earth in the little trench, my hands clutching my helmet, my shoulders hunched so as to protect the back of my neck under the flap, while I had the sensation that the broad expanse of my back and hips was already hurting as if the worst had happened, that my whole spine was exposed to the heavens, with nothing to protect it, and that all my flesh, that human flesh, so delicate and soft that a pin is enough to rend it, was perhaps going to be mangled in the next instant . . .

The shell burst, quite near. This time I saw it, I watched it. I saw God appear in the burning bush, a tall red flame between two yellow spurts of upflung earth. But I saw no smoke because, like a spring released, I was on my feet again. Everybody had leaped up.

Where was the officer? The overriding will-power had ceased to exist. The strong hand had relaxed its grip and, as a body, we fell apart. The men jumped out of the trenches and began to run. A voice could be heard saying: 'Wait, there's a wounded man here.' Another voice: 'There's a shelter ahead, to the right.' Still another: 'Stay here.' We did not know where to go, being ignorant of the lie of the land.

By now, we were advancing in single file further into the wood. And from one second to the next, we could feel the dwindling of the interval that separated us from the death about to fall and strike at random, perhaps to the right, perhaps to the left, perhaps in the place we were going to, perhaps in the one we had just left. It is an obscure, mysterious inspiration which guides you during such fateful moments, and you have nothing else to go by, since as a matter of fact there is no reason to do one thing rather than another. The other fellows began to scatter in various directions. Who would be the first to be killed? Suddenly I caught sight of the lieutenant. I realized the extent of the mistake he had made, and I was neither a child nor a booby. Yet I was drawn to him. I heard a voice prompting: 'He knows more than you do. He is the one to follow.'

He was the one I followed.

We came to a small trench and five of us got into it, including the officer. I glanced at my wrist-watch: 10.17; it was twelve minutes fast, so the correct time was 10.05; if the next shell killed me, I would have died on such-and-such a day at 10.06 or 7 in the morning. I looked up. In front of me I could see the lieutenant's back. He was standing with rounded shoulders and did not throw himself to the ground until the last moment. His leather shoulder-strap had slipped a little to one side revealing the part of the back of his uniform that it normally covered and where the blue cloth was not so faded as elsewhere. His hair had left a greasy mark on the top of his collar at the back. I saw this quite distinctly. Then everything was extinguished. Flat on the ground, screwing up my eyelids and still instinctively holding my helmet over the nape of my neck, I heard the horrible thing come down, straight down this time, straight on to the whole naked and exposed surface of my body. I was completely devoid of thought.

The explosion was very near. I felt a violent blow in the middle and the small of my back. I picked myself up, not knowing whether I was going to be able to stand or whether I would collapse; behind me there was a continuous howling; my sleeve and shoulder were bespattered with blood ... I got out of the trench and ran blindly forward.

At this point there is a gap in my recollections. Then I remember half turning back and seeing the lieutenant who had been in front of me in the trench, behind me now, upright, larger than life, looming like a ghost, red in the face, and howling; the sight was all the more hideous since it was an officer who was howling. Then the lieutenant was in front of me, being carried on someone's shoulders, and we were at the entrance of a pathetic kind of shelter. A man gave me a reproachful look because, on entering the shelter, I involuntarily bumped against the poor wretch who was being lugged in.

'Has anyone got his packet of bandages with him?' I hadn't mine, of course. I was soon outside the shelter again, because it was nothing but a miserable little hut. Another soldier, who came out at the same time as I did, said: 'Come this way.' I looked at him. He had a little blond moustache and a big Jewish nose. 'Do you know the wood?' I asked. 'Not at all.' Why, then, should I go after him, since he might lead me to a fatal spot? However, I went after him.

There followed an extraordinary scramble through the sun-flecked undergrowth. I had no idea where I was going. I followed the soldier with the Jewish nose and a third man was running along behind us. I leaped across ditches and plunged through bushes, holding up my revolver and my gas-mask case with both hands to prevent them banging against my sides. The monster gave its warning whistle and in a second I was flat on the ground, but my companion said: 'There's no danger. That one will fall short of us.' I believed him and raised my head and shoulders. The shell came down a long way behind us.

The three of us ran on through the wood, and my helmet was jumping up and down on my head. I took it off, and with a hand that was none too steady, I tightened the chin-strap. There was another whistle. Instinctively I shot my companion an inquiring glance. 'No, this one will fall ahead of us.' I did not bother to lower my head. The shell landed a long way off behind the lines. 'I was sure they would raise their sights,' he said. 'Let's go on.'

We had now reached the edge of the wood. Beyond us lay the road, camouflage, farmers working in the fields, the outskirts of the village and the whole, untouched countryside which was smiling, 'Land! Land!' We scrambled down a little slope and found ourselves at the edge of a field of tall wheat. We had almost won through to 'land' and to the whole future stretching ahead. Shells were bursting in the wood behind us. 'Let's run for it through the wheat field!' I shouted. But he answered, 'No, we'll crawl. Musn't give the others away.' We stooped down and advanced with long strides, half-hidden in the deep golden sea; after about ten yards, I stood up and ran for all I was worth; my companion did the same and beat me to the road. It was over.

We stopped, and he said, 'What about the lieutenant? And the other fellow who was wounded?'

I answered without hesitation, 'Yes, I know. The decent thing would be to go and fetch them. But it's too late now. It would be madness to go back in there, without knowing our way about. We would never find them.'

Shells were falling rhythmically on the hillock in the little wood. You could see the fine, flower-like, red and purple flame, and then the thick smoke, which was at first a light, cinder-blue against the dark background of the trees, then all of a sudden red, russet and progressively blacker when it was silhouetted against the sky, where it remained motionless for a long time before drifting off and melting away. The soldier with the Jewish nose was at a loss; I could feel he didn't want to go away. What was bothering him? Did he want to be quoted in dispatches or was he worried about 'the decent thing to do'? At that point, other men came out of the wood, slipped down the slope and crossed over the field. He put his hands to his mouth like a megaphone and called out twice: 'Do you need anybody?' For a moment, I wondered if he wasn't mainly interested in attracting attention to himself. As for the men, they heard perfectly well but they didn't even answer. He caught up with me and we walked towards the village.

'If I were a lieutenant,' I said, 'I would recommend you for promotion to the rank of corporal.'

'Why?'

'When we were on the run just now, you were in charge. When you said "This way", I followed and when you said "That one will land further on", I didn't take cover.'

'Oh!' he said. But he blushed. I saw him blush! And I felt the thrill of admiring him, of making him feel proud of himself and of humiliating myself to do him justice.

'What's your name?'

'Lepcigé.' (I write it as he pronounced it.)

There was a short silence.

'You're not Jewish, by any chance?'

'If you have any doubt about it, you can't have looked at me.'

'When were you called up?'

'Nineteen-eighteen.'

'Ah!'

I reflected that the man whose orders I had accepted was two years younger than I was. He didn't look it. With his colourless hair, his nondescript features, his short, pale little moustache and his huge nose, he was totally lacking in youthfulness. To tell the truth, he was frankly ugly. His fingernails were pretentiously pointed, and he had a thumb like a dressmaker's.

We had now reached the village and the village church. I nodded towards it.

'Excuse me. I'm going in there. I'll not be a minute.'

But 'Lepcigé' followed me and advanced towards the church. He stopped at the bottom step. For a second or two, there was some slight confusion. Then I put an end to it by saying 'I'll be back at once' and went in.

I went in. I felt no emotion, no uplifting of the soul; merely a sort of politeness. And I thanked the God of Battle who had made it possible for a relatively serious experience to remain always linked in my memory with a person whom I felt I could like.

Three men had been wounded in the little wood and one of them did not survive. The lieutenant died that same evening.

I said to myself, 'He was the one I chose as a guarantee of security.' I still saw what my last glance had seen ten seconds before the explosion: the mark left by the shoulder-strap on the back of the uniform, and the greasy stain left by the hair on the rim of the collar. 'One yard farther forward and I was the dead one.'

I reflected further: 'The private who was killed was killed because of the lieutenant. Anybody with common sense would have seen that we ought not to go into the wood, which was like a mousetrap, but instead scatter away from it in any direction. But I suppose the lieutenant would have felt himself to have been dishonoured. What price the theory that an officer must always have his men well in hand if—perish the thought—his men had run for it? And yet, if everybody had run for it and reassembled three hundred yards farther on or, better still, had found their way back to the village separately, they would all now be safe and sound.

'It is only fair, then, that the lieutenant should have been killed. He has paid for his stupidity. But he will be awarded the *Croix de Guerre*, posthumously, and will become the guardian angel of his family.

'And at the same time, he was a fine fellow; he had guts, more guts than any of us, more than I had. Brave, stupid, and guilty. How can you strike an average out of that?'

'I knew all this and yet he was the one I followed. But why? Because of his stripes? Even though I knew exactly what they were worth?'

'Everything is absurd and war more than anything else. No good trying to understand.'

II

When I find myself with a pen in my hand and a blank sheet of paper in front of me, I always have too much to say. And so it is with a surprise verging on amusement and an amusement verging on a smile that I ask myself, as I look at this sheet: 'Have I really enough material even for a short piece?' Yet for nine years[1] I have been saying to myself every now and again: I would rather like to have some record of it. Let us come to a decision. However slender may be the data in our memory, let us make our little story out of it, modestly. We shall have an opportunity to be richly copious some other time.

If a man like Maurice Leipziger happened to cross my path now (and it would no more occur to me to go and look for him than it did then), it would not take me long to realize that he was worth watching and might make the subject of an interesting book —perhaps a sort of counterpart to *Silbermann*. But at the age of twenty-two, I was only interested in myself and in the contemporaries of Pelopidas; perhaps I might sometimes stretch a point and go as far as AD 200. When I open the notebooks I kept during the war to jot down things that struck me, I find—as might well be expected—drawings of weapons, both for attack and defence. But these drawings, which are very detailed, represent the different varieties of Etruscan helmet, and the sword I described so carefully, giving each part its technical name, was the sword used by the Corcyreans during the Peloponnesian War. These are the things I was concerned with, as the bombs were falling. Scarcely a quarter of each of my wartime notebooks deals with the war. And there is not a single reference, direct or indirect, to Maurice Leipziger, although he made enough of an impression at the time for me to bring him out now from behind I don't know how many layers of shadow. Everything I say about him here has had to be drawn from my memory.

And precisely for this reason, I shall not say much. At this stage, I could talk about Leipziger with Jewish friends, question them

[1] Written in 1927.

about the Jewish people, and if need be, show them what I have written, when it is finished, and try to make a book out of it. I shall not do so. I remember a few remarks, a few scenes, and I shall put them down one after the other. In this account the reader should expect to find neither incidents nor plot and, least of all, a character study. If he does, he will be disappointed.

At the time I was attached to the Intelligence Officer of my regiment. I was stationed at L——, a mile and a half behind the lines; I slept in an Army hut, messed with the sergeants on the colonel's administrative staff, and made a daily trip along the front with the Intelligence Officer, carrying no equipment other than my cane, gas-mask, and revolver. I was also provided with a fantastic pass, according to which I was 'required, in the interests of duty, to move about the sector in all directions and at any time'; in other words, I enjoyed as much freedom as was possible for a private soldier in an infantry regiment at the front. I knew, of course, that this state of affairs would not last and that eventually a frown from a brass-hat would intimate that I was no longer *persona grata* and should go back to my place in the ranks.

The day after our fright, I had the pleasure of meeting 'Lepcigé', that is Maurice Leipziger, in the village. I had seen his name inscribed in copperplate on one of the lists prepared by the colonel's secretaries. Leipziger, native of Leipzig. He was obviously a German Jew. He had just been made one of the colonel's dispatch-riders—a temporary appointment, like mine. We took to each other at once.

I was rather weary of simple souls and, after only a week, had had enough of the non-com type in the mess at the colonel's headquarters. Although he hadn't had a secondary education, Leipziger was not uncultured, and he had a definite liking for culture. What he knew had been picked up from magazines; the authors he quoted were all popularizers; all his knowledge was second-hand. But whereas the ordinary half-baked type uses the language of the absolute, dear to the naïve, and glares with the fierce self-satisfaction of a cock on its midden, Leipziger had no pretentiousness whatsoever and was even more youthfully spontaneous than his years would have led one to expect; his laughter and gestures, for instance, were those of a very young man, who is working off through them what he cannot manage to express as he would like by means of language. At the same time, he never let it be forgotten that he had, as they say, a certain amount of book-learning. I don't know if it was through using his velocipede that he got ink on his fingers, but I know they were always ink-stained. I think he deliberately saw to it that they were.

When I was a boy, my parents wondered for a long time whether or not they should let me sit the *baccalauréat* examination. In their view, I think, it was not so much learning itself that was degrading as the fact of allowing their son to be 'examined' by strangers whose social origins were more than doubtful. Whatever the reason, they clearly had no great reverence for paper qualifications. This may be why, generally speaking, I disapprove of lower-class people who try to better themselves by passing examinations. And yet, as a matter of fact, whenever I meet one of them, I find the experience moving.

At headquarters, there was a distinguished 'cellist, who had won a first prize at the Conservatoire and had been put in charge of the regimental band. One day when I was saying that I felt so cut off from art in our rough, military life that I was never out of the museums during my periods of leave in Paris, he remarked in a jeering, contemptuous, almost insolent way: 'So that's how you spend your leave!' And he was a very talented artist. At the opposite end of the scale, when Leipziger arranged that we should meet during his twenty-fifth year so that he could prove to me that he had 'got somewhere', guess the place he chose for the assignment. In front of Rodin's statue of *The Thinker*! Naïve and cheap, if you like, but preferable to the gut-scraper's disdainfulness.

Another feature that brought me close to the young Jew was that he displayed what are called in French army dispatches *de beaux sentiments militaires* (magnificent fighting spirit). The war was in its fifth year and although everyone did his duty and on occasions more than his duty, I never heard anyone except Leipziger say: 'I'll not take my leave if the 23rd (his company) is going into action,' or 'I have rotten luck. I've always missed the really rough stuff.' And how well he described one of his fellow-soldiers, a married man of mature years, who had trembled in every limb when the colonel pinned the Military Medal to his tunic! You felt that he himself would have trembled in the same way. We were both at the same pitch of enthusiasm, neither of us having yet been seriously dashed by events. Labourers hired at the eleventh hour always flex their muscles ostentatiously. Could anything be more natural?

Leipziger's father was a trader in the Faubourg du Temple. I don't remember what he dealt in. But when Leipziger told me that his two brothers had been killed in the war, I was deeply moved. In every letter I wrote to members of my family, I explained that I had become friendly with a young Jew who was very Jewish, and who had lost two brothers in the war. In our part of society, people were convinced that no Jew was ever killed except in Barrès's articles, and it was held against Barrès that he had devoted an article to the part played by the Jews in the fighting; someone had obviously pulled the wool over his eyes. As regards the physical courage of the Jews, I have no opinion. The usual thing is to cast doubts on it, and I don't know whether or not this is right. A Frenchman who was in Russia at the beginning of the Revolution has told me that he was impressed by the bravery displayed in street fighting by Jewish mensheviks, who showed themselves to be pluckier than their Russian opponents. Whatever the truth of the matter, in 1918 I held the accepted ideas and tended to think that military gallantry was not a Jewish virtue.

At L——, whenever Leipziger and I were free, we met and went for walks together; we were inseparable. Yet I knew that it was only through lack of other resources that I took pleasure in his company and that once we were separated by the accidents of war, we would cease to exist for each other.

When, at the beginning of our friendship, he heard me pronouncing his name in the German fashion, *Lyptziguer,* he asked me to give it the French pronunciation 'like everyone else'. I wanted to settle for a compromise: *Lepzijhair*; but he corrected me again: *Lepsijhay*. This was further than I could go, but since I sensed that he felt strongly about it, I got out of the difficulty by taking care not to pronounce his name in his hearing.

One morning, when I was going into the trenches with Lieutenant G——, the Intelligence Officer, he suddenly said to me:

'That little Yid's got hold of you, and no mistake!'

When I protested, he went on:

'I tell you. He saw straight away that amongst all the privates you were the one who could be most useful to him after the war, and perhaps even now.'

I protested again.

'He's a pushing little blighter, always putting himself forward. But what can you expect, he's like the rest of them.'

'But he likes fighting. It sticks out a mile!'

'Who told you?'

'He did.'

'Oh, you know, when people's loyalty is not above suspicion, they make more show of it. On the Fourteenth of July in Algiers you only have to look at the houses to see which flats are occupied by Jews. They're the only ones with the flag out. What's more, Leipziger knows what your attitude is, and he pretends to share it to get on the right side of you. But he's another sharp-nosed one . . .'

'You mean he's clever?'

'Yes, there's that to it as well. But I was thinking of rats. You know how they desert a sinking ship . . .'

That evening I asked some of the other men in Leipziger's company about his behaviour under fire. They said that he had arrived too recently to have taken part in an attack but that, from what they had seen of him, he was 'like everybody else'. They immediately spoiled the effect of this compliment by making it clear that no one was prepared to trust him. 'But why not?' —'Don't you see, he's the sort that always gets a cushy job?' I think they had a vague notion that it wasn't *normal* for a Jew to be in the trenches with them. How did he come to be there? There must have been some mistake. One of these days he would slip off. They didn't seem shocked by the prospect, no doubt because they had never considered him as one of themselves. For Leipziger to go back to civilian, or half-civilian, life was just as legitimate as for a swan to return to its lake or a bird to soar off into the sky.

Shortly afterwards, Leipziger welcomed me with the genial, smiling face that he turned on every new arrival and which made me wonder sometimes if it wasn't just the professional smile of the floor-walker: 'Anything else, Madam?' And seeing him smile at me and reflecting that he must think my attitude towards him unchanged, whereas it was no longer quite the same after the lieutenant's remarks, I felt a twinge of remorse.

Men returning from leave were coming towards us along the road. Leipziger started off in their direction, just like a little dog that goes quivering up to strangers to make a show of friendliness. And he called out to them:

'Hi, lads! I'll show you where your new quarters are, if you like.'

'Go on. We don't need any help from you.'

The scene was like a little drop of 'Leipziger' essence. There was a slight affectation, perhaps, in his use of the word 'lads'; it didn't ring quite true; he sounded rather like a middle-class man being self-consciously 'pally' with the workers. But their heartless reply made me feel sorry for him.

'Why do you put yourself forward like that? Can't you just leave them alone?'

'But I wasn't putting myself forward! They can't know where their quarters are, because they've been changed while they were away . . .'

And so the young Jew was snubbed on all sides for trying to do somebody a good turn. And I was beginning to be influenced. 'Putting oneself forward' wasn't my expression. I had got it from the lieutenant.

Some of the other fellows spoke unfavourably of him.

'Once when we were coming back from leave, there were two

of us with him. We were trying to get put up for the night at a farm. At the first one, they wouldn't have us. At the second one, the man would have taken us, but the wife was against it, even though we offered to pay them for their trouble. At the third one, Leipziger rang the bell at the gate and when the farmer's wife opened the house door, he bellowed at the top of his voice:

"Missus, we've got some money for you!" It sounded pretty awful, I can tell you. We didn't know where to look.'

'But what happened? Did she take you in?'

'Yes, she did. But to blurt out straight away, "Missus, we've got some money for you!", that's no way to behave.'

No doubt, yet it is something to get results.

In Tunis (where I am writing this), I usually have my meals in a restaurant where there are three waiters: a Frenchman, an Italian and a Jew. The Frenchman and the Italian have nothing remarkable about them except that, like all waiters, they spoil your appetite by waving their filthy hands about under your nose. The Jew is different. The first time I said 'Thank you' to him and heard him reply 'At your service', I felt a sudden rush of pleasure at having at last come across somebody polite. The second time he said 'At your service', the pleasure was, naturally, less keen; it was no longer a surprise. The third time I suppose I hardly noticed it. On the fourth occasion, I felt a definite irritation, and by the fifth time, I decided to put an end once and for all to his 'At your services' by never saying 'Thank you' again.

The Leipziger story is not unlike that.

III

About that time, there was a sudden reshuffle. Somebody had obviously prejudiced the colonel against Leipziger, who was sent back to the trenches. The lieutenant and I would, in the course of our duties, sometimes spend the night there, and if I were free after the evening meal, I would go along to see Leipziger.

I remember those occasions with pleasure, as being my most idyllic wartime experiences. I feel an urge to indulge in a little description.

The trenches looked like deep-set, little roads and there was always a thick cloud of yellow dust hanging in the bottom like mist in a valley. On all sides were broad vistas of slopes, with other trenches and earthworks and bare, mutilated tree-trunks and a peppering of shell-holes like the marks left by smallpox on a human face. At rare intervals, little groups of men with yellow covers over their helmets were camping like gipsies in the dunes, or perhaps one of them, waist-deep in a shell-hole, might be taken for a shipwrecked sailor adrift in the vast rippling of earth and stone. The blind sun, the sharpness of the shadows, the brownish-yellow ridges set against the sky, all gave an impression of irrevocability. We lived only in the hope of change and the setting was symbolic of eternity.

Soon the air would become absolutely translucent and of so delicate a quality that the men, even, seemed sensitive to it; at first it was copper-coloured and then shaded into that lacquered pink that one morning in the Camargue I mistook for the first signs of dawn when it was, in fact, a flock of flamingoes. On the rim of the broad basin and blocking the horizon to our left, a steep slope rose up in a sheer wall. During the day-time, it was bathed in its own blue shadow, but the setting sun caught it for an hour. During that hour, it gleamed on the threshold of night, like a life that achieves happiness only on the verge of extinction.

Three or four times, in the heart of the featureless silence, a long bow would be drawn across the taut string of light and, in the distance, a puff of white smoke would spurt from the ground, suggesting—in a context so reminiscent of a gently surging sea—the sudden uprush of a shower of spray. Another, then another and several more would break with wave-like regularity. Then silence would flow back into place again, and flood the sky to its utmost depths.

Nothing further would disturb the dying day. The soldiers' idleness took on a sort of grandeur. As darkness began to fill the hollow, the meanest objects would be strangely illuminated; the corrugated-iron roof of a shelter, a cartridge-case, a bully-beef tin that had been tossed on to the earth-wall, or an oversize helmet above a thin, child-like face, would glisten as if they had collected all the last remnants of light left here below. The sound of a voice a long way off would ring out as if it were quite near, within the great crystal sphere, and it, too, would seem to be a mysterious expression of light. Sometimes, from the far side of the wall, which was another world, would come the slow, very slow, throbbing of a motor-cycle. We could picture the side-car carrying a wounded, perhaps a dying man, moving off very slowly behind the lines; we could imagine the motionless body, as stiff as a plank, swathed to the chin in blankets, like a life-size puppet and with a peony of blood at its mouth.

Shortly afterwards, the Americans took over the sector; it was like the sudden watering of parched earth. One day, three horsemen appeared in the village: a French captain, an American captain and, between them, 'booted and spurred, such a radiant bird', Private Leipziger! He was being as dashing as he could manage, but wasn't quite up to the mark; you can only show off properly on horseback if you have a long heredity behind you.

Leipziger had got out of the trenches again—Leipziger was speaking English—Leipziger was on horseback, looking down on everybody (he couldn't help that)—Leipziger was in riding-boots and spurs (where had he got them?)—Leipziger was an interpreter and, as such, close to the officers and on familiar terms with them.... A surge of resentment swirled through the village. The men tried to set me against him.

'He doesn't know a word of English. You know English, but if you'd offered to be an interpreter, they would have told you to clear off. He knows nothing, but he's a Jew, so he gets the job.'

I didn't see Leipziger until the next day and first of all congratulated him on his skill as a horseman.

'Where did you learn to prance like that? In the Faubourg du Temple?'

'This is the first time in my life I've been on a horse!'

'You mean, the very first?'

'Cross my heart!'

I admired him. Not many young city-dwellers who have never

been in the saddle would suddenly jump on to a horse one day and ride gaily off. And in this case, he was a private accompanying two captains, and was running the risk not only of appearing clumsy or falling off—not to mention the danger of shell-fire—but also the possibility of being put to shame through proving inadequate as an interpreter; and all this in an atmosphere of watchful hostility.

But I was struck by something quite different. Leipziger *faisait un nez*,[1] which, in his case, amounted to one of nature's curiosities: as if his appearance had been altered by an optical illusion, he seemed to have some twenty centimetres of nose hanging between his cheeks. He explained what had happened:

'Anyway, it's all over. Sacked from the colonel's staff after a week. Sacked as an interpreter after two days. The captain told me that I didn't know English well enough. Would you like to test me?'

We talked together in English. He knew the language perfectly.

'It was Hulot (a sergeant) who put the idea into the captain's head. He told him, in so many words, that I wasn't intelligent enough to be an interpreter. I replied: "That's not true, sir. I'm educated. I was in business with my father. Question me about my job, and you'll see whether I am intelligent or not."'

'What did he say?'

'He said: "Sit at that table and draw up a —— (the author has to leave a blank here, because he knows nothing about these things; let's say it was a contract between X and the army for the supply of certain commodities, or something of that sort). And don't go out of the room, eh!" I drew up the document. Then he said: "Now write me —— (another document of the same sort)." I did so. He read it and said: "I never said you weren't intelligent enough to be an interpreter. But I can't keep you in the job, because it's causing a lot of ill-feeling."

'The captain isn't a bad sort. He must have seen that I was hurt, because he called me back and said: "You wouldn't be any better off as an interpreter. On the contrary, you'd be more exposed. If you want to serve with distinction, do so in the ranks. Surely it's not difficult to be like everybody else!"

[1] 'Was making a nose', i.e. 'was down in the mouth'.

'Do you know who they've made interpreter? Blancoud!'

Blancoud was an elementary schoolteacher and a clerk in the colonel's office. I have nothing to say against him, but you only had to look at him to see that he didn't know English.

'It's no good,' Leipziger concluded, 'they don't like intellectuals.' I had been impressed by his story. The persecution of a righteous man is a serious matter. But his last remark irritated me. I was depressed to see that he really thought himself an intellectual. On another occasion, he had said to me: 'When I was in training camp, I lost all my personality.' He also thought he had a personality! Incidentally, there are lots of people who aren't Jews and who think they have personalities. 'Develop your personality' is the advice contained in little booklets which explain how you can become a man for six hundred and eleven francs a year.

Leipziger refrained from any acrimonious remarks against the captain. I had already noticed that he never spoke of the officers except with sympathy and respect, even when it seemed to me that he had reason to complain of their attitude, and that had been one of the things that made me warm to him.

'So,' I said, when we parted, 'you came away on good terms with the captain?'

'Of course. I sold him my riding-boots.'

What an anticlimax! The matter had ended in a business deal! With Leipziger, you never knew whether you ought to admire him, respect him (with some feelings of friendship) or keep your distance.

The next morning, before going back into the trenches, he came to say good-bye. He had a box of *Camels* under his arm. It was the beginning of the period of *Camel* preponderancy, which was such an important phase of the war.

To begin with, he offered me one. It was his habit, when he took a cigarette out of the packet, to tap it on his match-box to shake down the tobacco, with a gesture that seemed to me supremely pretentious, and each time I was pained, because I had been taught that this *was not done*. But on this occasion it was disastrous. Leipziger took from his pocket a small bottle of perfume, such as I have seen since in shops in Tunis, and scented the end of his cigarette. What a tarty thing to do! Talk about Oriental luxury! It was as if the Tiber were looking at the Orontes, Cato of Utica (yes, Cato of Utica, no less) at Ben Hur!

When, after putting two packets of *Camels* in his pockets, Leipziger handed me the box, which was still three-quarters full, saying 'Here you are', I asked without a moment's hesitation, 'How much?' 'What do you mean?' he said, 'I'm giving them to you!'

He went, leaving me with mixed feelings. How kind, how thoughtful he had been! 'Yes, but it may be a case of giving a penny to get a pound...' Another remark of his had displeased me and put me on my guard: 'At first, I was really scared of you.' This was a piece of gross, *greasy*, sticky, flattery. And yet, he was obviously preferable to everybody else.

It was to describe my uncertainty about him, my self-questionings, my half-hearted feelings of friendship, that I began writing this account. Was Leipziger a brave man or was he trying to avoid danger? Was his affability the sign of a good, or of a calculating, nature? I was as unsure of his quality as the non-expert is of the value of a piece of porcelain: it may be worth several guineas or only five bob.

'But surely,' it will be objected, 'some things are clear to the naked eye! We thought you were more of psychologist than that.' I can only answer that I am a writer, a novelist and, like all of them, a psychologist on paper and blind in actual living.

One thing was missing from our friendship. We had never scrambled painfully together along the sandbag wall (the papers called it 'leaping out of the trench'); we had never gone forward together behind an artillery barrage, with bullets gurgling around us and shells landing like so many tons of bricks, amid the female screams and terrible bleatings of the freshly killed; never gone forward side by side, or a few yards apart, unhurriedly, as if we were at a beat, with the appalling calm of someone who has been told to jump from a boat and walk on the sea, and who then realizes that he is actually walking on the sea: for, to go from our trenches to the trenches opposite on the shifting surface of the shell-shaken earth, with its suddenly spouting waves, was exactly that; it was walking on the sea. If Leipziger and I had done this once together, I would have known. 'Known what?' How he behaved under fire, and that would have satisfied me. Whether or not he wanted to get something out of me did not really worry me much. But what I *needed* to know was how he behaved under fire. This would have allowed me to make up my mind about my feelings towards him. Since the war I have occasionally come across men whom I had seen behaving well under fire. Whatever they might do against me, I would never do anything against them.

IV

Wounded. Fini the war! A delightful evacuation. The staring eyes of dazed men in stations at night, among red glintings. A station where English ladies offered me a sandwich and three *Three Castles*, that I took as a pauper accepts a piece of bread; it's no good, you can't behave like Mucius Scaevola all day and every day; there's a time for everything. In hospital: for the first and last time in my life, I was looked upon as a deserving character. Compliments from my family: how sunburnt you are! What a broad chest! Being at the front is a real fresh-air cure! One day in Paris, playing truant, with the feelings Protesilas must have had when, after death, he was allowed to come back on to earth for a few hours before going down into Hades again. Inability to resist buying a small, very expensive antique, as if spending were a victory (during the seven months in the trenches, there had been no possibility of spending). The look of mingled pity and love that a woman gave me when she heard me say to the taxi-driver: 'Gare de l'Est.' And then, clippety-clop all the way round France to catch up with the regiment. Towns empty of Frenchmen and full of Italian workmen and American cavalry (with the sound of horses' hooves clattering on wooden bridges). Pont-Sainte-Maxence, a Roman name I am very fond of, and where the church contains a *schiacciato* angel, that looks like a Victory. Frenchmen and Americans in the stations shooting at each other with their revolvers. Toul cathedral in the rising sun, pink and yellow like the Parthenon and with its base hidden in the mists from the Moselle, so that it looked as if it were floating in mid-air; and if the sight doesn't make you believe in God, I don't know what will. 'So you've come to join your regiment in Argonne! Well, it's in Belgium.'—'Where?'—'Who knows? Dismiss!'

The smell of Belgium. Each wartime memory has its smell. The Forest of Villers-Cotterêts with the moving smell of rich earth freshly dug during the making of shelters. Valmy smelt of rust (why, Heaven alone knows). In the Vosges, the sky was a solid mass of trees, of magic murmurings accompanied by a delicious pine smell. Noyon smelt only of blood, that is of sugar and flowers. And in each sector there was a typical wartime smell, the smell of the dawn that we are unaware of in our civilized lives. The smell of Belgium was the sweetish smell of fair, oily skins, mixed with the smell of tobacco. For anyone coming from France, Belgium was also a sky full of Englishmen. So there were other planes besides the German ones!

And suddenly there was Leipziger. To get him to myself, I said:
'Should we go to the Social Club?'
'Yes.'
Why was it that, by this decision to do the same, very simple, thing together, we seemed to be proving straight away to each other that we were in fundamental agreement?

Yet we had not seen each other for two months, and I had no more written to him than he had written to me, although he must have known about my being wounded. These sudden separations are one of the good features of war. We would feel attracted to someone and the turntable at a junction, like the wheel of fate, would save the friendship the bother of beginning, that is of going sour one day, and would leave us with only the memory of a happy meeting. If the friendship did begin, the accident of a switch or a death, causing separation, proved in any amount of cases how easy it is to do without even the people we find most likeable. Hence a constant cleansing of the soul which remained free of the sentimental mould that grows during the idleness, and dangerous freedom, of peacetime.

I knew that the regiment had had a rough passage and I asked Leipziger how he had got on. He said he hadn't taken part in the attacks because he happened to be in hospital with flu. The lieutenant's remark leaped back into my mind: the rats that desert a sinking ship . . .

Partly crippled by my wound and feeling that I would never be much use again in the infantry (I was about to apply for a post with the Americans), I no longer had that keenness for the war that I had been so happy to share with Leipziger only two months before. But he, too, as it happened, seemed to have changed, to be more depressed. When an Underground ticket I had stuck in my tunic pocket during my day in Paris fell out by accident, it caused a film of melancholy to come over his eyes (and, it must be admitted, with good reason). England being the order of the day, since we were in contact with the English, he quoted Stevenson:

> Give us grace and strength to forbear and persevere.
> Deliver us from mean hopes and cheap pleasures.

He sang that extraordinary English soldiers' lament which, so far as I know, had no counterpart in the French army:

> I don't want to go to the trenches no more,
> Where —— and whizz-bangs are galore.
> Take me over the sea where the Allemand can't get at me.
> Oh God, I don't want to die!
> I want to go home.

So unequivocal a lament, by crystallizing too clearly the feeling it expressed, must have tended to strengthen it.

As we were going through an area exposed to shellfire, I said that we would be wise to bear a little to the left, but he answered: 'Oh, you know, if we have to die . . .' and carried on. I did so too.

Now, as I am writing this, I remember the lieutenant's other remark: 'He pretends to share your feelings, to get on the right side of you,' and I wonder if Leipziger, seeing a change in me, had not toned down his 'magnificent fighting spirit' to be able to go on responding to my mood.

The Englishmen in our vicinity were mainly officers. We both had a fondness for Englishmen of this kind; Leipziger because he hoped that by rubbing up against them he would learn something and broaden his mind; I because they kept themselves to themselves and only liked what was of good quality. After two years of French unbuttonedness and three months with the Americans, I had had my fill of democracy, and was pleased to see people who knew how to behave.

Leipziger was so struck with the English that he said an astounding thing to me. He told me that, all things being equal, he felt safer with them than with the French. He went even further: 'When I see the lists of the dead in their newspapers, I say to myself: "So they get killed too!"' Such was the effect of placid pipe-smoking, sleek-bellied horses and carefully tended leather on a young fellow who was in a subordinate position but could sense and respect higher things. Perhaps he also felt, unconsciously, that people sustained by a powerful tradition do not die.

For my part, whether or not contact with the English was a guarantee of immortality, I should not have liked to fight in the war, except in the thick of my own clan; it seems to me that I would have got no benefit from the war if I had spent it rubbing shoulders with foreigners. What possible communion can you have with them? Yet, if there is another war, I should like to serve three-quarters of the time with the French and one quarter with the English (always supposing—it is a delightful dream—that the English are with us in the next war). Curiosity is not one of my strong points, but I confess I am curious to see those strange specimens of humanity at grips with high tragedy. How on earth do they behave in such circumstances?

Leipziger made another remark on a deeper level than his usual pronouncements. We were watching the English cavalrymen coming back from watering their horses, 'baited like eagles having lately bathed', their legs dangling like those of the horsemen on the Parthenon. Leipziger stared intently at some of them, as one might stare at people one never expected to see again, and said: 'I'm choosing the ones I'd like to save from death.' There was nothing vulgar about such a sentiment.

Just as, in the French sectors, a motor-cyclist never stopped near him but he entered into conversation in order to get a free lesson in mechanical engineering, so in the new sector he took advantage of any Englishman to improve his knowledge of the language, learn technical terms and collect information on any and every subject. He wormed his way into their society with a self-confidence which, in his case, was spontaneous and not at all like the simulated self-confidence shown by very young French officers, subalterns for instance, who were inclined to stand on their dignity. Leipziger never tired, either, of being helpful, and it was clear to me now that he was not disinterested. He might, on occasion, have been swayed by sordid motives, but I could see that most of the time his aim was a very legitimate one: he was always eager to see, know and assimilate something new. He was so active and busy that he reminded me of the habit the Moroccans had before 1912 of forcing any Jew they met in the streets to dance for them, holding his skull-cap between his teeth, under pain of a good drubbing: among these apathetic Englishmen, Leipziger danced just like a mellah Jew. Together we were a remarkable sight, because I remained stiffly incurious, as distant as a polar ice-field, and for that reason well equipped—much better than he was, in fact—to get on with the English gentlemen in the sector. But how do two stiff gentlemen ever establish contact? I think that if I had been thrown up on Mr Crusoe's desert island, Mr Crusoe and I would have gone on for years crossing to opposite sides of the street whenever we met, each of us making it a point of honour not to be the first to address the other.

Here is another detail to show that we did not speak the same language. One day Leipziger told me that someone in the company was spreading the rumour that I was an ex-officer reduced to the ranks. They couldn't understand why I was only a private and, since I didn't want to look as if I were showing off, I gave no explanation. The reason was that, to become an officer, I should have had to spend some time in a training-camp and I did not want to leave the firing-line, since I was living under the 'threat' that the war might end without my having seen enough of it. (Moreover, I was pleased to share the men's lives and had no desire to be in a position of command, which would have cut me off from them.) And so I found myself rather in the position of those *ancien régime* officers who served in the ranks in the Princes' Army in 1792. The story retailed by Leipziger annoyed me, as might be expected, and I showed my annoyance. But Leipziger was surprised: 'The other fellows take you for an officer and you're vexed?' In the offensive invention, 'an officer reduced to the ranks', all I saw was the phrase 'reduced to the ranks'. All he saw was the word 'officer', and it made him gape with admiration.

The regiment moved into still another sector. My memory contains a vision of us marching through a ruined and abandoned town behind the tempestuous music of a band, and watched by two dazed old women, the only witnesses of our triumph. I see a village where we were received as heroes in the evening, and that we left in the middle of the night without anyone taking any further notice of us or a light appearing in a single window, and I remember the melancholy look in Leipziger's eyes, as if he were wondering what we had done to fall from favour between nine in the evening and two in the morning. And long, terrible marches, which perhaps were only terrible for me because I had a gammy leg and also because all that sort of thing had lost interest for me, now that I had been crossed off the fighting list.

There were no longer, as in France, little boys to carry your gun (I still remember the one who said to me: 'I take three steps when you take one', and said it with pride because it is very true that, in a democracy, there is more to be proud of in three than in one). But Leipziger was there with his constant cordiality. He relieved me of part of my kit and got it carried in cars, as if it were his own, because I wouldn't *ask*. He would pick up and bring me veined stones that could be found on the roadside, because I had said that they looked like ancient marble and, in the midst of our wretchedness, provided both a memory and a foretaste of the good life.

(During one of those moments of profound melancholy and solitude such as we all experienced during the war, I remember seeing a Strasbourg porcelain plate hanging on a café wall and suddenly losing my feeling of loneliness. For a second or two, I dreamt of buying it and carrying it in my knapsack. I had a feeling that it would protect me.) When we came to a stopping-place, he would go on ahead to get me a good billet. I could have had anything that was in his possession; I had only to say the word. I wonder if the reader understands the nature of the emotion such gestures aroused in me, coming as they did from someone of whom I was still not sure. I had deciphered the meaning of his advances to the Englishmen: he always expected to get something out of them. Were the advances he made to me of the same kind? Yet since he had got to know me, he had had time to find out exactly what I could, or could not, would, or would not, give. Was it possible he thought that by being a little more obliging, he would strengthen his hold on me?

We stopped in a village and I would often take a book and go and sit by myself on the outskirts. Several times I noticed Leipziger doing the same thing and I respected his solitude. I have never seen any soldiers, except Germans and Russians belonging to the Foreign Legion, go off on their own like that, with or without a book: Frenchmen, alas, are *sociable*. Leipziger's desire to escape in this way could be explained by a certain delicacy of soul, but I am also inclined to think it was a consequence of his non-French blood.

We set off again, this time *en 'dur'*,[1] to use the dear old wartime term. Since we were among the first to enter the compartment, Leipziger settled himself and, pointing to the other empty seats, cried: 'Hurry up, stake your claim!' I was, of course, preparing to take a seat very quickly. 'Stake your claim' froze me in my tracks. Leipziger shouted again more loudly and then again, and his noisy, insistent, impatient repetition of the words disgusted me so much that even if a bushel of pearls had been scattered on the floor, I would not have lifted a finger to take advantage of the situation.

[1] 'On the hard', i.e. in a train with wooden seats.

When everbody had got wedged in, I went and sat on my kit in the corridor. For a long time, I saw his gaze gravely fixed on me, beautiful in its gravity and in its innocence, because it showed so naïvely that he was trying to understand and was not succeeding.

I thought I had taught him a lesson. An hour or so later, he taught me one.

Night was falling and the carriages were unlit. We passed grounded balloons, looking like monstrous slugs or like great black warts on the face of the earth; ruined villages; churches of which only the centre parts survived, since artillery fire had raked them from all sides and removed all the frills; churches gnawed away like things that have lain a long time on the sea-bed; gnawed away, in fact, like village churches swallowed up by the sea. Leipziger had changed places and sat with his back to me (who knows? perhaps to show that he was offended), and I could see only the top of his cap above the partition against which he was leaning. But suddenly I heard his voice that had been silent for a long time. He was reciting:

> *Dans le vieux parc solitaire et glacé,*
> *Deux ombres ont évoqué le passé.*

Often, during our walks together, he had begun to recite Lamartine or Musset in this way. I would immediately start imitating a dog howling at the moon, the squalling of love-lorn cats, etc., until he stopped. I can't stand people who think there is poetry in alexandrines, because they have been taught that there should be, and who laugh at the finest poetry when it occurs in real life. But that evening, while the Jew was reciting Verlaine to loud-mouthed little Frenchmen and gradually forcing them to listen quietly—all this in semi-darkness, among the ruins, and as we were on our way to offer ourselves, one and all, to death—I didn't imitate a tom-cat on the tiles; I was on his side.

I am writing this account unemotionally; otherwise, I would use a less simple style. The scene, highly coloured as it was, yet worthy of respect, would lend itself to a purple passage for quotation in anthologies, but I shall not resort to artifice in describing it. It lasted fully ten minutes, which is a long time. The fable does not say how long Orpheus was able to charm the wild beasts; I think that after ten minutes they must have gone back to their usual pursuits. I shall only explain what the lesson was that Leipziger taught me: to take the plunge and recite poetry to these uncouth soldiers so that they listened to it as if they were moved by it, needed the same confidence as he had shown in jumping on to the horse or button-holing English officers, and he took the plunge, whereas I would have remained on the edge, through fear of ridicule or failure. In all respects, he had more faith than I had: more faith in himself and more faith in mankind.

The Verlaine recitation ended badly, in my opinion at least. When Verlaine had been exhausted, a typically Jewish fit came over Leipziger; he went into raptures about Wilson: 'He's not a man, he's a God' [sic].

The next day we stopped somewhere and I was separated from Leipziger. And in the evening we took the train again, but this time we were in cattle-trucks.

I was in the same truck as Leipziger. When darkness came on, the men settled down on the floor to sleep and began arranging themselves like the interlocking pieces of a jig-saw puzzle. Leipziger, when he lay down, squeezed himself to one side and signalled to me with a look that he had made a place for me. I imagined the innocent pleasure it would give him if I lay there and, instead, went and slept at the other end of the truck.

The next morning when we got to our destination, we were disbanded just before dawn, in that pre-dawn cold which goes so well with the bitter taste in the mouth at that ungodly hour. He joined his company and I joined mine. Did we speak to each other that morning? Did we say good-bye? I haven't the faintest recollection. I think we didn't and that the journey ended in din and confusion.

Nor can I remember in what circumstances or from whom I learnt the bare fact that he had been killed ten days or so later. Since I can find in my memory no trace of any emotion caused by the news, I suppose I felt none. I must have made it plain by now that I had no feelings of friendship for him.

Even so, the first time I went on leave, I called at his house in the Faubourg du Temple. The concierge confirmed the fact that his two brothers had been killed and told me that the father, broken-hearted at the loss of his three sons, had recently died too. Leipziger's only surviving relatives were his mother and sister, who happened to be out that day.

'Poor Mr Moses! He was always so nice to everybody!'

'Mr Moses . . . ?'

'Maybe you only knew him as Maurice. That's what he used to be called. It sounded better for the people here. But his real name was Moses.'

Four years went by. I had been demobbed. Undoubtedly the feelings Moses Leipziger had aroused in me were not feelings of friendship. But the very uncertainty of my interest in him gave that interest a tremulous quality, so that it persisted like friendship. It seemed to me now that I could have asked him frankly about many things I had not even touched on in our conversations together. I would have said to him: 'I know what I'm fighting for: a fuller and nobler life. But how can you fight for a nation and a race you don't belong to? You bear the name of a German town; what are your feelings towards the Germans? What exactly are you up to?' Now I would no doubt understand that he could want to be both in the firing-line and out of harm's way, that he could be helpful by nature and helfpul through an ulterior motive, and that his courage and his helpfulness, although they might as a result appear less impressive, were still valuable qualities, deserving of respect; I would no doubt understand that there were times when he would have sacrificed his life for mine and other times when he would have left me to shift for myself, and that this in itself was something. But all these truths had been obscured for me by the stupidity of youth: twenty is an age at which you understand nothing at all. It appears that some people are sorry to be no longer twenty. If so, they are people who don't mind being unintelligent. I blush for what I was at twenty. When I realize what I was like between seventeen and twenty-seven, that is during the years that are referred to, I think, as youth, I wish I could spit on my former self.

One day in 1923, I went back to the Faubourg du Temple. I had not been curious about Leipziger when he was alive, but I was now that he was dead. I wanted to talk and ask questions about him. To think that I hadn't a single photograph of him, whereas I had so many of other wartime comrades who didn't interest me in the least! To think that I didn't even know what his handwriting was like! (When I reproached myself with having treated him rather harshly, I would remember that he had not written to me during the two months we were apart, and his indifference would dull my remorse. But at the same time, I would say to myself: 'If he had been cultivating my friendship only for what he could get out of it, he would have written to me . . .')

Mme Leipziger had moved. I wrote to her new address. I recalled the bond that had existed between her son and myself—making it rather closer than it had actually been—and even went so far as to quote certain moving particulars. I added that I would be glad to talk to her about him and asked if I could go and see her. A fortnight went by without my receiving any response.

The end of the story is so unreal that, were I writing anything other than a strictly truthful account, I do not think I would have dared leave it in its original form. When, after three weeks, I still received no reply, I went to Rue Demours, which was Mme Leipziger's new address.

The door was opened by a woman of about thirty, with a pronounced nose: Mlle Leipziger, presumably. With as much charm as I could command, I told her my name, said that I had written a letter and—with some incipient embarrassment, perhaps, because her welcome seemed ominously chilly—restated the purpose of my visit. All this took place in the entrance-hall, almost on the doorstep, and the lady displayed no intention of asking me to come farther in.

'Yes,' she said at length, after listening to me in silence, 'my mother received your letter. But she is ill at the moment. When she has recovered, she will write to you.'

That was all. Standing in front of me, blocking all avenues except the exit, without a word or a gesture, she intimated in the most forceful manner possible that the interview was over and that I could go back where I had come from. Which I did pronto.

Walking along the street with, I suppose, a sorry expression on my face, I could find only one explanation for being cold-shouldered in this way. I reflected that, since the war, the families of dead soldiers must have had lots of visits from more or less genuine 'comrades in arms' of their dear departed, who wanted money or help in finding a job. Having lost three sons, Mme Leipziger had perhaps been particularly exposed to this kind of nuisance. It was quite clear; they had taken me for a cadger.

I have paid four visits to the families of dead soldiers that I had known only at the front. Only once did I meet with an attitude which seemed to me to be on the same moral level as my wartime relationship with the dead man. The comradeship between Leipziger and myself, imperfect as it had been, from all points of view, yet not without that glow of nobility that touches everything connected with the firing-line, and ending on a vision of a woman with crudely coloured hair standing with one hand over the doorknob and the other over her purse—was full of significance. Almost always when someone we have *chosen* brings us into contact with his or her family, that is with people we have not *chosen,* and who are therefore likely to arouse in us nothing but indifference, dislike or disrespect, there is conflict, and this is so natural that it would not be worth mentioning, if an institution such as marriage did not make this inevitable cause of dissension and trouble into a social necessity. My reception by Mlle Leipziger was not merely an illustration of this law; it was also expressive of another law, that of the depreciation everything undergoes in surviving from wartime to peacetime. The door Mlle Leipziger closed in my face also closed on the whole order of things that should be kept intact and could only be blighted or soiled by any compromise with the people and things of peacetime. As the inscription reads on Cellini's medal for Clement VII: *Clauduntur belli portae.*

Mors et Vita, 1932
(Written in 1926)

EXPLICIT MYSTERIUM

THE REFLECTIONS you are about to read were entrusted to me by a writer who was anxious for them to be published. 'They are,' he said, 'notes that I jotted down from day to day at a time when I had very good reason to believe that I wouldn't see the year out.' 'Congratulations!' I said, in the off-hand way in which we judge another man's work, especially when it springs from the innermost depths of his being. 'Congratulations! I've read what you have to say. It really appeals to me. I love to see you galloping in to the attack on Hope with the colours of the Void streaming from your lance. It would make a good subject for a picture: *The Knight of the Void!* Delightful! But if you are entirely sincere in what you write . . .'

At this he stuttered with rage and shouted: 'Can't you see that what you have just said is a downright insult and would entitle me, at the very least, to refuse to have anything more to do with you? What's more, your criticism is of the cowardly kind that can't be answered. It is exactly the same as saying of a writer: he's a bore. No reply is possible. And, pray, why shouldn't I be sincere? When the surest way of producing good writing is to use the page in front of us to collect what spurts out, while it is still warm, and when this is the easiest method, since all that is required is to let the pen flow of its own accord, why should we allow some demon to prompt us to imagine and express feelings we have never experienced? That is hard work, and risky work, too, because, if you fumble about in the unknown, you are in danger of writing badly and inaccurately.'

'Forgive me,' I said, 'but you have a healthy, well-fed look. I hadn't imagined you in a *moriturus* attitude. And I had never heard of you being in that position.'

'What do you know about my life? When I thought I was going to die, do you think I shouted the fact from the house-tops? Was it even necessary to think of myself as a dying man for any length of time? If the belief had lasted only a month or so, even if it had lasted no more than a week and I had written my notes, in abysmal sincerity, during that one week, their value would be in no way diminished.'

'You didn't shout from the house-tops. But, precisely for that reason, are you not afraid of the public thinking that by publishing these notes now you are trying to make up for not having shouted?'

'Statements which self-consciousness prevents us uttering in conversation can be published unashamedly. We trumpet to an audience of fifty thousand people confidences that we would not whisper in a friend's ear. This is a very strange thing. It is as if the printed word became something remote from us.'

'The public will not bother their heads with such subtle distinctions. All they will notice is that you devote thirty pages to explaining that you are going to die and then fail to do so, which is a first breach of good manners, and then publish your thirty pages, thus committing a second breach. Believe me, if you want to go on being considered as a reliable character, don't publish these notes under your own name.'

He accepted my advice and we agreed that I should include them, anonymously, in the present volume.

But I could feel he was profoundly hurt. He kept repeating a remark said to have been made by M Briand: 'Must we die to prove our sincerity?' and he added: 'Should I have put a note at the end, quoting the doctors' certificates and the police guarantee of their authenticity?' But I thought to myself, as I watched him lighting a cigar: 'He can say what he likes. A man who puffs away like that has no right to go on about his latter end.'

It took me three days to get used to the prospect of being dead before the end of the year. By Thursday I felt I was over the worst—

until the time comes to conclude the business, when there will, obviously, have to be another crisis.

After the first three days, I needed three more to recover complete freedom of mind such as I had enjoyed before *I knew*. So the announcement of my approaching death has caused me an upset lasting, all told, about a week.

The sword of Damocles symbolizes a threat. It ought rather to symbolize use. Damocles must have lived under his sword exactly as if there were no sword there. He probably joked about it: 'That confounded little sword of mine...!'

I have heard it asked how old men can go on living so peacefully when they know they are so close to death. I understand, because I can, and I am still young. You get into the habit.

When you see how much money it costs to die and you remember how inexpensive all the most exquisite things in life were...

A wounded man fights against his wound, against his doctors and against people, who either fuss over him or think there is nothing wrong.

You can hardly stand on your feet, but people invite you to dinner and are offended if you don't accept.

When I'm slow at getting into the tram, the people behind jostle me: 'Hurry on, there!'
Pass it on to the next man. When the patient who is dying of a lung complaint coughs incessantly on the other side of the wall, I can stand it for a little while, then I lose my temper: 'He's doing it on purpose!'

There are recipes for dealing with unhappiness. Stendhal gives one: 'When unhappiness occurs, there is only one way to blunt its sharp edge. Resist it with the utmost courage. The soul then revels in its own strength and contemplates that, instead of contemplating unhappiness and bitterly experiencing it in all its details.' This is definitely a *practical* recipe, which is genuinely effective. There are others, too.

I should have liked to collect all those 'thoughts' and all those reflective passages in which great minds, or simply averagely good minds, have expressed ideas likely to make dying easier for those who do not believe in life after death. I would have published them in a cheap, popular edition, under some such title as *A Handbook on Decent Dying* or *How to Die with Dignity*. This would certainly have been a good action.

At the moment, I do not find such an anthology a serious lack, but it would have been very welcome. To put it together now would mean a great deal of work; it should have been ready to hand.

I have always been very moved by Paul Drouot's account of how he saw Major Madelin weeping on his stretcher as he was being carried away, fatally wounded. I seem to remember that, according to Drouot, the Major was weeping about 'those he was leaving behind him'. At once my hackles were up. 'That's what they say! It was the horror of death that was making the poor fellow weep. But people have always to be given a halo, at whatever cost.' Well, I now believe that Madelin and all those in the same plight are in fact weeping because of 'those they are leaving behind them'. I doubt whether anyone who knows he is going to die can weep about his own death, about himself. Perhaps in the complete physical exhaustion at the end.

A girl asked me once if I had ever seen soldiers weeping over their fallen comrades. I told her I had often seen men weeping at the front: soldiers weeping over other soldiers, officers weeping over officers, soldiers weeping over officers and officers weeping over soldiers.

She seemed very surprised, and her expression betrayed slight disapproval. Men weeping! Not very manly behaviour, particularly when they were weeping about something other than women!

I say to myself: 'What a dreadful thing to die at the age of . . .' But my next impulse is to correct this: 'Don't use exaggerated expressions . . .'
I find it dreadful, yet *calmly* dreadful.

The hero feels pity for all suffering except that which is undergone because of himself.
If I remember rightly, Marcus Aurelius complains gently about the good suffering the same fate, after death, as the wicked. This is a complaint I don't like. What need have we that justice should be done to us?

We meet people again after an absence and try to read in their looks whether or not they think we have altered.
Let us rise above this sort of thing.
Battlefield, hospital and monastery are places where men need no longer seek to impress. Whatever may be said against these places, it is to their credit that they raise man to a higher level by making him humble again.
During the war, when a position had to be abandoned, we would burn all the documents relating to it, so that the enemy could not use them against us. On the verge of death, you burn your private papers, so that your friends cannot use them against you.

I struggle with all my might against any emotional softening caused by physical pain. Our conception of life can be altered by a good lunch. A change due to suffering is on the same low level.

Louis XIV brought his death-bed scene to a quick close: 'Farewell, gentlemen, I am afraid of touching your feelings. Think of me from time to time.' *I am afraid of touching your feelings.* What a magnificent sense of respect for others.

'Ordinary people in Russia are convinced that the presence of onlookers around a death-bed increases the dying man's sufferings and makes it more difficult for the soul to escape from the body (the same applies to childbirth).'

How true a belief this is, in my view!

It is incredible how much exhaustion a patient is caused and how many risks he is made to run through the mere fact of having a doctor.

You may be suffering from bronchitis and lung trouble and have been warned again and again: 'Take care not to catch cold!', but the doctor, before using his stethoscope, makes you strip to the waist in a room where the heating is only moderate.

People with pneumonia are made to lie half-naked on the icy surface of the X-ray table.

'The main thing is not to tire yourself,' the doctor says. Whereupon you have to go and see him and the fatigue caused by the effort of going out poisons your whole day. It would not be so bad if you did not have to wait. Waiting an hour and a half at the doctor's would put a strain on even a healthy person's nervous system. How much greater must the strain be on someone whose nerves are already on edge through physical weakness!

A day which promised to be quiet and enjoyable is completely ruined through the prospect of having to see the doctor.

A lot of people, on the verge of death, utter famous last words or stiffen into attitudes, as if the final stiffening due in three days' time were not enough; they will have ceased to exist three days' hence, yet they still want to arouse admiration and adopt a pose and tell a lie with their last gasp: 'See how well I breathe my last!' This is called heroism. I call it disgusting. If a complaint rose to my lips, should I stifle it to please the gaping onlookers and make them admire me? I would rather complain more loudly to give a last demonstration of my low opinion of other people and what they think. There is a feeling which is at the opposite extreme from pride; it is self-respect.

'To be a hero and a saint for oneself' (Baudelaire). For oneself. And to show oneself to the world in the guise of a coward or a clown. For the admiration of the world covers you with slime like the trail of a slug.

The great mystery is not death but life. The manuscripts of our medieval 'mysteries' end with the words: *Explicit mysterium,* 'Here ends the mystery.'

Explicit mysterium.

While waiting for death, you feel both calm and curious.

Any injustice suffered comes in useful. The small return for what you gave comes in useful. Everything which might have been sadness becomes the foundation of a finally discovered peace.

And people shout at you, like that top-hatted cad at the riding school when you were twelve years old, 'Don't hold yourself so stiffly!' People can't believe that if you keep a straight back (more or less), you do so instinctively. For them, such a thing as sagging does not exist; there is only stiffness. What is dignity they term pride. A clear indication of what they are themselves.

The pleasures of the world, the pleasures we loved so madly, slip unmourned below the horizon. How can this be? It is incomprehensible. How can we show enough gratitude—and to whom should we show it—for the total absence of rebelliousness, for the enjoyment of this absurd state of affairs?

A little while ago, I wrote that we needed a collection of quotations to put new heart into people about to die. Now, I no longer feel any necessity for it. Were the quotations by men of genius, that fact itself would make them appear 'literary'.

For years, there has been this swinging to and fro between the belief that one would go on living and the belief that one was about to die. Sometimes on the crest of the wave, sometimes in the trough, yet always relaxed and yielding, as if cradled on the surface of some blissful swell. . . .

There have been three passions in my life: independence, indifference and physical delight. How satisfactory to feel that passionate indifference has remained until the end, to see people, subjects and problems being snuffed out inside me, one after the other, as city lights are extinguished after midnight, one by one, and to murmur, 'It's getting late inside. . . .'

I do not smoke, because my spirit needs no solace. If it needed solace, I would smoke. But it doesn't.

Antoninus, on his death-bed, gave *Aequanimitas* as the watchword to the tribune on duty. 'Then, turning away, he seemed to fall asleep' (Renan).
Very moving, almost too moving. It is sentences like this that we should impress upon our minds in case a time comes when we need support.

Intelligence, heroism, ambition, poetry, art and work, all these things certainly have some value. But for me they are of secondary importance, definitely secondary—compared to what I have always called, and always shall call, the Sovereign Good, which is loving someone. If intelligence were taken out of my life, it would only be more or less reduced. If I had no one to love, it would be ruined.
As for being loved, not only does it serve no purpose, it almost always brings disaster. It must be admitted that this is one of the risks you run in loving someone.

I love the lightning which flashes above the skyline, without touching the earth. But I love the earth no less passionately. 'And to think that I shall have to leave all this behind.'[1]

The heart misses a beat. The pain is purely physical, not mental. When life returns, we feel no jolt, no retrospective emotion. How can one fail to wish for a sudden death, in preference to any other

[1] Cardinal Mazarrin's words to the doctor who told him he was going to die.

sort? Four seconds of anguish for a life of bliss. And avoid all the labour of the death agony.

Not only am I not intimidated by the interruption in my heartbeats; I treat it as an amusement, a game. Once the spasm is over, I enjoy the sort of amusement you get in riding when, after clearing a difficult obstacle, you feel the horse's hindquarters collapse under you and then, suddenly, find yourself trotting along again as sedately as before. After the spasm and the jump, the same inner smile which steals invisibly over your face.

Suffering has no meaning and raises no questions. It just is, like storms and floods. It is, in short, an absolute.

At death's door, proclaim that the great difficulty is physical suffering.

I wake up in the middle of the night, switch on the light and make these notes. This *amuses* me.

When a man is dying, he becomes more and more involved in the falseness of society. His relations make 'sacred' promises that they have every intention of getting out of on the ground that he was not altogether in his right mind when he insisted on them. His heirs cajole him to his face and jeer at him behind his back. The doctors, with fixed grins, assure him that everything is going perfectly (were he at death's door, they would tell him that he was just letting his nerves get the better of him). The patent medicines consist of nothing but powdered chalk. Useless treatments put money into the quack's pocket. The night nurse dozes off and swears, on waking, that she has heard the clock strike every hour. The priest fools around in a complete phantasmagoria and harries the dying man to get him to do the same. And that is not all. Nature, too, is false. There is the sudden mysterious improvement which occurs at some moment or other in all fatal illnesses. This is the terrible deceitfulness of nature. You think you are making a fresh start, but in fact everything is at an end.

How well I understand those people who, when illness strikes, hide themselves away like sick animals and refuse to see anyone. Such apparently inhuman will-power, which adds solitude to anguish, seems at first to be peculiar to heroes; in fact, many quite average people are capable of it. Even some ordinary people have no wish to close their eyes for the last time with their faces set in a social grimace. They seem quite forsaken; but one is not forsaken when one still has oneself—the self, that only haven of security.

In any case, well-bred people die quickly so as not to disturb present company.

From Socrates to Clemenceau, men on their death-beds have always said: 'Keep the women out.' And yet a dying man is mourned only by women.

Since the beginning of the world, and as old as the sound of the sea—their eternal mourning for Adonis.

But let Tacitus shed his cruel light on the subject: 'It is woman's duty to mourn the dead, man's to remember them.'

Everything is just as it should be. I don't need to force myself to say this. If I had to, I shouldn't say it.

Talthybios in *Agamemnon*: 'I am happy, and were I to die, I should not bear the gods a grudge.'

Oedipus in *Oedipus at Colonnus*: 'In spite of so many misfortunes, my advanced years and the greatness of my soul make me conclude that all is well.'

So far gone already that the actual crossing over now seems no more than a formality.

A few more remarks, like birds flying up out of a well.

I have never known the sort of things that can be learnt. Nor the sort of things that can be understood. I have never understood anything, not a thing. Made a guess, occasionally. But even so, I was still in the dark. I walked about in star-studded ignorance. For me, the world has been one vast, unknown country. Snatches of knowledge, superficial views, unfounded opinions—and the sum total of that is expected to make historic statements! All the things

I've had no inkling of! The new-born babe has tightly clenched fists, as if he were saying: 'I'll take on the whole world!' The dying man is open-handed. He says, 'Look, I'm leaving and I'm taking nothing with me.'

Everything has been brought about by chance. Chance has been responsible for my work, since it was by chance that I met certain people and not others, was present at certain events and not others, read certain books and not others, saw certain landscapes and not others. My experience of the world and my books are the products of slightly organized chance.

Physical sensations are like stars. Points of light surrounded by darkness, which is sometimes dimly lit, as if by the Milky Way, but even so it is still darkness. Oh stars!

The same is true for everyone. Upbringing, marriage, the choice of a career and often the choice of a 'faith'—are all a matter of chance. It is through chance that, from among the various individuals of which each of us is composed, one emerges rather than another. Everybody knows this more or less, but I am blowing the gaff.

That man has lived a good life who began by believing he was something and ends by believing he is nothing.

You hear it said: 'Between truth and us, there is ourself.' But *from* truth to ourself, what is there but ourself?

Don't try to explain to me what I understood long ago.

It has been said that the Greeks had no deep understanding of death. But, since we cannot possibly know anything about it, what is there to be understood? Death can only inspire unwholesome fancies.

Hesiod: 'You must not allow a child of twelve to sit on tombstones. By so doing, you would only turn him into a spineless man.'

Memento quia pulvis es. The truth is precisely the opposite. Once we have worked out our attitude towards death, the only sensible course of action is never to think about the subject at all. Only men incapable of thinking about life, think about death. Since death provides no subject for thought, they are quite happy. What distinguishes all 'thoughts on death' is that they never contain any thought.

If there was one place where men gave little thought to the after-life and, comparatively speaking, to death, it was at the front.

'Preparing for death'. There is only one way to prepare for death; it is to have your fill—in soul, heart, mind and flesh. Up to the brim.

And there is only one form of immortality worth wishing for—the immortality of life.

The doctor prods you when you are at your lowest ebb and poisons you with his breath which reeks of spirits and cigars.

It would be mortifying now not to die. I used to feel a similar slight disappointment (fearing the sea as I do) when it became absolutely clear that the crossing would be calm right to the end.

After all, it is natural to be curious. At last we are about to know! How superior we shall be to all the living!

What I see as depressing in individuals may become more cheering in the mass. This is a well-known, if unjustifiable, phenomenon. I am depressed from time to time, for instance, when I reflect that our experience of the Beyond remains useless for others. At last we know, but a second too late! What a pity that there should not be, for the tiniest fraction of a second, simultaneity of life and death so that the dying could say: 'There is something' or 'There is nothing'. Prometheus gave men the fire of hope. We could give them another kind—the fire of no more hope.

On the floor above, people are laughing and stamping their feet. The stamping is mostly done by children who thus express their joy at having to die between the ages of twenty and thirty, some of them in the next war, the others of tuberculosis.

The parents also are stamping their feet to express their joy at having brought their children into the world for this purpose.

The drawback of infirmities or diseases is that they prevent man exercising his divine power of fulfilling himself in the present. Dreaming of the future—a servile attitude.

On the battlefield, in hospital and in a monastery, you are more or less sheltered from humanity. At the front, men are rid of their wives, their relations, their acquaintances, etc. (Of course, they will never admit that this is one of the advantages of war. But just hint at it, when ex-servicemen are together, and you will see them smile . . .) In hospital, visitors are allowed in only twice a week and at fixed times to send your temperature up by 1·2 degrees; in a monastery, you can always find the god of solitude, failing the one you went there to seek. It was on a bed of suffering, two months ago, that I spent the most delightful hours of my life.

Socrates, when dying, said: 'And now, nothing but music.' Please let us avoid any symbolical interpretation. We take 'music' to mean music. The old scoundrel of the intellect wanted to cleanse his mind of sixty years of ratiocination. What a surprise! When it came to facilitating the transition from life to death, he turned to the *unum necessarium*, to poetry. The unexpected last testament of the thinker was the strumming of the cithara and the touch of Phaedo's hair.

A superb remark by X, after the death of his friend Y: forty years of friendship; Y this and Y that, all the outward signs of real friendship.
X, as I said, watched Y die slowly of cancer, and suffer a long drawn-out, painful agony before he finally expired. 'You may think me heartless,' he said, 'but I may as well be frank. It didn't affect me one little bit.'
He also said, 'Up to two years ago, whenever I saw healthy, cheerful, handsome young men in the street, and reflected that

they would be killed in the next war in a few years' time, I used to be horrified at the thought. Today I can't see the tragic side of that either.'

X is seventy. His is the strength that comes from old age.

By accident, I find myself looking at a photograph of the crypt in Palermo where the skeletons of monks of former days—about a hundred of them—are hung against a wall, still wearing their habits. Poor devils! Some of them may have had some spark of higher feeling, and for three centuries now they have been hanging there like ridiculous puppets or decorations in a Montmartre night-club. Their bogey-man parade is only likely to scare women and children. What is it supposed to mean? That the monks were mortal? Surely we knew that. That we shall all die? So what? At the sight of this sepulchral reach-me-down, only the feeble-minded will experience anything other than disgust and contempt for the vulgar people who thought of it.

Just as when you leave a town, you feel disdain (absurd disdain) for all the people who are staying behind and carrying on with their daily business, so I glance contemptuously at letters telling me of things which are to take place in six months' or a year's time. I always have such a wild desire to escape, to send everybody and everything to the devil, that it gives me pleasure to leave, even if it means going for good.

Don't buy any new clothes.

People are not severe enough with anyone who is suffering and the sufferer himself is too ready to believe in his own greatness.

Physical pleasure is the reality I have always put my hand on in moments of turmoil, as one snatches at papers in a rising wind. Let everything else blow away! A constant and ungovernable reflex.

EXPLICIT MYSTERIUM

More than the thirst for sacrifice, more than inspiration, more than pity, more than grief, more than music, the power of physical sensation has raised me above the earth, as mystic love raised the saints, and has enabled me to cast an occasional glance over the wall. Occasionally, it has turned me into something other than myself. It represents all I am worth. With what force and constancy (although I am so changeable) have I known this, from the very beginning!

Lying naked on the bed, after making love, with a naked body across my outstretched left arm, a powerful body, with a root-like smell, and of whose mass I was conscious as if it were a statue that had fallen from its plinth, I would conceive my thoughts and my dreams and they would go out from me like armies. For a while, I would retain command of them. But soon their spearheads would begin to elude me and they would vanish into a region of shadow.

When I was eighteen or so, like everyone else at that age, I wrote some last reflections in *bouts rimés*. I remember only the concluding verse:

> *Que je voudrais pouvoir dire ces mots un soir,*
> *Et puis, les yeux tournés vers la face de l'Etre,*
> *Sans regret, mais non sans un gracieux espoir,*
> *Avec simplicité m'étendre et disparaître.*

> How I should like to say these words some evening,
> And then, turning my eyes towards the face of Being,
> With no regrets, but not without a gracious hope,
> With simplicity lie down and die.

Simplicité—gracieux—sans regret—the words fly towards me like cooing doves. Only *espoir* fails to take wing.

When I was twenty, I also wrote the following two lines in a poem:

> *Les dernières barques menées*
> *Par les Eros musiciens.*

> The last boats guided
> By love-gods playing melodious airs.

Again the same conception of death as graceful and gracious.

Death introduces a little dignity among the living. Spite and ridiculousness cannot exist in a pure form around a death-bed. And, in such a situation, even the flimsiest people acquire gravity.

Death introduces a little gentleness among the living; people make up their quarrels, make good resolutions, etc.

Death also gives us more elbow-room. By removing people we have got to know too well, it opens the way to fresh adventures.

And how much art and literature would lose, if this particular *pedal* were missing from their orchestras.

And how much love and physical pleasure would lose, without the consciousness of the threat of death.

Lastly, the greatest of death's benefits is to bring completion. By outlining men in sharp silhouette, it enables us to see phenomena as wholes, to draw conclusions, and so helps us to think.

I can imagine a religion in which death would be represented symbolically as oil, because it is the oil in the machinery of the universe.

It is physical suffering which has all the appearances of evil, which is useless, inexplicable and apparently unavoidable. It is this which spoils the prospect of death for me.

I have never exerted myself except in the pursuit of pleasure; of that I have always wanted more. What I like about my life is that it has all happened to me as if in the effortlessness of sleep. I can't stand people who strain to do things. What cannot be done easily should not be done at all. Dying should, then, be carried out smoothly (and I hope nature will not steal a march on me).

'And with this death make life.' Exactly. Death is for me a source of vitality.

You hear people talking about the 'oriental' conception of life, in which death is said to occupy a more important place than in the 'western' conception. In so far as I am entitled to speak about the

East, knowing, as I do, only the Arabs and Berbers of North Africa, I have never noticed this. On the contrary, the North Africans do not dwell on their own deaths or on the deaths of others. Their indifference to death reminds me of the attitude of Homer's Greeks. Their funerals have nothing formal about them. Their cemeteries have neither the pretentiousness nor the impressiveness of European ones, where death preens itself and where the grave-mounds are as round and as adorned as auditors' bellies.

An Arab funeral in the streets of Algiers lacks dignity, I agree. It is taken at the gallop. It looks like a film that the operator has speeded up. But, when all is said and done, is it not more seemly— I mean: does it not seem more reasonable—than a European funeral procession which brings seven trams to a halt for ten minutes, because it is crawling along the tram-lines, whereas, by moving to the right and putting on a little speed, it could easily leave the lines clear? But the tram-drivers would never dare insist on that. They would be put to shame in no uncertain tones: 'Have you no respect for the dead?' etc. And yet the people in the trams—the midinette on her way to meet her boy-friend, the office-boy running an errand for his boss, the business brute who has a business luncheon appointment at midday—may be engaged in paltry activities, but what they are doing is still something, whereas the corpse holding them up is nothing, because, if there is an after-life, its soul has gone from it, and if there is no after-life, it is worse than nothing.

Throughout the world, ever since the beginning of time, people have worshipped the dead. The fact does not impress me. There is a fine line by Herriot:

> *Le vrai tombeau des morts est le coeur des vivants*
> The real tombs of the dead are the hearts of the living.

Let us remember the dead in our hearts. Let us honour them in the only way worthy of rational man, by being as they would have wished us to be. If necessary, in less important matters, in connection with which it is not essential to have our own personal opinions, let us incline towards the opinions that they would have had, while making, of course, our own reservations. Otherwise, everything becomes rank superstition. The fact that a man happens to be dead does not entitle him to the recognition we would have withheld had he been alive. To respect a dead man merely because he is dead is to prostitute respect, which should be reserved for ability and virtue.

I am shocked beyond expression to see, as happens nowadays in France, half the people in a crowd keep their hats on when the tricolour goes by, whereas the whole crowd, to a man, salutes a passing funeral.

I note with interest the following custom which existed at a certain period in ancient Rome: during a funeral, a clown would imitate any ridiculous aspects of the dead man's former behaviour.

I am shocked beyond measure, exasperated and incensed (as only stupidity can incense us) by that false intellectual distinction according to which the sight of death proves that life has no reality in itself, and therefore no value. 'How narrow are the horizons of the earth and the flesh! What a prison we are in!' Well, if that is what you think, don't be surprised to find me dry-eyed the day you escape from prison. A pleasant journey, Mr Softie!

I have a strange habit of always seeing the good in everything, of making everything out to be acceptable.

If my appetite for life declines, I say: 'That is what I shall be like when I am old. When I see how little it would matter to me if I had to go now, I can tell how little it will matter when I am old. Everything is for the best!'

If I suffer physical pain, I say: 'Well, it's only natural. I have been happy enough! Things have to even themselves out.'

If I had to die now, I should say: 'The odds were eight to ten in favour of my being killed at the age of twenty during the war, so I am n years to the good!'

And if war were to break out now: 'What the hell! We've had a decent breathing-space since the 11th November—n years of peace, n years' leave, that's not to be sneezed at!'

There are apparently—do they wear badges? do they get reductions in fares for group travelling?—societies of *néantistes* (believers in total destruction). Just one of their meetings would be enough, I think, to revive in me a longing for the after-life, for half a day at least.

It comes to the same thing whether you are given a Christian burial, are cremated or thrown into a pauper's grave. No need, then, to specify in your will which you want.

Since the end of the war, whenever I have felt tired or lethargic because of the heat or some other cause, I have only had to open a war book and go and see a war film to be cheered up again at once by the thought: 'We lived through that and here I am complaining because it's ninety-five degrees in the shade!' And so war, which is sometimes said to diminish life, can be a source of vitality, even when it survives only as a memory; in the same way, it gives me pleasure now to think back to the wartime hospitals, because what I chiefly remember about them is the indifference with which men faced their own, and others' deaths, and, consequently, the roughness which surrounded the process of dying. Both indifference and roughness are just what I need to encourage within me at this moment. (Of course, there were many exceptions. I am referring to a general impression.)

At X——, where we used to have bets about which of us would pop off first, Y, who was actually dying, used to simulate rigor mortis as a joke, pulling the sheet up to his chin and putting a handkerchief over his face; he was playing at being a dead man, and he was one. And here is an example of how a man's last breath can make people roar with laughter. F gave up the ghost, soundlessly. In the next bed, there was a little Parisian who was watching him die. The other patients were looking across inquiringly to find out how far gone F was, when suddenly the Parisian brought his heels down on the bed, lifted his face and his eyes heavenwards and, with outstretched arms, imitated a few wing-beats. F was on his way to heaven! Everybody burst out laughing. Afterwards, they all felt ashamed, but there was no getting away from it; they had laughed. (I wonder if the little Parisian's piece of mimicry was his own invention. If so, it was brilliant. But I rather think he had seen it done before somewhere. A great many of the apparent flashes of inspiration which delight us in children and in working-class people are, in fact, parrot-like imitations.)

The men were as hard as nails, particularly the young ones. If a patient gave a groan—'Shut up, we can't get to sleep for you.'—'I'm done for.'—'I'll give you what for if you go on about being done for! Would you talk like that if you were done for? We're just asking you to let us get some sleep, that's all.' And the tone in which it was said! If they had ripped out his liver, it couldn't have been any worse. During the night, he called to them all in turn, like a sinking ship sending out SOS messages in all directions: 'Paupaul! Jacquot!' They were fast asleep, or pretending to be. And so he died, surrounded by his comrades, his brothers in arms, men he called by their Christian names, by the shortened forms of their Christian names, and he was more forsaken than if he had been alone in a desert; worse than forsaken, rejected, snubbed. In the morning, they were all astounded and rather remorseful. Always surprised by things; surprised at being wounded, surprised at having to die, surprised that others should have to die. There was no light in their profound darkness; I mean no light of understanding, for there was sometimes a light of generosity. They no more knew how abominable they had been that night than they had known, a few days before, how magnificent they had been in the trenches. They never understood anything, and that was why things went so well.

A sick or dying man who called out 'Mother!' was no more thinking of his mother than a man who says 'By God!' is thinking of God.

I saw so few men ask for a priest that I think the proportion must have been lower than one in twenty.

A young Breton was dying. 'Is it true that you're a Breton and have no religious feelings?' 'My religion is to have my pocket full of pennies and my belly full of drink.' Which, when suitably translated for the national records, becomes: 'On the point of death, the brave son of Armorica expressed a desire to kiss the flag and was heard to murmur: 'Gentle Jesus! France! Mother!'

M, feeling that the end was near, handed me ten francs. 'Will you give them to N (the nurse) when he comes back from leave? I owe them to him.' M hovered between life and death for three days. On the morning of the fourth day, he had the look of a man restored to life, fancied a roll (?) and asked for the ten francs back. 'So you've got a new lease, old man? But what about N and his ten francs?'—'Let him wait!'

(But maybe N would have preferred to see M dead so as to get his ten francs back?)

From all this can be derived the comforting impression that death is not as bad as all that, that its terrors have been exaggerated. Between 1914 and 1918, death got the better of millions of men. But before dying, they showed their contempt for death, which is as it should be.

I have read a little book published by a Christian society and entitled 'Consolations by the graveside'.

Given its aim, it is very well done, and I should be surprised if any mental defective, who happens to be 'mourning a dear one', did not find in it some relief for his sorrow.

Death is not an end but a beginning. Our 'dear departed' are in Heaven. Soon we shall be reunited with them for all eternity. But what if their lives and even their deaths have been ungodly? Even so, we must not despair of their salvation because, at the moment of death, God works 'hidden mysteries of His pity'.

This last point is supported by a wealth of authorities and even examples. There is no end to the list of free-thinkers who are *known* to have been saved at the last moment. The argument leaves the reader with the impression that there are no lost souls at all; that some arrangement can always be patched up on the final pillow, and that just men and evil-doers walk into Paradise arm-in-arm.

The book is an anthology of prose passages. Bands of saints and bishops, to say nothing of Pascal, Bossuet and Bourdaloue, testify in favour of the doctrine. In favour of part of it (the death-is-a-beginning idea and the reunion with the dead) are Hugo, Lamartine, Rousseau, etc., not forgetting Cicero and Epictetus.

The reader cannot help saying to himself: if famous men have professed beliefs like these, they can have done so only for philanthropic reasons. No doubt they thought it was up to them to console 'wretched humanity' (for I can't bring myself to believe for one moment that they were trying to reassure themselves). And when you really want to be consoling, you say whatever comes into your head, provided it appears to have some consoling power.

But is it enough to wipe away tears and cure funk?

Among the supporters of the hope-at-all-costs doctrine in this small volume, we find, in addition to Saint Thomas and Pascal, M Octave Feuillet.[1]

'Ah!' M Feuillet exclaims. 'At the spectacle of the lifeless body of a loved one, what heart could be so hardened, what mind so blighted by doubt, as not to dismiss for ever the odious thought that the word "immortality" might be nothing more than an empty sound devoid of meaning!'

I am quite familiar by now with this sort of outflanking movement by which what is obviously noble is rechristened baseness and the dogs sent yapping after it. But each time it leaves me flabbergasted.

The soul's longing for infinity, a longing which proclaims its weakness and impotence, is the surest sign of its unworthiness of infinity, which will be for ever denied to it.

But even if there were a chance of life after death, and of course there is, we ought to stake everything on the supposition which gives us the best opportunity of living with dignity and courage, unlike those people who cringe in hope. But such courage is always relative; a man may need courage to go to the dentist or sail in a boat, and at the same time feel quite at home in a universe where there is neither God, punishment nor immortality.

[1] An indifferent nineteenth-century French novelist.

'But can that which must come to an end be great?'—What if it knows it is coming to an end and is quite satisfied to do so?

'But everywhere, in the most primitive countries, people have always believed in the life after death, and still believe in it.' Do Papuans and Botocudos provide an intellectual guarantee? Perhaps not.

'Does this mean I shall never see my dear Ernest or my little Caroline again . . .?' Counting one here and another there, you can be sure that thousands of millions of people have believed they would never see their Ernests and their Carolines again. If they could face it, there is no reason why you shouldn't.

'But I'm so full of life, of . . . etc. How can it be the end of me?' You poor fool, take a look at yourself. You can see in your face that you are only good for extinction.

'But my sublime faith, my glass of beer, my absorbing activities helped me to forget . . .'—To forget what?—'What do you mean, forget what? It's obvious you don't know what life is like; I meant, forget our vale of tears, of course. I was able to bear it only by thinking of the great rewards in the world to come.'—A slave breed, that's what you are, always living in hopes, always living for the day of emancipation. You say that absolute death fills you with horror. Well, I say that your despair fills me with horror. Sometimes horror, sometimes mirth. You say the world is a vale of tears. For anyone who laughs as I laugh when I see your despair, there is no vale of tears.

'No, no, it cannot be true! It would be too ghastly.' We shall not utterly perish, because that would be 'too ghastly'; there can't be another war, because that would be 'too ghastly', and so on. In one of the ancient religions, the world was represented as resting on the back of a bull. It seems to me to rest on the back of an ostrich.

'Oh, if there is no life after death, at least let me prolong my stay on this earth!'—But I thought it was a vale of tears, a prison?— 'I will produce some sublime work, and through it, I shall conquer death. But is my work really sublime? There's the rub. Let's change the subject. Oh, but I have a son! With little Jackie to survive me,

I shall never be completely dead. And I intend to endow a religious foundation, which will perpetuate my cherished name.'—Our turn to say, let's change the subject.

A world without God, a world without final justice, a lawless, will-less world, a world without mask or mist, a world where objects cast no shadow, an unaccommodating world—only this, but how completely this—is the world worthy of man!

'Blessed', perhaps, be those who inscribed hope on grave-stones. But honour to those who have removed it.

Mors et Vita 1932
(Written in 1931)

FOREWORD TO 'SERVICE INUTILE'

I SHOULD LIKE to say a few words about the circumstances in which *Service Inutile* was written. M Jean Guéhenno, in an excellent book which does him great credit,[1] has warned men of forty or thereabouts that this is an appropriate age at which to take stock of the past. But I am not concerned here with recalling past memories. I merely wish to provide a few connecting links between the various writings in this volume, to set them in their context and help to explain their meaning.

I shall not refer to myself in the third person as 'the author of these pages, etc.', because that is childish hypocrisy. I shall say 'I', because that is the way to be natural. (In any case, the phrase 'the author of these pages' makes me think of a waiter in a café; if you forget to tip him, he doesn't say 'me', he says, '*Il n'y a rien pour le garçon?*'—Is there nothing for the waiter?) I shall write this preface with deliberate restraint. I shall put into it neither 'music' nor 'colour' nor rhetorical effects. In short, I shall invent nothing with a view to enhancing my own reputation—a most praiseworthy intention. Supposing I had been tempted to do so, I have just re-read Chateaubriand's *Mémoires d'outre-tombe* and the three volumes of Hugo's *Actes et paroles*. Fifty years of Chateaubriand's histrionics followed by sixty years of Hugo's; aristocratic histrionics followed by lower-class histrionics, very different in quality it is true (with the Viscount showing up very much to his advantage), but akin in their posturings, their playing to the gallery, their obvious tricks, their pathological self-bloatedness and their indescribable shamelessness, so much so that the reader who enjoys either cannot be a really genuine person. . . . But enough about them! I would rather go to the opposite extreme and make my writing too

[1] *Journal d'un homme de quarante ans.*

dry and colourless. We have had enough of flowery language and phoneyness.

The year 1924, during which I published *Les Olympiques* and *Le Chant funèbre pour les morts de Verdun,* brought me fame and cured me of any liking for it. I was able to see the sort of thing fame was, and that was enough. I sensed the truth of the remark, which Montalembert, I think, made, in the first flush of success: 'Fame? In what way does fame make you any happier?' It was also the only year when I felt that my books were the object of wholly sympathetic interest, and the feeling is perhaps one for which I am temperamentally unsuited. I saw a broad and easy path ahead of me and jibbed at it. So I disposed of hearth and home, put my remaining possessions into store and, completely relieved from now on of all the earthly encumbrance of a place of residence, left France with two suitcases which, for nearly ten years, were to be my only luggage. As it happens, since my departure on the 15th January 1925, which was a turning-point in my life, I have spent seven years and two months outside France (counting both short and long absences).

I have described the feelings which prompted me to clear out in *Aux Fontaines du Désir*. I need not explain them again. In a word, I wanted (1) to live a life of enchantment; (2) to be uncommitted. In addition, I had a great lust for human beings. I immediately obtained all I wanted and was immediately fed up with it. An essay, entitled *Le Carnaval de Madrid*,[1] expresses the essence of what I was going to reiterate for the next three years: 'That which has been achieved has been destroyed.' This essay dates from March 1925, two months after my departure. Nothing could be more edifying—and I say so seriously—than this experience of mine, which might have been sponsored by one of the fathers of the Church and had as its conclusion Pascal's remark about the uselessness of ever going out of one's room.

I shall not apologize for the very physical details I am now about

[1] Published in *Un voyageur solitaire est un diable*.

to give. The body is too much part of the soul for one to apologize for speaking about it.

Towards the end of that year, which I had spent partly in Italy, partly in Spanish Morocco, but chiefly in Spain, it so happened that I was knocked over by a young bull when I was practising on a *ganaderia*[1] near Albacete, and its horn made a gash in my chest near the lungs. While the news of this event was causing mirth in Parisian night-clubs during the festive season, I was spitting blood. A *chansonnier* called Bonnaud, giving a list of his New Year wishes for 1926, sang:

> *Espérons . . .*
> *Et que c'raseur de Montherlant*
> *Ne publiera qu'un seul volume.*
> *Espérons mêm' qu'il s'ra posthume.*
>
> Let us hope . . .
> That that bore Montherlant
> Will publish only one volume
> And let us hope it will be posthumous.

It almost was. I was in hospital when *Les Bestiaires* came out. I had typhoid fever and two attacks of pneumonia; I spent four months of 1926 in various nursing homes. Finally, when I was convalescing in the autumn at Tangier I suffered from the after-effects of a war wound. I had been mentioned in dispatches as being 'severely wounded'. Of the seven pieces of shrapnel which had lodged themselves in the small of my back, it had been possible to extract only one. After being in pain for a few months, I had ceased to feel anything, so much so that after the war I played football and ran the hundred yards. At Tangier, I was forbidden to ride, etc. I was to be forbidden more and more things during the following years. To cut a long story short, I leave the reader to imagine what it was like to be 'fifty per cent unfit' for a man who had never had to think about his body and had derived one of the greatest satisfactions of his youth from his exuberant energy.

In *Service Inutile*, the reader will not find more than five or six

[1] A breeding establishment for fighting bulls.

pages dating from the years 1925-27. I was too preoccupied with myself, too busy worrying and trying to save myself from despair, to give much attention to anything else. I had, incidentally, taken notes during these critical months and out of my many deaths made life.

I know people who judge me solely on these two volumes of essays. But you can't judge a man on what he does and says in a state of crisis. That would be doing him an injustice, just as surely as if you judged him on what he said in his sleep or under the influence of drink.

The crisis expressed in *Les Voyageurs traqués* began to ease in 1928. For no obvious reason. I suppose it had spent itself, as love spends itself; and that it had run its course. Why do you stop loving a woman? Because, I suppose, your system feels a vague impulse to move on to something else and to avoid falling asleep in one particular state when a thousand different ones are beckoning, including the exact opposite of the present one. I suppose the crisis came to an end because I was tending to stagnate in it. When I look back on it now, it seems incomprehensible, just as incomprehensible as the fact that, six months ago, we were sobbing for a woman whom today we cross the road to avoid. There is no point in apologizing for these transformations or in trying to explain them. 'I was like that then. I am different now. That's how human nature is. So, everything is all right.' How could the crisis be defined? It had been, first and foremost, a rather coarse urge to satisfy my sensuality. Then a sort of outburst of delayed adolescence. Up to 1925, my experience had been limited to school, war and the sports ground, three things which did not add up to a complete life. Life was really given to me only in 1925, and I admit that I took certain liberties with it. 'Barbarism must have its day,' said the Abbé Bremond. Barbarism came and went. The crisis had perhaps also been what certain authors call 'the crisis at the age of thirty', half-way between the crisis of adolescence and the other, later one, on the brink of old age. I don't know whether this 'crisis at the age of thirty' is a Loch Ness monster or a reality.

In 1929, serenity returned. But I should make it clear, as regards the metaphysical crisis—why are we alive?—that it had been not so much resolved as integrated into my personality, with the result that I was now able to live with it. In this volume, the fundamental attitude expressed in *Aux Fontaines du désir* is everywhere implicit. Formerly, the question: 'What's the use?' would plunge me into despair; now it soothes me.

There emerged from the crisis, if not a new man, certainly a better one. In 1925 I had taken the first step towards a spiritual life, which is the renunciation of all worldly interests. I had accepted conditions which were those of a spiritual way of life, and something resembling the spiritual life had occurred. Like Tobias's angel, I had seemed to be feeding on the fruits of the earth when, in fact, I was enjoying divine sustenance.

I lived the full life of the senses and, having thereby purged myself of the desire for it, I was free to lead a spiritual life. 'You can detach yourself from the good things of this world only if you have overindulged in them' (Saadi). This happened in a general way and also on particular issues: as soon as a desire was satisfied, that is to say purged, an exhaltation of the spirit would begin within me; it was as if, my being having been drained of sensuality, spirituality promptly began to blossom in the vacant space. 'Before God can come in, things must go out,' as a religious writer has said, with reference to this automatic movement. At the time, I saw quite clearly that these achievements were no more than an approach, and I told Catholics so, but they would not believe a word I said.[1]

---

[1] 'No book published since the war has been greeted with more unjust irritation than *Aux Fontaines du désir*', wrote Paul Souday, and I remember Mauriac's remark: 'If your book is a gaping wound, you will always find a motionless circle of flies on it.' I think Catholics have a better understanding of the work today. A sentence from it is quoted by Father Sanson in one of his sermons; another appears on the title-page of an anthology of Christian mystics (J. Chuzeville, *Les Mystiques allemands*). And Canon Ollier writes, '*Aux Fontaines du désir* can be considered as the first step on the road to the highest form of spirituality, both because of the disgust it expresses for the vanities of this world—a disgust which is the leitmotiv of the book—and because of the impassioned search for Unity evident in so many passages, in particular in *Syncrétisme et Alternance*, several sentences of which could have been taken straight from the mystics: those referring to 'sovereign adherence', 'the state of pure love, which can exclude nothing and makes everything equal' ('We see unity at last'), etc.

Before 1925, I lived violently. I was steeped in such principles as *sine caritate Romani*. My character now became more gentle. In the trenches, on playing fields and on racing tracks, I had seen violence practised only between equals, a healthy violence. In North Africa, I saw it practised by the strong, the Europeans, against the weak, the natives: that, I think, turned me against violence for the rest of my life. And I began to develop a liking for the defeated.

Before 1925, I was not averse to the idea of getting on. I was moderately ambitious. Now ambition, go-getting, seemed paltry things. This was not virtue on my part. The simple explanation was that I no longer had any desire for the 'advantages' that ambition strives for. I saw that social vanity is the canker devouring the European world. All vanity had died within me; this at first produces a peculiar sensation, perhaps not unlike the feeling of a patient who comes out of the anaesthetic to discover that he has lost a leg. It is in such circumstances that you can gauge the place that vanity occupies in man. You were propped up by vanity. When it disappears, you are at a loss for a long time; you feel rather out of your element in society. Perhaps only those who are writers themselves will realize what it means to spend, of your own free will, seven years and two months outside France, including one stretch of two and a half years, especially during the great post-war period of literary activity; only they know how much care, concentration and daily effort is required to keep a literary reputation going (moreover, they make no bones about it: So-and-so is not ashamed to imply that it was from Victor Hugo that he learned how to minister to his own vanity); only they can appreciate the degree of self-denial implied by a complete and prolonged disappearance, such as mine was. Before 1925, I had welcomed fame. Now I was living in the exile of a completely disinterested life. Sunk in the peace that is ensured by an earnestly preserved incognito, neurotically anxious to pass unnoticed and to display no feature that was in the least out of the ordinary, I was, in short, making as much effort to reduce my social importance as is normally devoted to developing it. I had decided to forego being in the secret of the human comedy—that is, its superficial secret—in order to understand its deeper secret.

Before 1925, will-power played an important part in my life. I had seen that it can achieve practically anything within reason. I had seen, in external matters, how easy everything was for me, how easy everything is. If I take the Christian view for a moment, this will-power within me was obviously satanic: God does not will, nor does a Christian. Lucifer fell from Heaven because he had a will of his own. After 1925, my will became that of the universe (in other words, God's will). I held that any action, unless it was prompted by charity, was ludicrous. The inspiration of *La Rose de Sable* sprang from these sentiments. From cover to cover, that book stresses nothing so much as the vanity of will-power and of action. That is one reason, amongst others, why the book is Christian in inspiration, but not suitable for a community viewed in terms of patriotism. My will lapsed. Hope disappeared with it. 'And there was a great calm.'

Before 1925, I was constantly on my guard in everyday life; I had safes, locks and a revolver. Later I saw the kind of life led by a few men I respected; they left their doors open on principle. I felt ashamed, and decided to trust mankind as I trusted wild beasts. No unsophisticated person has ever given me cause to regret my decision.[1] We shall see how long this state of things will last.

Before 1925, I had the same attitude to money as other people of my class. Now I believed that money ought not to 'work' any more than man should work; that the spontaneous generation of money has a nasty smell about it, and that the interest you fail to draw in this world will be credited to you in another, higher sphere. I once heard a Marseilles workman say of his cigarette that was burning itself out in the ash-tray: 'It's God that's smoking it.' Well, let us suppose that God draws the interest we don't draw and that he is grateful to us for it. It is a good thing to lose a certain amount; the sensation is a wholesome one. So, in 1925 I stopped investing

[1] I cannot, of course, say as much for the French middle classes; during the last five or six years, dishonesty has become a rule of life with them.

my money, and since then I have consistently maintained this attitude, believing it to be important, not only for the reasons I have just stated, but also because, by running counter to business and industry in the modern sense of these words, it symbolizes a break with a social order which deserves condemnation. Later, I had the great pleasure of learning what I did not know at the time, that the canon law of the Christian Middle Ages forbade usury (in spite of the Church's disapproval of the 'buried talent') and that the Moslem canon law still forbids it.

Before 1925, I accepted the idea of getting married for reasons of social propriety or even social interest, and I had been on the verge of this kind of action. Now it seemed hateful to me. I also became convinced, through one experience after another, of something else: if, as a bachelor, I already found the humbler preoccupations of life a constant nuisance, what would it be like were I a married man? There is a serious way of being philosophically minded, of being religiously minded and of approaching artistic creation which is incompatible with marriage, at least for certain kinds of men: either my wife would be neglected and would suffer, or the deepest part of myself—my soul—would be ruined, or more probably still both would be seriously damaged. Lastly, I wished to remain free to accept any of the possibilities hanging over me: either war, or (if I became a believer) the total form of the religious life, or (in the absence of religious belief) still greater austerity—or again, other, new adventures. In short, I realized in time the madness of forging new bonds for myself, when I had set out to achieve detachment. And once married (given my ideas, I could obviously only marry someone poor) I should be lost; by 'lost' I mean, obliged to earn money. I therefore sacrificed the possibility of marriage. Some day, perhaps, one of my books will give an idea of the fresh crises I went through in doing so. But now, supposing I had no other reason to be happy, the thought of the abyss I avoided would be enough to ensure my felicity.

Before 1925, I made do with a coarse mixture of paganism and idiosyncratic, decorative Catholicism, a Catholicism totally devoid of Christianity; with this I indulged my imagination; Jesus Christ was no more than a plaything. Then came the period of *Les voyageurs traqués*, during which I sported a few fake blasphemies in the Spanish style. I pulled God the Father's beard. Lo and behold, it came away in my hand! At first, I was rather startled. But he winked at me and said: 'It's a false one that I put on for the benefit of self-important people who, otherwise, wouldn't take me seriously.' Then, rubbing his hand over his cheek, he went on with a satisfied look: 'I'm still young, am I not? And I deserve some credit for it, I think, when you consider the prayers I have to put up with and the run-of-the-mill elect that I can't avoid letting in.' By this little fable (a pure invention from beginning to end), I mean that God, when he is in the mood, can behave like a mischievous little boy.[1] That is how I know I shall always be able to get on with him. I no longer claimed to have the faith of a Christian, but my feelings were to a large extent those of a Christian; I was keeping my distance, but I respected religion.[2] *La Rose de Sable* is a

---

[1] God says to the Jews: 'Except ye turn, and become as little children ...' He calls the Greeks a nation of children: 'O Greeks, you will always be children!' (the Egyptian priest to Solon). To the Hindoos ... But let me quote a Hindoo writer (Mukerji, *Brahman and Paria*):

p. 54: *To achieve the soul of a child, that is the aim of Hindoo religious education.*

p. 56: *One day, the Saint put his hand on my shoulder* (a child is speaking):

What do you intend to do, child?

I don't know. What do you wish me to do?

Can you play with the Lord? Do you realize that if you could play with the Lord, that might be the most extraordinary thing anyone had ever done. Everybody takes Him so seriously that they make Him deadly boring.

This passage, in my opinion, can be put on a level with the greatest mystical statements.

[2] In 1929, I wrote in *Pour une vierge noire*:

'I am not a believer but, do what I may, I remain a Catholic through having been baptized as such. I do not wish to take advantage of the Church's stretching of the term; I am, quite obviously, outside Catholicism. From this position, I look back on it, in varying moods, and I take from it what suits my spiritual and my poetic life, including the practice of religion up to a point. In short, I make use of it, in a human way.

I believe I have a healthier and worthier view of religion than I formerly had, or was willing to have. The judgement is the only thing which grows younger with age. But above all, there is nothing like getting away from

(continued overleaf)

book which sounds Christian. In 1929, I made a retreat at Montserrat and spent Holy Week at Solesmes; I wrote part of a play, *Don Fadrique,* which was Catholic in inspiration, and a scene from which is included in this volume; under the title of *A Catholic Family in the Nineteenth Century,* I began writing the life of my great-grandfather, Henry de Riancey, a journalist and politician who was active in the Catholic party during the last century; I went off to Rome to work at this book in an appropriate atmosphere. And I may add, with a smile, that during my four years as a dissenter I did not fail to pay my annual subscription to the Montserrat brotherhood, of which I was a member. . . .

I had settled the material organization of my life in what was, I am fairly sure, the ideal way for a writer. I spent, on an average, three months a year in Paris (usually in the summer, so as to avoid bores) and the rest in North Africa. There, sometimes in the sandy desert, sometimes in the desert of the big towns, drunk with the sort of hatred I feel for everything approaching entertainment; always living under a false name, keeping strictly to the discipline of 'seeing no one', going for three weeks at a time without a single

---

something for enabling you to see it properly. I know what I am talking about, having spent my life coming out whereby I went in. And I can see that if, some day, I happened to be smitten by 'grace', I should take my place in a line that I would be tempted to call the heart-line of Christianity, because I seem to see it running through the heart of Christianity, like the sap through a tree: it is a tradition stretching from the New Testament to Port-Royal, by way of St Paul and St Augustine (does it not pass very near Calvin?). I give as its motto Bossuet's cry: "Teaching of the Testament, how severe you are!" and as its symbol a perpetually narrowing road.

'The attempt to reconcile Pan and Jesus Christ will always be a sovereign exercise for stimulating the imagination of the non-believer: it leads you to excite the mind and quicken the blood by reading the biographies of certain popes who bore the mark of the Beast. These accounts are incomparable elixirs of life, capable of raising up the dead. Compared to such popes, all your Neros are naively simple. But what if one is a believer? When the Catholic Church mixes up Jesus Christ with the Fatherland, Jesus Christ with money, Jesus Christ with sport and what have you, and puts the three Lusts into gala-dress to act as handmaidens to Jesus Christ, the sight fills you with a thick and acrid poetry if you are outside the fold, but turns you to stone if, for one moment, you put yourself in the place of one who loves the crucified Christ.'

fixed obligation, having my correspondence delivered away from home so that I should never hear a ring at my door, with no other cares but work, reading and reflection, tempered by the breathing in of life and by carnal knowledge, in a region of the world where nature and the flesh alike are pleasing to me: a natural, innocent life, during which I was often alone with animals, always took my time and was always at leisure; never doing or writing except what pleased me and when it pleased me; and having to consider no one.

It was a life hampered, materially, only by the problem of servants. It may be asked why I bothered to have servants. Because, unlike the majority of men who lead the life of the mind, I have always thought—haunted as I am by the passage of time—that I should not do for myself what someone else could do for me. If, like so many men who lead the life of the mind, I had done my own housework, I should always have been thinking that the hours spent on it might have been better employed for cultural purposes, for my inner development or in playing with a ball. If manual labour is obligatory (during wartime or under a Communist régime), well and good. But as for doing it spontaneously, no. On the other hand, since 1925, and more precisely since I saw what horrible little tyrants so many Europeans turn into in the colonies, I have had a dislike of being looked after by others, feel guilty when I give an order and have never had servants in my house except when I have been able to treat them as comrades, granting them all they ask for, including all the freedom they want (rather, I think, as the Moroccans treat their slaves). It follows that their presence has sometimes been troublesome.

I have explained the details of the life I led, and which was full of the private celebrations I provided for myself, because it is during such long empty days—empty of all trifling pursuits—that one comes to understand, and take possession of, oneself. Herein lies the origin of creative work. As soon as you have scoured away all frivolous accretions, life stretches on endlessly before you. A cluttered life, during which you are tugged this way and that, is a short one. In a life freed from all except essentials, you get good measure; an eighteen-hour day during which you only do the things that matter (always a pleasant task) is something worth having. I should not be in my present situation of being able, literally, to refrain from writing another line during the next ten years and still bring out seven complete but unpublished books, if I had not evolved this sort of existence for myself.

And furthermore, a writer who has neither a lawful wedded wife nor legitimate children, who has no home in the accepted sense of the word, no worldly goods, business interests, ambition, desire for money or fixed habits, can produce natural work—I mean work that he does not need to fake so as to win fame, or feed his children, or satisfy his better half. But I won't labour the point, since I know that the public doesn't care a rap whether a work is natural or not, or whether it is merely the sorry instrument of necessity and passion.

It is an obvious fact that, from a temporal point of view, you lose heavily by leading this sort of existence. The same men who, in Paris, would come rushing round on all fours in response to a phone call, do not even answer your letters if you are in Algiers. But there are other advantages again, apart from those I have mentioned, in placing yourself in a posthumous condition. You find out who your real friends are. You find out to what extent your work can stand on its own feet. You see other people doing things and you yourself—although able to do as much—doing nothing: this is a satisfying spectacle. You feel, and know yourself to be, forgotten and this fills you with a mysterious joy; the flattering tongues have ceased to wag and the encircling silence already foretokens the symphonies of eternity. You learn to accept insults from those who know you are too far away to retaliate and, in any case, devoid of social power; soon you approve of such insults, because they are part of the natural order of things; the day comes when you even like them, and perhaps even provoke them. When you come up again after plumbing these depths, you are proof against many things. It is not possible to gain much hold over a man whose ideal is death in life—or at least to be dead to the world, since such a death is, in fact, the true life.

I have no changes to make in what I wrote as early as 1924 about the non-possession of goods and chattels (*Appareillage* in *Aux Fontaines du Désir*). It is a well-known fact that the non-possession of goods and chattels is the first step towards spiritual freedom. Wherever I live, everything except the cell devoted to work is a burden to me, a source of irritation and remorse. There may be a few *objets d'art* (I say *objets d'art* and not *objets de luxe*, because luxury has always made me shudder with disgust and scorn), but they might as well not be there, because they could be taken from me without my feeling anything more than a passing irritation. The police once warned me that a servant of mine had been stealing things from me for quite a time. I knew about it and had been letting him get on with it; my *objets d'art* had become so many dead weights and he was relieving me of them; and he got far more pleasure out of the money he made from them than I ever got from looking at them, a pleasure which, moreover, he deserved more than I did.[1] That a thinking, sensitive, creative man should have to give up time to looking after his domestic interior and to 'social duties' has always seemed abominable to me. Death will come upon us and we shall be still just as ignorant; we shall have fathomed nothing —what a mockery!—and we shall have sacrificed a third of our existence to the pursuit of the trivial and the frivolous. 'Away, then, to the desert!', we say to ourselves. But I've changed my

---

[1] At that time, I was spending a lot of money rather stupidly and he, poverty stricken as he was, saw this. He was stealing from me but I thoroughly deserved to be stolen from.

The police warned me that this same servant had planned a thoroughgoing burglary of my flat; he and his accomplices intended to relieve me of all my silver. I dismissed him because, after all, we have to make some concessions to society, but I made no official complaint and even remained on good terms with him to the extent of taking him on again from time to time and sending him financial help for years. When he died, he spoke of me with his last breath.

The evening before, or a day or two before, the date fixed for the intended burglary, the police inspector shadowing the servant heard him say to his pals, in a café: 'I'm pleased, because I've given the boss a surprise. I've springcleaned the flat while he's been away'. He was going to burgle the flat and yet he was devoted to me. People unfamiliar with such apparent contradictions and *who don't consider them as being perfectly natural have no understanding whatever of human nature.*

mind on that score, because in the desert you have to fight against everything—heat, flies, sand, scorpions, the putrefaction of food and water, etc., and this struggle whittles away your life just as much as social obligations do. That is why I think the conventional idea that you 'find God' in the desert is all rubbish; your thoughts are elsewhere. Failing a monastery, you are more likely to 'find God' in an hotel bedroom in a big city, because it is there that you are most thoroughly cleansed of all sordid pre-occupations.

Non-possession, or some small measure of casual possession, of goods and chattels, non-investment of money earned, the cutting down to a minimum of social activities, personal non-imperialism (neglect, or intermittent, absent-minded cultivation of anything that might enhance your prestige in the eyes of the world: negligence can sometimes be a great virtue!) and, lastly celibacy— these are features of a way of life recommended by all religions and all philosophies, and which was mine for eleven years, including the wildest part of the post-war period in France. I was criticized for this, not by people who will always be ready to criticize me whatever I do, but by those of my friends who would normally give the wisest counsel and who were certainly well-disposed towards me. They felt they could not rest until I was back in the usual Punch and Judy show. When they talked to me, such expressions as 'playing a part', 'taking one's place' or simply 'occupying a position' would occur again and again. That was what I ought to have been doing and I was crazy enough—crazy and cowardly enough—not to do it. 'Cowardly!' As though abstention and absolute detachment did not call for greater strength of mind![1] They kept repeating: 'Don't forget that races are won not by horses that are free to roam but by those which have accepted reins and spurs and the bit.' What they forgot was that some people do not see life as a race, and even regard the conception as childish and vulgar. I received letters accusing me of leading 'too simple' a life, of 'not living up to my station', of being 'too egalitarian'—all of which gives an unforgettable glimpse of human values as seen by society.

[1] 'Not to take when able to take is the essentially virile act.' (*Aux Fontaines du Désir.*)

People are for ever trying to bring out the least good side of our characters—the very people we might have expected to encourage us to follow the straight and narrow path. When, in 1929, I would not allow an early work, *L'Exil*, to be translated into German because it showed a French mother preventing her son from joining up during the war, the French Right-Wing papers declared that my scruples were stupid. When I gave up the idea of bringing out *La Rose de Sable,* because the novel might do some disservice to France, the only man who told me I had 'lacked courage' by not publishing the novel was a fellow-writer of nationalistic tendencies. And it has always been my experience that, whenever young men or girls want to take holy orders or the veil, criticism and opposition come from their Catholic environment. I have always noticed, too, that whenever a young man with no money marries a penniless young woman, it is people of their own kind—'respectable' people —who greet the marriage with haughty, derisive laughter. Not to mention the fate of those saintly individuals, whom we ought to revere on bended knee because they have given all their wealth to the poor and whom their despicable 'heirs', taking advantage of 'the bond of kinship', put away in the loony bin, with the unanimous approval of right-thinking people.

I have said that by 1928 the *Voyageurs traqués* crisis had begun to show signs of abatement. In 1929, I was still groping, as can be seen from *Pour une vierge noire*. Here is a curious example of my uncertainty. I had become more genuine, and perhaps esteemed that this called for some distinctive garb. I quite seriously considered joining the army, and asked one of my colleagues in Algiers, who had some influence with military personnel out there, to inquire how an unfit, ex-private of thirty-three could set about transforming himself—there and then, I suppose—into a regular officer. I cannot have received much encouragement, because the affair went no further.

It was in 1930 that I regained my stability. Since 1930 I have been very happy—and that makes more happiness than the three weeks claimed by Goethe, and it was achieved much less ostentatiously than his. It was not happiness that fell from the heavens; it was my own work and I paid for it. That is why I am not ashamed of it, supposing one could ever be ashamed of being happy. I may add that almost all the happiness which came to me was obtained in guises other than my true identity. It is the obscure life which gets the full force of the sun. During my years of crisis, I had published only a few feverish and disjointed extracts from a private diary. In 1929, I wrote *Moustique ou l'Hôpital,* a novel which has a working-class setting and shows how people die when they cannot afford to buy tonics. In 1930, I began *La Rose de Sable,* my first 'real' novel.

Life is a wonderful thing. When you turn it over and examine it thoroughly, when you see *that which is,* you feel like getting down on your knees. *That which is*—three remarkable syllables! Life is certainly an extraordinary thing, more extraordinary than genius. It always holds something in store to startle us. When we ask a question of it, it rarely gives the expected answer. I have a passion for asking that kind of question. There is a proverb which says: 'The old woman didn't want to die, because she was still learning every day.' Like the old woman, I am still learning every day. Joseph Kessel attacked Paul Morand for using as the title of one of his books, *Rien que la Terre* (Nothing but the earth), saying, more or less, 'What blasphemy! I'm sorry for people who have that attitude.' Kessel is right, but I had agreed with Morand. For three years, I had proclaimed, like him, 'Rien que la terre!' I was like a man just starting on opium. It appears that opium, although a key to Paradise, begins by making you ill, so that you need a period of initiation. The three years described in *Les voyageurs traqués* was my period of sickening apprenticeship in the art of mastering life. Now all that is over. I have learnt, once and for all, how vast life is and how it makes you want to go down on your bended knee. When I sink into the hideousness of extreme old age, I shall still have the sovereign and impregnable knowledge, the divine knowledge, that I did what I have done—that I have not wasted my time, but cleared away from my path all that had to be cleared away and allowed nothing to hold me back. I shall surely die in peace! (Touch wood.)

FOREWORD TO 'SERVICE INUTILE'

Poor, foolish youth, how confused it is in face of life! But now, when the first wrinkles are chasing each other across your brow, what confidence you have in life. What complicity between life and you! What conspiratorial smiles! 'I know you, you old rascal!' Now you can be sure that life will never betray you, never has betrayed you. You have always risked everything, and never made a false step. You have always walked on the edge of the abyss, and never slipped over. It was never God who was holding your hand; it was always a human being, some frail, little human being (for I have never been alone, I have always been passed from hand to hand), and the human being did not let you down. If the whole of my novel, *Les Célibatiares,* had to be destroyed, I should like to save one sentence from it: '*Les hommes ne nous font jamais tout le mal qu'ils pourraient*' (Men never do us all the evil of which they are capable). Yes, it is true, they are not really as wicked as all that. How many had only to raise a finger to send me hurtling into the abyss. They did not do so. I thank them for it.

I wrote once, a long time ago: 'I don't give a damn for happiness.' This proves how music can mislead you. The thought came to me while I was listening to music, that is to say when I was not myself. In actual fact, I was made for happiness. I had been born with a keener and more demanding sense of happiness than is usual in my fellow-creatures, and thanks to my lucky star, I realized this in time. I was made for felicity, for a felicity ever loftier and ever more profound. Such felicity I have enjoyed and still enjoy.

As the desert sky can be veiled by a sand mist, my happiness was clouded over, during long periods, by the awareness of some great issue which was not as it should be: the injustice shown by one class to another and by one race to another. Then, after suffering through the oppressor, I saw him being oppressed in turn and I suffered afresh. I suffered through France when I considered France as a colonial power, but later the trials that France was undergoing because of her enemies or because of her own behaviour destroyed my lightness of heart and my freedom of mind, whenever they happened to return; for days and days, I could not 'get a grip on myself', because I was thinking of the misfortunes of my country. You can always find something to suffer about, if you are fond of suffering. But I have no fondness for it. Unhappily, and quite against my will, I find endless, preposterous causes for suffering. I admit that, sometimes, I have felt weary of my tendency to take so much to heart questions that are really foreign to me; weary —when, by rare good fortune, my private life and the life of those dearest to me was following a very happy course—of being saddened by the fate of my country, or by the social problem, or by the racial question, all of which leave most men crassly indifferent.

I did myself an injustice in quoting only the three lusts as incentives for my departure in 1925. I was prancing with impatience to go to Morocco and achieve some action worthy of myself. Since the Armistice, I had been shut away with my war memories (idealized out of all proportion, I dare say), like Don Quixote with his books on chivalry. Everything that can be imagined going on in the brain of a boy of nineteen was going on in mine, and I was twenty-nine. I have always been a bit backward for my age. During the whole of the autumn of 1924, I practised riding and shooting at Gastinne's. But once I got to Africa I realized that if there was any duty to be done, it was not to smite 'the infidels' but rather to defend them. That was where justice, and even courage, lay. From the very beginning, the native problem was the only one which caught my attention in North Africa. In March 1930 I began *La Rose de Sable* and spent two hard years over it. Hard, because I worked at it persistently, and sustained work is not my strong point; but I was compelled to do it; having embarked on a social theme, I couldn't just follow my own whims; I had to see things at first hand, talk to people, check thousands of details and also my own judgements. Hard, mainly, because I was divided against myself; the conflict between patriotism and justice is a horrible thing. By the spring of 1932, I had finished *La Rose de Sable*. It was a work fired essentially by charity.

To write, and not to publish, is a very pleasant position to be in. I had prolonged the pleasure. I had made it last three years, counting *La Petite Infante de Castille* as my most recent appearance in print, and that—apart from some thirty odd pages—had been by way of

FOREWORD TO 'SERVICE INUTILE'

a relaxation. Meanwhile, I could have brought out *Les Jeunes Filles* or a selection of essays. But after such a long silence, I was prepared to make a come-back only with *La Rose de Sable*, which was the book that meant most to me. People kept repeating that I had nothing more to say and from now on could only be referred to in the past tense, and I admit I was not displeased at the prospect of bringing out an eight-hundred-page work to contradict the sorry picture of myself that was being put about by my literary friends.

So I came back to France (April 1932) and it wasn't long before I was writing in the newspaper *La Liberté*:

'I am horrified at the progress that has been made in the space of two and a half years (the length of my last absence) by everything except integrity. In future, mind and conscience will speak a language increasingly incomprehensible to the majority. I wonder how mind and conscience will be able to resist the attacks made on them from all sides, with the help, moreover, of the social and intellectual *élite*; for whereas the German *élite* has saved Germany from the consequences of her defeat, the French *élite* is doing its utmost to sabotage our victory. The situation is urgent and critical and I am all the more conscious of it, through having been plunged suddenly into it after a long absence.

'Our country is undermined from within and attacked from without. By surreptitious infiltration, the foreigner has established himself within our gates. Our national feeling is weak and indeterminate; I notice a total lack of public spirit and an anarchistic conformism which itself displays all the stupidity that it ascribes to right-wing conformism. There is no indignation, no hint of any lively reaction, from anybody; France is a soft cheese, which anybody can cut into and hack about at will. I have sometimes been accused of being lacking in love, but I feel indignation which is a form of love.'

Would it be right to publish a work which criticized both the principle of colonialism and its application by my own countrymen, at a time when the country needed all its remaining strength to defend itself against the enemy without and its own government within? I hesitated for several months, cut out passages that were too starkly authentic, and imagined I could produce a softened, that is to say, a false, version. Finally, reverting to my true self, I gave up the idea of publishing it altogether, just as a nation will run one of its own warships aground, rather than let the enemy make use of it.

Instead of *La Rose de Sable*, and although I had a presentiment of the sort of welcome such a change of programme would receive, I decided to publish reprints of two books which might have a beneficial effect. As I expected, my literary friends were more tearful than ever; I hadn't published a new work for four years, and here I was falling back on reprints. However, I had in reserve the two volumes of *Moustique* (600 pages), the two volumes of *La Rose* (800 pages), *Un voyageur solitaire est un diable* (200 pages), not counting the first sketch of a book on animals and the hundred or so poems of *Almouradiel*. But I was quite happy to let so much manuscript lie fallow; one should always have something in hand. So I set to work again and wrote *Les Célibataires*.

That was how I spent my time during the years when I was writing *Service inutile*. And let me say again that I have given only a bare and rapid outline to explain these essays and put them in their context. In short, what had I done? I had lived. I had given pleasure to myself and to those I loved, and to others I had done less harm than I might. I had been myself, at a time when the world was saying threateningly, 'You will not be forgiven unless you lie.' 'It is an absolute, even divine perfection,' writes Montaigne, 'to know how to enjoy one's being honestly.' I had seen things as they really are. I had kneaded the stuff of life, in an existence warm with adventure and in which everything was sound and true. I had produced, along with my healthy fruit, some wizened ones and some dead leaves, which is in accordance with the laws of nature. Let God, if he exists, pick out what belongs to him; it is certainly there. Ought I to have done something else? Cut a figure? Given up what I could do fairly well, because I did it instinctively, in order to strain to do badly something that was not really in my line? Ought I to have renounced the sort of happiness which has no purpose other than itself? I had been like an untrammelled stream, which neither turns mill-wheels nor sets factories working, but where children bathe and animals come to drink and which, for better or for worse, fulfils its little task upon this earth, always supposing that streams and men have tasks to fulfil—in my view, a highly preposterous and ridiculous supposition.

March 1935. Never has war and revolution seemed more likely or closer; you feel you could put out your hand and touch them. French excitability is going to have a field day. This gives a not unpleasant piquancy to life. 'Troubled times are very enjoyable,' someone said to me, with his nostrils quivering as he sniffed the odour of approaching doom.

Ever since the 11th November 1918, I have believed that war would break out again, and very soon. *La Relève du Matin,* which was published in 1920, ends with the words: '... in five years' time, during the next invasion of France.' And why was there to be this new invasion? Because the French 'have begun to play the fool again'.

As recently as three years ago, when I brought out *Mors et Vita,* men for whom I feel respect looked me severely in the eye and said: 'I don't want my sons to go through that.' Their intention was *to teach me a lesson* because, in their view, to think war inevitable, as I did, was to wish it so. 'Alas, it is, then, the same thing to foresee a misfortune and to wish for it?' exclaimed Savonarola long ago, since *eadem sunt omnia semper.*

No, my fellow-Frenchmen are so convinced that we are heading for war (at least, they were convinced a week ago; they can be terrified or reassured at will), that it wouldn't take much to make them think me sceptical: 'But can't you see, it's absolutely obvious!' But they don't want to prepare for war. What they want is to remain absorbed in their petty interests and petty pleasures, with their eyes tight shut and their ears plugged, right up to the very last moment: to be precise, until the aeroplanes begin dropping bombs. The Press, which for once deserves praise, can give warning after warning. In any newspaper, the article on 'German armaments' is the one everybody skips.

Some Frenchmen feel in exile in their mother country. The cause is, partly, the attitude France has taken up in face of the danger; rightly or wrongly, this attitude does not seem to them very virile. These internal exiles—Henry Bordeaux spoke of *émigrés de l'intérieur* (internal émigrés)—watch the gap between them and their fellow-countrymen growing with every month that passes. Occasionally, they make an effort. 'Come, come! I want to feel in harmony with other people!' It is true that, from one point of view, the carefree attitude of the French can appear admirable. Let us make haste to adopt that point of view. In any case, a nation which complains loudly of its poverty and is stupefied by the pleasures of living is a sight worth seeing. The French are a mysterious people.

> *Qui craint le grand méchant loup?*
> *C'est p'être vous,*
> *C'est pas nous!*
> *Vous voyez si on tient l'coup.*
> *Tra la la la la.*

> Who's afraid of the big bad wolf?
> It may be you,
> It's not us!
> We don't let him get us down.
> Tra la la la la.

I propose an alternative reading:

> *Y a des 'Marne' pour un coup.*

> There'll always be another Battle of the Marne.

Good luck, little pigs! Go on believing in miracles, you who are said to believe in nothing. After all, it is really funny that I should find myself preaching to you. Am I not exactly like you? Just one more minute of happiness! In the times in which we live, every day gained is a victory. A day will come when it will be said that people who did not live in France between 1930 and 1935 cannot have known the delight of living.

FOREWORD TO 'SERVICE INUTILE'

I have gambled with my life many times since 1925. But never in so carefully deliberate a way as on certain occasions in 1927. I gambled, and when the result was life and not extinction, I was at first taken aback; I had bet on extinction. I had to adjust myself to living. I put my confidence in nature and my destiny, with both of which I am on good terms (they have never let me down) and I sketched out a programme of work extending over a number of years. I mention this because some people think I like war and am secretly longing for it. Were I to die in a war in the fairly near future, I should suffer a double death; I should be deprived of life and of the chance to give my life a meaning.

And yet the desire to live until I have fulfilled myself is not so strong as to make me long passionately for the few years needed to give a sense to my little appearance on life's stage. It is understandable that a young man of twenty should be revolted at the prospect of death. But a man of forty or thereabouts? If he has not had his fill of creation by the age of forty, he must have been a prize ass. There are worse things than dying, and one of them is to agree to live a base life. On re-reading this book, I am struck by one remark in particular: 'We must feel at home in nature.' Yes, that is a sound observation. I think I should still feel at home in nature, even if nature were taken from me.

There is also the revolution to be considered. It is undoubtedly 'necessary'. At least, if we adopt a lofty standpoint. If we take a humdrum view, I think very few changes would be needed to allow the present régime to weather the storm. If we take a lofty standpoint, obviously *quid divinum* must descend upon France. It should be easy to see by the kind of lament that rises from all the essays collected in *Service inutile* whether or not their author is satisfied with the present order of things.[1] It appears that the

[1] There are two kinds of patriotism. That which consists in believing that everything done by one's country is right; and that which consists in thinking that everything done by one's country is wrong. Mine is the second kind. I must observe, however, that the severe criticism of the French expressed in most of the essays in *Service inutile* strikes me as excessive, now that I am correcting the proofs in Paris in the summer of 1935. Almost the whole book

(continued overleaf)

revolution will be carried out for the benefit of the people. Well and good, although I don't believe it for one moment. Not for the benefit of the genuine people, the masses, sandwiched between the clever ones at the top who are pulling the strings and the pals at the bottom who are harming the cause. When I was a young man, I used to spend two hours a week doing social work among poor children; I would encourage them to read, which was rather silly, or I organized games, which was better. During the war, I refused to be anything more than a private, so as not to be cut off from the working classes and obliged 'to keep my distance'; and so as not to have to lead them to their deaths in accordance with plans that I had not myself drawn up. When, after demobilization, I went in for sport, my aim was not to compete stupidly with the chronometer but to be with the lower classes again. I found myself with them once more during my wandering life, and with people more humble, even—with colonial natives, who are working-class pariahs. I refused to invest my money; 'Dilory, the tramp',[1] was my financial mentor. I refused to have a home, because I did not want to have any *property*, except that which was *proper to me*, that is, my head and my heart. I turned down the money that a government was offering me—along with its instructions—to celebrate, conquests unworthy of praise, because one can't hymn an evil even if it is a necessary evil. I wrote *La Rose* on behalf of the natives and *L'Hôpital* on behalf of the working classes. I am quite ready, mentally, for social upheavals, just as I am ready on the material plane, having nothing to lose, but I have little doubt about the fate

[1] A character in the Comtesse de Ségur's books for children.

---

was written outside France; this may mean that my vision of France was slightly distorted. During the four months I have spent in Paris, I have been impressed rather by the good sense, the willingness, the niceness (the politeness, even!) of ordinary people. When political parties can, with impunity, preach hatred as violently as they do at the moment, one wonders whether, instead of reproaching France with a lack of vitality, it would not be fairer to admire the extraordinary strength she needs to defend herself on her own —yes, with no help from any source—against the evils that her internal enemies are trying by every means to inflict upon her.

a revolution would hold in store for me. In my great-grandfather's generation, three members of my family were imprisoned for political reasons and two were assassinated, so I knew that I would end up in front of the firing-squad. No matter, I put my trust in the working classes, just as when I was in wild country, I would leave my travelling-kit with rather hostile-looking strangers, and the only little light in my dreary day would be the gesture I had made in thus placing a bottomless trust in my fellow-men. Trust is one of the divine possibilities of man.

Nothing could be more natural than to end up in front of the firing-squad, with or without famous last words. However difficult the times may be, they are only obeying the laws of nature. The insanity of war is more terrifying than the insanity of peace for the flesh, but not for the mind. It all comes to the same thing in the end. Nations threatened by their neighbours, traitors in governments and civil wars have always been part of the scheme of things. The events hanging over us run true to classical form and the thought that humanity has been monotonously repeating them since life first smiled on this earth should teach us to be reasonable and to look forward to them calmly.

In any case, none of this affects a certain part of ourselves, which is the essential part; nor can it trouble a certain kind of peace that lies within us, the peace which is beyond all intelligence and all love. If I make an effort of will, I see myself, or think I see myself, at such and such a point in time and space and I invent for myself the duty of taking my share in the passions of the age. But however much we may condescend to engage in external matters, we still find ourselves asking the question: is this duty justified? Where is reality? How can the contemplative life be reconciled with the social? How can one make an honest gesture of belonging—how can one belong—if one does not belong? The physical man in me sees impending events through the narrow end of the telescope and then the spiritual man looks at them through the broad end. In the one case, they seem bigger than they are and, in the other, tiny and infinitely remote. But the two visions cannot be simultaneous. Does this mean that we should fall back on the expedient of alternating between them? On even dates look at things from the point of view of immediate necessity and on odd dates from the point of view of eternity? Can such a series of contradictions, like certain electric currents, give an illusion of continuity? And if so, is such an illusion enough?

Each phase of life presents its own particular problem. The problems are solved in succession and we pass on to the next. 'Are solved' is the way to put it; we don't feel that we have solved them; they seem to have solved themselves of their own accord; there comes a day when we notice that our bloodstream is no longer feeding them and that, for us, they are now dead problems. 'For us' only, because I think no problems are ever solved. Once past, they become, strictly speaking, incomprehensible to us. When I was an adolescent, they all presented themselves at once, which is normal at that age. In the trenches, they were reduced to a very simple form; how to do a little more than one's duty and, at the same time, avoid being wiped out. Then, during the period described in *Les Voyageurs traqués*, everything was swallowed up by the problem of happiness, which finally stated itself in the form of the dilemma: to do or not to do? Then the problem of happiness died the death in its turn, and my new trouble was the problem of life and art: how could they be brought into line with each other? How could I avoid feeling frustrated at not living, when I was busy working, and uneasy at not working, when I was busy living? This dilemma presents itself daily, and can only cease when fatigue, old age or illness make living impossible. Then, in Africa, I could not reconcile two duties I found in flat contradiction with each other: my duty towards France and my duty towards the individual. And now there is a new conflict arising within me, which again concerns France; the conflict between the mother country where we happen to have been born and that other, inner mother country we have created for ourselves.

Action and non-action will meet in eternity and will be eternally intertwined there. But what of the present? The soldier-monk! It is around this rather disturbing character that my thoughts are now gravitating, in so far as I have thoughts. As a soldier, he braces action; as a monk, he undermines it. *Aedificabo et destruam;* I shall build, and then I shall destroy that which I have built. There we have an epigraph for this book—an epigraph for my life.

Service Inutile, 1935
(Written in Paris, March 1935)

THE SAMURAI'S UMBRELLA

THIS PAPER was read in its present form (except for two paragraphs which were in a different position) on the 11th January 1938, at a meeting of the *Rive Gauche* group, as an introduction to a lecture by the German publicist, M Otto Abetz, on 'German youth and the question of happiness'. The meeting was held under the auspices of the *Comité France-Allemagne,* but it is probable that the attitude expressed was not quite the same as that of the *Comité*.

The swastika originated in the four-spoked wheel and the disc that was used in ancient times to represent the sun. It was the emblem carried by the last pagan armies in the fourth century during their battles with Constantine's armies whose symbol was the Christian cross; the two emblems are again face to face in present-day Germany.

The Greeks called the sun *panderkes* 'the all-seeing'. The seeing of all things as they are has a name: clearsightedness. And clearsightedness is, in my opinion, the greatest quality of the intelligence because it brings the character into play. I cannot say whether I am going to shed a ray of lucidity on the problem of the present attitude of the French towards the Germans but at least I am going to try.

What lies ahead of us, Germans and Frenchmen? There lies ahead the possibility of another war. It is, no doubt, a very strong possibility.

Some people find this possibility very chilling. 'It's impossible,' they explain. 'It would be too ghastly, etc.' This reaction is not worth discussing. There are also people who say: 'If only the *élite* of both countries, especially the intellectual *élite,* or the ex-servicemen, or the young people, could get together, they could strengthen the cause of peace.' I feel obliged to say that I don't believe this for one moment. I do believe that if the politicians, diplomats and financiers of both countries got together at a given time and with precise and limited aims—I emphasize these two conditions—they could at that particular moment prevent war for a certain length of time. But I don't believe that the getting together of either the *élite* or the masses can further the cause of peace. It will take more than mutual understanding between two nations to stop the leader of either attacking the other, if he thinks his country will derive some benefit from war. Even though the two nations should happen to be on the most friendly terms, a six weeks' Press campaign would soon set that right. When we say, 'If only the French and the Germans got to know each other better, the risk of war would be lessened,' either we are trying to deceive others, or we are deceiving ourselves.

Finally there is a third attitude. 'Let the French and Germans get to know each other better, not in the hope that this understanding may avert war, which it is incapable of doing, but simply because it is a good thing, because they've plenty to learn from each other, because it's good from the human point of view that they should understand each other, respect each other, indeed make friends across the frontiers. Should war break out, perhaps something of this would remain: for instance, in the treatment of prisoners. But this is a pure hypothesis and of small importance; France and Germany ought to get to know each other for the reasons that make it advisable that all great nations should know each other. There are, in addition, those mysterious reasons for attraction which arise from hostility. Such is the third attitude in face of the possibility of another Franco-German war, and it is the attitude I myself share.

I don't find it in the least inhuman that an individual belonging to nation A should feel an intellectual affinity with, or even friendship for, an individual belonging to nation B, and yet at the same time say to himself: 'In six months he may well kill me.' I don't find it at all inhuman that an individual belonging to nation A should admire the leaders of nation B, or even be in sympathy with them and yet say to himself: 'In six months they may well hurl their people against mine.' The leaders of nation B are playing the game as they understand it. It's up to us who belong to nation A to play our game, that is to be strong enough to win the day. This is a healthy attitude. It has all the vigour, grandeur and innocence of stark nakedness.

I have often expressed this attitude since the First World War, as the readers of my books know. Before Hitler came to power, German university professors often asked me to go and speak to their students. I thought it proper to warn them of what I would say if ever I went to Germany. These professors were mostly Jewish. My reply chilled them. They wrote back saying, 'You discuss Franco–German relations as if war were possible. That is dangerous. We must work on the assumption that war is impossible.' I replied that war was possible, and that I always based my assumptions on things as they are, in which case it was better that I should not meet their students. But I had already set down in black and white the talk I would give if I visited the German universities. It was published in *Mors et Vita* and I shall give a short extract from it now. Here, then, is what I intended to say to the young Germans:

> Gentlemen, we must admit the possibility that one day it may again be our duty to kill each other. This eventuality must be calmly faced: there are worse things than dying. Let me say, in passing, that of course there is no question of 'fatality' in Franco–German relations. A serious-minded man shrugs his shoulders at the word 'fatality'. Here, as elsewhere, it is a question of will-power. Which side will the will-power be on, the French or the German? On that point let us keep our thoughts to ourselves.
>
> Just as our former hostility does not in my view exclude friendly relations in the present, so our present friendliness does not seem to me to exclude the possibility of hostility in the future.
>
> Neither war itself, nor the right to wage war, gives me the feeling that a higher order of things is being impaired, provided the combatants are of comparable strength; nor do I have the feeling that a higher order of being is impaired by our moving, almost overnight, from friendliness to warfare, and to appalling warfare, at that. It is a wise and sensible manner of loving

human beings and human situations, and one that has often been preached throughout the centuries, to love them as if they were possessions that might easily be lost: and if this maxim had not existed, we should have had to invent it in order to apply it to the sort of peace we have today. There is another well-known maxim, although one that is rarely respected (especially its second half), according to which you should treat your enemy as if he might one day become your friend, and your friend as if he might one day become your enemy. I think this is an excellent maxim; I have almost always lived according to it; it has stood me in good stead. The man is strong indeed who can keep his attention fixed on conditions which are the exact opposite of the state in which he happens to find himself, and who considers them not only possible, but even equally good.

Homer's Greeks declare that when they fight, they feel no hatred. After his great combat with Ajax, Hector suggests bringing the struggle to a close and adds: 'Let us exchange illustrious gifts so that the Trojans and the Acheans may say: Bravely did they sustain the struggle, yet they parted *good friends.*' When Achilles kills Lycaon he calls him *philos* and says to him 'Die, friend!' If another war should break out between us, let this phrase stand as its epitaph.

Let us strive, then, gentlemen, to give tone to the ghost-like peace which exists between us. But at this point, I stand down. First of all because there are specialists in the subject who will harangue you more ably than I can. Secondly because I don't believe in the effectiveness of words in the cause of peace. I think that for the last fifteen years they have done no good at all—they have even done harm in so far as they have reduced peace to a mere word—and a platitudinous word at that: and the platitude has been puffed up with so many words that it must finally explode. With this, Gentlemen, I leave you. Perhaps we shall meet again—perhaps in peace, perhaps in war. If in peace, we shall look at each other with pride: we shall have done much for our fellow-men. If in war, and in a war for which we are in no way responsible, having failed to achieve the good of our fellow-men, we shall try to discover some good for ourselves; no experience in life should be wasted—not even that. For if war has its smoke and its flames, it also has its light. 'Light bearing' like the archangel you have heard of.

* * *

I have found the following anecdote in a Japanese book. A Samurai was on his way towards the place where he was going to fight a duel with another Samurai. He had put up his umbrella, because it was raining. Suddenly he saw his opponent who was also going in the same direction, but had no umbrella. Whereupon the first Samurai invited the second to take shelter under his. And so, conversing politely under the same umbrella they strolled towards the appointed place, and there, taking out their sabres, they proceeded to do what they had come to do and were both killed. When I tell this anecdote to Frenchmen it makes them laugh because laughter is the reaction of present-day Frenchmen to anything noble. Nevertheless, Franco–German peacetime manifestations are, in my view, so many conversations under the umbrella.

L'Equinoxe de Sepscribre, 1939
(Written in January, 1938)

THE 7th MARCH 1936

THE MAN WAS SITTING at the table, in the shabby hotel room, under a centre light that was both too high and too dim. When he heard a step on the stairs—heavy and slow—he got up and opened the door. A young soldier came in. The man smiled.

'I would know your step anywhere. But you're dragging your feet a bit, old chap, since you got those boots . . . Anything fresh?'

'I don't know if I can see you tomorrow. We may be confined to barracks. There's a rumour that we might leave the day after tomorrow for L——.' (This was one of the 'security' fortress-towns on the Alsatian border.)

'Because of the scare about the military occupation of the Rhineland. But . . . is it as likely as all that?'

'Don't you read the papers?'

'What! those filthy rags! Never. A day without newspapers is a day of purity, liberation, deliverance.'

'But in unsettled times . . . ?'

'That's just when you shouldn't read them.'

The young man had removed his cap and overcoat and taken a seat. He was nineteen years old, but looked even younger. He was badly-shaven, spotty, and along his damp forehead his cap had left a red mark. Already, the little room was pervaded by the rank smell of leather and grease coming from his boots.

'I suppose when you're up there I'll not be able to go and see you?'

'I don't think so.'

'Do you expect to be there long?'

'They say five or six months.'

'What a crazy idea of yours it was to rush straight into the most risky outfit! Just as if there weren't enough regiments in France

143

without choosing frontier-protection . . . I've told you often enough . . .'

He had said it 'often enough' but his son just replied 'what difference does it make?' And the man who understood his own fatalism, failed to understand fatalism in his child.

The young man didn't reply this time either but took from his pocket five packets of service cigarettes and set them out on the table. His father had taken a fancy to these cigarettes, and wouldn't smoke any others. He smiled and put three francs on the table: the boy pushed one franc back.

'A pal sold them to me and he only charged me eight sous a packet.'

The man smiled, rather touched.

'Hopelessly unselfish, as usual! You know you won't get on in life if you don't like money. They'll make you pay for that! But you must get used now to the idea of asking me for the things you need. I don't know what L—— is like. It may be a god-forsaken frontier town where there's nothing to be had. When I'm here and can ask you definite questions "Are your socks in good condition? Is the food good?" you sometimes condescend to answer me. But as for writing to tell me there's something you would like, you wouldn't dream of that. Why?'

'It never crosses my mind.'

'You're a silly ass, my boy. You might at least grasp the fact that I'm doing myself a favour when I give you something . . .'

Yes, hopelessly unselfish, honest and nice—in all respects. Not an ounce of malice, or graspingness, or meanness in his make-up. In 1936, in France! What a miraculous survival! 'A thousand shall fall at thy side, and ten thousand at thy right hand: but it shall not come nigh thee' (Psalm xci). How can he fail to be trampled on sooner or later? The whole horde will ride roughshod over him. The man loved his son, but it was perhaps not so much because he was his son as because he could respect him absolutely.

They talked of one thing and another. Not a word, however, about the German occupation of the Rhineland, or the seriousness of the situation. The man was barely forty, and he had been brilliant in his day. But for a number of years now he had ceased to express opinions about important matters, or things that were of vital concern to him. He would have had too much to say, and he would have said it to too little purpose. He had become so taciturn that in the little Alsatian garrison town where he came every month from Paris to spend a few days with his son, he eventually noticed that he was arousing curiosity through never speaking to anyone. 'Perhaps they think I'm a spy.' The son hardly spoke either, but for a different reason. During the six months he had been slogging in this 'active' garrison, his main experience had been one of fatigue. When he said to his father: 'I won't come tomorrow. We've got shooting practice seventeen miles from here. That means a thirty-five mile march during the day. I'll be too tired,' the father did not press the point.

At the moment they were discussing military matters. The father was surprised to see his son take such an interest in them and was naïvely disposed to think how unfair it was that such a knowledgeable young fellow should not have been made a corporal. To keep the conversation going, he asked questions about the new weapons, although he had no real interest in them and made a point of showing that he knew something about them. When he was ignorant of something, or did not remember, he would apologize, saying, 'That didn't exist in my day.' On this particular evening, he even related one of his wartime memories, touching it up a little.

Then, for ten minutes, the young man explained to his father how much more convenient and economical a lighter was than matches. He went on and on, taking his to pieces. 'Perhaps I shan't see him again for months. How long exactly? And if the Germans occupy the Rhineland, what will happen?' The man imagined the worst. He was well aware that this evening their relationship should be marked by a certain seriousness. But his son had never had much to say for himself: a word now and again, very few gestures, impassive features; he rarely laughed but only smiled, a thin smile which gave a curve to the line of his lips. Something about him suggested a young Hindoo God, a remote *bodhisattva,* a denizen of another world. The man put his emotion into words, but only silently. He was paralysed by a kind of inhibition. And already—for he had been a soldier, and would be a soldier again—there existed between them the embarrassed self-consciousness of fighting men.

'Are you having dinner with me?'
'It's not possible tonight.'
'Your girl?'

The young man did not reply, but smiled. He never told a lie. If he were asked an indiscreet question he did not bother to reply; if he wanted to admit something, he smiled but said nothing. The father did not feel hurt in the least. He found it perfectly natural and normal that his son should spend the last evening before what might be a tragic separation with a woman, instead of with himself.

Finally the boy got up to take his leave. As usual, he spent some time in front of the mirror, pulling his coat into position, polishing his belt with his handkerchief and setting his cap at a 'cute' angle. And as usual the father smoothed out his coat for him under his belt at the back. He would have liked to say 'Don't walk too quickly in the street so that I can see you for as long as possible'. But he didn't say it.

'I'll wait for you at midday, here, for lunch. If you don't arrive by one, I'll know that you're confined to barracks and that you leave for L—— the day after tomorrow—and I'll go back to Paris at the same time. In which case, don't forget to send me your exact address at L——. Good-bye, son.'

'Good-bye.'

Their hands barely touched. (The young man's hand which used to be so clean and transparent was now rough and always slightly grimy.) For one moment the man wondered whether he shouldn't kiss his son. But he didn't. His son knew he loved him. When you really love someone, there's no need to kiss him or tell to him so.... Only women have a mania for constant reassurance.

The man moved over to the window. There were plenty of soldiers walking about in the street. He tried to pick out his son —but couldn't recognize him. 'Yet he must have left the hotel by now. Perhaps he realized he had forgotten something when he was half-way down the stairs. Or perhaps he has met someone he knows in the entrance hall.' His eyes were glued to the crowd below. Ten minutes passed thus. Finally he left the window. 'I haven't been able to pick out my son and I may never see him again.' He remained motionless for a long time, seated at the table. What he sensed of the future was coming towards him, bearing the face of grief, and he felt crucified in advance.

In the restaurant there was only one diner besides himself, a young man of about twenty who was gobbling his way through a detective magazine. A German voice came from the radio. The man did not understand German, but made out the name of Hitler. 'If I went nearer the set, I'm sure I should learn something.' But the inhibition he had felt a little while before continued to paralyse him. 'And yet this young fellow doesn't seem at all upset. Of course, it takes a lot to drag a Frenchman away from his detective muck. In fact, this is beyond human possibilities.'

The waiter, who, since he had been eating there had never once spoken to him except for strictly utilitarian purposes, came up and said:

'So they've taken it over again . . . Cologne, Mayence, Kehl. We must put a stop to this. Things can't go on like this.'

It was certain now. His son would not come tomorrow. He had been caught up in the terrible mechanism which grinds on until it lands you in the grave. Their parting had been a real, wartime one. At the front, a man is ready to sacrifice his life for a comrade, but he leaves him for ever with a mere 'good-bye', without even offering to shake hands.

'If he hasn't come by one o'clock tomorrow, I'll go to the barracks.'

Why, at nine o'clock in the evening, did the church bell start ringing? The first two peals happened to be on the same note. 'Could it be an alarm-bell?' A little later voices started singing in the street. 'Are they going to sing the "Marseillaise"? In that case it's all up.' The noise of singing changed into something unrecognizable.

'If I went down to the square or to the station, I would get news.' But he was already undressed—it would mean putting on his clothes again.

Late in the evening there was a great noise of motor-cycles in the street. 'I could always ring for the waiter. He would surely tell me something.' All he had to do was to stretch out his hand. He didn't do it. He was still in the grip of the same inhibition—the immense, obscure, tragic French inhibition of the year 1936.

He awoke at two o'clock in the morning and went straight to the window. The hotel overlooked the station square: from the window could be seen the station, the railway line, the countryside. Everything was still in the pale, pure night. Not a soul to be seen. There was a light in the station-master's office: apart from the lights on the track this was the only one. No, there was nothing out of the ordinary. No extra trucks on the line. None of that painful chugging that could once be heard when overloaded trains were going up to the front, as if each one were climbing its own Hill of Calvary.

He thought he wouldn't be able to go off to sleep again, but he soon sank into slumber. It had been just the same in the past when he used to say to himself 'I'll never be able to get to the end of today's march. I'll collapse.' And then he would do one, two, three days' marching.

He woke again at six o'clock and went once more to the window. The station square was as deserted in broad daylight as it had been in the middle of the night. Then a youth appeared on the scene and started to play, all by himself, with a ball, like a cat playing with a roll of paper. 'If only I were as carefree as he is!' *Except ye become as little children*. Yes, Lord, but how can I? I who remember, imagine, foresee and know . . .

While dressing, he returned several times to the window. Now the square was beginning to liven up. Local citizens were quietly smoking and laughing. A workman made for the station carrying a fishing-rod. Seeing these little indications of normality, the man of forty felt very like his son, who, when he was frightened once during a storm at sea, had been reassured on hearing one of the ship's officers whistling.

But when he got outside, the atmosphere in the station was no longer the same. Strangers came up to each other to ask what was in the papers, or went to sit on a quiet seat to read the news. Two helmeted soldiers were on guard at the entrance to the platform.

'Leave is cancelled isn't it?'

'Yes, sir.'

'I suppose the troops will leave tomorrow?'

'Tomorrow? They all went off during the night in lorries. Ninety-six lorries. All the cafés were combed to round up the men.'

Deceptive, quiet little station: it was not here but elsewhere that suffering had to be endured. If he had rung for the waiter during the night when he heard the motor-cycles coming and going, he would have known. He would have gone to the barracks. He would perhaps have seen his son helmeted, and with all his kit taking his place in the lorry which was to take him to ... for simplicity's sake, let's say the front. He would at last have lived through that experience which had been latent within him for so many years like a cancer. And yet he hadn't made the simple gesture of stretching out his arm towards the bell. He had slept—just as France had slept. 'Sleep, thou who art made for sleep' said Don Quixote to Sancho. Neither his nerves, nor his forebodings, nor his love had given him any warning.

To have foreseen this for so long and in the end to be taken unawares! If you wait too long for something to happen, your attention slackens.

He hated newspapers. Often he did not look at one for a fortnight at a time. Now he was standing in the middle of the street, reading three at once. There was nothing but lies in them and he knew it, but he swallowed them. After reading an agency dispatch in one paper, he read it from end to end in two others. He didn't spare the expense at lunch-time—claret and two brandies. There was no point in being abstemious, since death was imminent. As he left the restaurant he caught sight of an NCO belonging to the same regiment as his son. He thought of going up to him and asking if by any chance anyone belonging to the 3rd Battalion, 9th Company was still in barracks. But he went past the NCO without speaking to him. He stopped, turned round, and was undecided whether or not to retrace his steps. But again, something paralysed his will, and he moved on towards the hotel.

He knew perfectly well that his son would not come at midday. Nevertheless he went up to his room and waited—if waiting is the proper term. He had said, 'If you haven't come by one o'clock——' He was still there at 2.30. It was now certain that the boy had gone and yet when he heard a step on the stairs, even though he knew by the sound that it wasn't his son's, he pricked up his ears. 'When he's dead, I'll still hear him coming upstairs.'

He went out, walked through the Sunday town, that looked almost deserted now that the troops had left. He passed a few pretty girls who seemed to him to belong to a totally different *order of things*: he almost bore them a grudge for being so pretty. Soon he reached the country where he had gone for walks during the last few days, and, on hearing the noise of machine-gun fire in the distance, used to say to himself 'Perhaps that's him'. A long grey stain running by the side of the road came into view. It was the military cemetery.

He went in. The statue of a naked man towered above the graves —grotesque, worse than grotesque, misshapen, teratological, quite unspeakable. It had been created by an 'artist'! A municipal councillor had welcomed it! The population of a town accepted it! It was a revelation about the aesthetic sense of the French. But the cemetery itself was tidy, clean, well-kept with its thousands of white crosses and Moslem tombstones, divided by a pattern of red gravel paths.

On one of the tombstones the man read—really did read—his son's name. 'What are the chances of him still being alive in two or three years' time? Let's say one in fifty.'

When his son had volunteered he had said to himself that if war broke out he would join the same regiment. Now he no longer had the same urge. On the one hand was the bottomless pit of things not worth saying, and, on the other, the bottomless pit of actions not worth carrying out. In present-day France every noble impulse is promptly dashed like the leaping telegraph wires you see from an express train, and which are suddenly brought down to earth again by a stupid post. France is a nation in which everything noble and spontaneous is considered suspect; every time you would like to protest against some mean action, you find you can't do so because the majority are conniving at it.

The First World War had been for him the comrades' war. Now the fathers' war was beginning. He thought about what it would be like to be there at that moment, if he had had no children. His wife had long been dead. His mistress was more of a convenience than an object for affection. Were he to die, her future was assured. What he earned in 'business' was sufficient for his needs, which were modest. The emergency which threatened, whether it turned out to be international or civil war, would find him ready, having left no untidy ends, and having, in the expectation of the event, filled in the time by doing all the things he liked best in this life; the work of preparation itself—putting his house in order before the leap into the unknown—had had its savour, compounded of a sensation of virility, and a sensation of repose. He didn't mind what the outcome of the crisis might be: in the last fifteen years he was a middle-class Frenchman who had seen all his ideals shattered, his religious faith, his belief in his country, his social convictions. For a while, he had wrestled with the angel, fought against his tendency to take the fate of his country to heart. Then he had overcome it and the struggle had ceased. Now he was a man who 'wouldn't let the wool be pulled over his eyes', and he was proud of the fact. Anyone who believed in anything at all, he considered to be a fool. All he wanted was to be left in peace to jog along at his own pace for the twenty odd years he still had to live.

Furthermore, this sense of doom vindicated two fundamental characteristics of his nature: his retiringness and his indifference. Long before the threat took a precise form, for years he had lived with the feeling that the end of the world was at hand, and had withdrawn into his shell. He had stopped seeing his family (because of his mistress); he had allowed his friendships to decay; he had deliberately reduced his business commitments, and had renounced all ambition. Now that the danger was acute he was exultant. He had been right not to buy such and such a piece of land, since land was going to be shared out, or such and such a house, because it would have been nothing but a drain on him all this time: he had been right not to spread his interests, because that would have exposed him to disaster; he had been right not to wear himself out making money, because by one means or another, either legally or by force, it would have been taken from him; right not to have a luxuriously furnished house since his house was going to be obliterated by bombs; right not to have started such and such an undertaking because it could already be classed as a failure; right not to trouble to understand which way the world was going, since, as far as one could tell, things had got to such a pitch that nobody could understand them any more. In that month of March 1936, all the things which worked in his favour and made him freer, less anxious, less vulnerable than his fellow-countrymen, were the very things he had failed to achieve through carelessness or faint-heartedness. And so the threat, although still a source of pain, was in some respects not unpleasant for him. Each one of us—and this is our whole intellectual effort—constructs a philosophy to justify his way of life—that is to say his deficiencies, weaknesses and vices. Let the world come to an end, we are easily consoled if we can say, 'You see how right I was.' You take the sting out of an event by forecasting it.

That was the situation—or rather that might have been the situation but wasn't. Because of a single act in his past; because of his son who was going to fight and perhaps die, for an order of things that the father had renounced. It was as if he had destroyed the world, and then, by having this son, had re-created it. One by one he had severed the ties which bound him to the world, as if they had been the tentacles of an octopus: but one still remained and through this one remaining contact his life and the life of the world continued to intermingle. He had been bound by twenty chains but what was the point of having cut away nineteen if the twentieth had only to hold fast to keep him in captivity? Buddha said, when a son was born to him: 'A fetter has been forged for me.' What was the use of being indifferent to his own death, when he was afraid for someone else who might be killed? What was the use of having abolished hope, with regard to his own concerns, if he were going to go on hoping desperately for another? He had given the world this terrible hold over him; it could threaten him through the object of his love. They held him, the wretches, they *had got him*; he, too, was one of the herd; he could no longer sink back into cowardice as it was in his nature to do. 'When he had meningitis at the age of fifteen, crazed and horrified at the thought that he might die, I said to him, "My little fellow, you've got to stay alive you know. I have deserved to have you stay alive—do you understand—deserved it." Then I thought I had earned this right by all the trouble, care and sacrifices, even financial sacrifice, I had accepted for the sake of his health and his education. Now, it is because of a sacrifice of quite a different order that I "deserve" that he should live. In bringing him into the world I destroyed the harmony between my life and my beliefs.'

For a long time a lark trilled invisibly. Then it could be seen in the whitish sky hovering with quivering wings, the only living thing in the whole countryside, climbing in stages higher and ever higher, madly absorbed in its singing and its ecstasy like a mystic dancer, until suddenly it fell straight to the ground as though something had hit it, and the song was cut short, ceased, existed no more. The man imagined everything he might have read in the papers twenty years ago, and perhaps with pleasure, about the 'gallic' lark singing high above a cemetery and symbolizing 'hope immortal' etc. Today, what struck him was not that the ecstatic song could still be heard among the tombstones, but that it should have stopped abruptly, as if strangled. Was there another symbol to be found here? God Almighty, we've had enough of symbols, and literature, and 'happy phrases' to justify what cannot be happy. Now, a single sentence sprang from the heart of the war: '*Only* let him not be killed.'

Evening was drawing in and the man returned to the hotel. A

Sunday silence reigned in the empty room. There came the sound of a dog's bark, a child's voice, a woman's laugh—again women were laughing in the hour of tragedy, just as they had done twenty years before. And he saw from time to time on the landscape visible through the window, smoke from a hidden train which seemed to engulf the houses, as if it were smoke from an exploding shell.

The next morning, when his bag was packed and he was giving the usual final glance around the hotel room, he saw the empty crumpled cigarette packet which had dropped on to the floor when he put the cigarettes into his case. 'He gave it to me.' He picked it up, slipped it into his pocket and went downstairs. In the refreshment-room at the station, a solid group was standing in front of a public notice. What memories of the First World War the large white sheet evoked! He went nearer—it was a list of the afternoon's sporting results. Farther down the room a captain was sitting at a table with a platinum blonde: she was smoking, sprawled against him, almost on his knees. The captain, pencil in hand, was bent over a newspaper doing a crossword puzzle. On reaching the Gare de l'Est, the man who expected war to break out in a week's time took a taxi, but went neither to his bank, nor to his mistress's flat, nor to church, nor to his home to put his affairs in order, nor to a chemist to buy a gas-mask, nor to the Recruiting Office to find out what his fate would be. The taxi stopped at the entrance to the Palais Royal. In a shop there he bought 38 francs, 75 centimes' worth of medal ribbons: the *Légion d'Honneur*, the *Médaille Militaire*, the *Croix de Guerre*, and various commemorative medals. When he held the packet in his hand, his face which had been so sombre during the last two days, and almost tragic in expression, finally relaxed.

L'Equinoxe de Septembre, 1938

(Written in 1936)

A GOOD THING TO LIVE IN 1938

'Here, all cowardice must die'
Dante *Inferno* III

I DON'T KNOW how I shall manage to write this article, since everything I have to say is so simple.

In France, the tricolour flag over the door of a shop usually indicates that it is a Jewish concern. But it can happen that the Swiss flag hanging outside a café is the sign of a Nazi meeting place. A few weeks ago I was in one of these places where Nazis living in Paris devote themselves to doing as much harm as they can to France. A passing Frenchman came in not realizing what sort of a place it was, even though it was in a rather inaccessible spot. Soon he scented the 'blond ass', the Aryan German. I caught his hostile glance and was not in agreement with him.

If you feel that these blond individuals have already got the upper hand, this hostile glance is understandable. It is less understandable if, as a Frenchman, you feel that you are their equal and as strong as they are: there is no bitterness between equals. Our blond friends play their game: let us play ours, that is as it should be. Are we morally strong enough to fight them? (on the material plane we are). If so, let us do our duty and come what may.

The totalitarian spell-binders, great and small, prevent those who prefer happiness from falling into inefficiency: there is a minimum level of virility below which it will be impossible to sink. Germany has been placed next to France just as Xanthippe was put next to Socrates—to give us the chance to achieve self-control. The totalitarian spell-binders, great and small, prompt the lovers of liberty to appreciate it in a more subtle way, and the partisans of a certain type of culture to come together for its defence; an entire moral universe is brought more clearly into focus through the need for opposition. 'Go' says God to Ravana (Lucifer) in the Hindoo myth, 'go and become my enemy. If you turn men away from the straight and narrow path, I shall come down to earth to destroy you and save humanity. And by destroying you, I shall free you and bring you back up to Heaven.'

Lastly, they keep alive a feeling for the precariousness of existence and not only do they add zest to life by investing it with a touch of anxiety (the vinegar in the salad) but they help to keep alive awareness of the relativity of all things—an awareness which is the very essence of intelligence and also of wisdom. Those who are to come 'like lightning out of the East' play the same role as was formerly played for Christians by Him who was to come 'like a thief in the night': they teach us the art of total renunciation. Every fresh alarm is an opportunity for what is called in military parlance 'rallying the men': let everything be always in readiness, let everything be always in order. Ready for what? And in order for what? For renunciation. Let everything, according to the Old Testament formula, be considered as already lost, our goods, our possibilities, the flesh of our flesh. And that is as it should be, because everything—human beings and civilizations—ought to be risked, just as everything should be challenged. You only have a right to what you are prepared to risk.

And so the totalitarian spell-binders help to bolster up the very civilization which is fighting them and slandering them (because it is usually through fear that people commit slander). I think back to those sacred wars of the gods, related by Hesiod and Nonnos, in which the two factions, by the very fact of their antagonism, contribute to the general harmony. Asclepios, although Zeus hurled a thunderbolt at him, nevertheless remained a tutelary divinity, worthy of possessing his own temples. Prometheus and Kronos were enemies of Zeus, yet one finally settled in Heaven where he was reinstated by Heracles, while the other reigned over the Islands of the Blessed. The Titans were conquered but not damned; both Gods and men continued to invoke them, and soon they, too, were set free. The Greek gods—and later the heroes of Valhalla—made their peace in the evening after spending the day

A GOOD THING TO LIVE IN 1938

in mutual slaughter like rival teams when the match is over. There is a place for everyone in the great world family: there is no 'obscure region' in the world, just as there is none in the individual; everything which exists has a fundamental justification. Similarly our 1938 theo- or mythomachy, the struggle in progress between imperialisms and mystiques in the world of today, and so many other naïve divisions occurring at the same time on more restricted stages, should be viewed in the light of *rerum concordia discors*. I need hardly point out that the necessity of opposing forces, which was virtually a dogma with the Ancient Greeks and the basis of one of their most celebrated Mysteries, is in keeping with modern science which believes that in Nature, in mineral life, in organized life, nothing occurs except as a compromise between opposing forces, through the contradiction inherent in complementary laws, in short through the existence of an alternating movement: there is no end to the manifold forms of this regular ebb and flow, a rhythmic action of the systole and diastole, which ensures the circulation of life throughout the whole of creation. Probably this was the conception of the universe which lay behind a statement made by one of my friends during a ticklish crisis in French life, a few years ago: 'It must be admitted that difficult times are very pleasant.' This remark was thought badly of, but people were mistaken: it is the remark of a philosopher wearing a guise of casualness.

That is why I say to all those who would have preferred to live under Pericles or Louis XIV—damn it all, 1938 is very nice, too. People moan about the corruption of the times but all corruption, whether of the mind, the conscience, or the flesh, fertilizes the ground it covers. People moan about the hardness of the age: riff-raff flap their wings and cheep: 'Love, love.' It is true that we are living through tough times; provided you don't speak to a little girl in the street (you would be lynched) or don't set fire to some old farmer's deserted storage shed (five years' hard), or don't kick a dog, you can kill, steal, lie, betray, perjure yourself, etc. and the whole population, as one man, will turn a blind eye, thanks to the important daily papers and also perhaps to a certain trend in public education. French people only display indignation about offences which are not really offences at all. But it is because the age is immunized in this way—it is the age of Mithridates—that it can bear to withstand its ordeals, resorb its tumours, in short, assimilate and recuperate with an ease and a power of oblivion which, in any organism, are the hall-mark of health. For France to have survived the nervous shocks she has been submitted to during the past five years, she has had to be quite indifferent to the fate of, say, Chinese children. Everything is interconnected.

I was reading the other day, with disgust, some poems recently published by a French author. Over his daughter's cradle he 'begs forgiveness for her existence and for all those born in these times, forgiveness for the birth of each child'. And the tearful bard talks about 'the arrogance and hardness of this iron age', and he asks himself 'Is the world of today not living in a death-bed atmosphere?' Don't you think that there would be very little harm in releasing from this sad life those who ask forgiveness for having, and having given, life? And what is meant by a death-bed atmosphere? The death-throes of the world? Yes, of course. And its birth as well. Everything is constantly dying and being reborn—bodies, nature, even perhaps ideas. Surely we knew that? This age is like all ages. Like all ages, it has its dominant features. These dominant features (the decline in international morality, the acceptance of might as right, mithridatism, the unreliability of justice, unbridled hypocrisy and falsehood, etc.), are simply variations of mood in the history of humanity. They are only important in so far as they characterize the age in which we happen to be living, so that we have to reckon with them. If it were true that our civilization is in its death-throes, I should not bemoan this situation, because one thing would cancel out the other. Life, which is Protean, will take another form. There is no shortage of spare civilizations ready to take over. Those who go on lamenting about the devastation caused by wars and revolutions are those who do not feel within themselves any ability to create something new. Let people lament, if they want to, but let them get it over quickly. 'And now, we are going to start again from the beginning.'

* * *

A GOOD THING TO LIVE IN 1938

Yet through the extraordinary confusion and complexity of the world of 1938 runs the gold thread of individual behaviour. In a prose study entitled *The 7th March* 1936, I described the type of man who is entirely approved of by the French of today: I mean— the dead-dog-drifting-with-the-current type. But there is another type. There are cases of the individual who keeps a firm eye on himself, and continues to will himself to be an individual. His personality is absolutely clear-cut; he has himself well under control, he administers himself ably, and feeling as much at ease in a strong nation as in a 'gamey' one, he resists, takes care of himself, holds fast and carries on.

Dans un si grand malheur que vous reste-t-il?—Moi. (In this great misfortune, what have you left?—Myself.) Welcoming danger, because he is too aware of his unity and his permanence to have any fear of losing, or of losing himself—believing moreover that the best way to fight death is to integrate it into your conception of life, by deliberately running risks, adhering indomitably to his own opinion, living indomitably according to his own law (however odd it may be) and the stern rules of his own private immorality: he is the sturdy statue that the fire gilds but does not destroy, and at the same time his body is well oiled (like the statues of antiquity), so that it can slip through the fingers of history (for we have already made a note of all the emergency exits). Oh, those 'historic' Saturday nights between 1936 and 1938 when the totalitarian sorcerer, on the summit of the Brocken, hurled the bent lightning of his sabbaths! Under an iron, godless sky, man is alone with his passions and his deeds. Absolutely alone: no one will telephone him to warn him that the mobilization notices will be posted up at two o'clock in the morning: he will learn the news, when the street lamps are still gleaming in the wan dawn, from the voices of the night-shift workers hurrying home on their bicycles, and of tubercular little twirps whose faces predestine them to the infantry. 'From the womb of the morning, thou hast the dew of thy youth.' Utterly alone, and as indeed he must be—utterly abandoned. Terrifyingly ahead of his own people, like Vigny's Julian: ahead of rhetorical phrases and anthems and 'any kind of joke' (Nietzsche), stripped bare, scraped clean, as sharp as steel—proud, unbelieving, and utterly sober. He feels sorry for his own people; they, too, have been abandoned, by him! He is not yet quite sure whether he is going to fit in with events 'just a little, a great deal, passionately, or not at all'.[1] Nor is he quite sure which he will finally choose of his various overlapping loyalties (loyalty to his geographical fatherland, to talent, to courage, to culture, to shared passion). He will let himself be guided by his obligations towards himself, and will decide according to them. Who knows, perhaps he will give himself to some cause! But in giving himself he won't quite commit himself: he won't play the game, but his game, or rather he will play them both at once, which is the great game. He will merely pursue his own individual adventure and the working out of his own personality, through unforeseeable circumstances; it is not so much a question of remaining alive as of living a superior life; not so much a matter of getting the better of the enemy as of the war; war is— almost entirely—something to get the better of.

So, we are about to witness something new. Whatever it may be, we shall derive some benefit from it, just as we did from waiting for women who did, or did not, turn up; in either case, there was some advantage to be gained. At any rate, it will be a time for action (action in its most perfect form: a game)—and it is only in action that you get to know yourself, as my old owl said[2] in one of his more inspired moments. I appreciate will-power, but I also appreciate necessity. Will-power and necessity: it is up to me to weave together these two strands with all the skill of a virtuoso. It is up to me to play the game and to avoid being manœuvred or cheated. It is up to me to try to be a credit to mankind. 'Hail, then, oh grim visage of the day of battle.' In the night sky which is armour-grey, an enemy bomber tries to set his nerves on edge; his nerves are not set on edge: he is saving up his excitement until the last minute: he will sleep the sleep of Alexander (how soft is the last bed before the shaggy earth) and the thought that this night is full of anguished creatures incapable of sleep does him, in fact,

[1] The French counterpart of 'she loves me, she loves me not. . . .'
[2] Goethe.

a power of good: he laughs at the thought and falls off to sleep in the middle of it. And tomorrow he will awaken and there will be nothing; I mean nothing but life. But at least he will be one laugh to the good. Such are the 'glorious Saturdays' lived by a few Frenchmen between 1936 and 1938 (*sabado de gloria* is the Spanish name for Easter Saturday) and if we call them 'glorious Saturdays' it is because they allow the individual to accomplish himself in triumphant deeds; in the future there may be others in which he will be able to pursue self-accomplishment in international war or social conflict—a double triumph for the individual, since they force him daily to wrest his life from death, and at the same time provide him with competition, being phenomena governed by their own laws. All this, I say, is a good thing and as for those squeamish ninnies who beg forgiveness for having brought children into the world of 1938, I say, let them clear out and leave room for people who think the world a good place to be in. Make way for the sons of the earth!

I am writing these words under the auspices of the *Association des Ecrivains pour la Défense de la Culture*.[1] And yet, as I re-read them it seems to me that, apart from a sentence or two, they would be just as suitable for *Der Angriff*[2] (or just as unsuitable). To enter the enemy's world and realize that you are in harmony with everything you find there, is a very significant experience. Every system offers a complete solution of the problems of the universe. Two antagonistic doctrines are merely different deviations of the same truth: in passing from one to the other, you do not substitute one ideal for another any more than you assume an object to be different because you contemplate it from varying angles. Hence the fact that the orthodoxy of one century consists in the heresy of the preceding one. I was waiting one day in the street for a member of the fair sex whom I had arranged to meet at 3 o'clock. At 3.20 she hadn't yet arrived and my heart began to swell with hope at the thought that I might be rid of her for ever (she knew neither my name nor my address). At 3.25 she turned up; I had made a point of giving

[1] A Communist organization. [2] A Nazi newspaper.

her a fair chance. At 3.35, in a hotel bedroom, I sensed she was armed, and I said to myself that, should she begin shooting, I would not lift a finger in self-defence, because I didn't mind being killed by her. I was not in love with her, since only a quarter of an hour earlier I had been prancing with joy at the thought of losing her for good. And yet the vague feeling I had for her was strong enough to lead me naturally into giving a proof of supreme love in being unwilling to defend my life against her. This story is no more a 'typically Parisian' anecdote than the stories in Les Jeunes Filles are 'typically Parisian', whatever some people may think. It is a story which ought to be the object of an effort of understanding, and not simply laughed off. The effort to understand ought to be made, even though the fact appears quite beyond human comprehension. It brings us into contact with the equivalence which is at the heart of one Mystery, just as that alternating movement we have already referred to is at the heart of another mystery. We have written elsewhere: 'Action and non-action will meet in eternity and there embrace eternally.' This is an imperfect truth. The yea and the nay, all the yeas and all the nays, all already united and fused together in time as they will unite and fuse together in eternity. All is one. And this oneness is good.

L'Equinoxe de Septembre, 1938

(Written in 1938)

THE SEPTEMBER EQUINOX

Henry de Montherlant joined the auxiliary 'forces' in 1916, at the age of twenty, and after being appointed to a staff post behind the lines, asked to be transferred to active service with an infantry regiment of the 20th Army Corps, which had the reputation at the time of being the 'toughest' in the French army. He was seriously wounded in 1918, being hit by seven pieces of shrapnel, and was given a complete discharge.

At the time of 'Munich', he was therefore a civilian, and it was as a civilian, but wearing military uniform, that he went to the Maginot Line, where he could join up at once, should war break out.

In the event, after having had two attacks of pneumonia in 1937 and 1938, H de Montherlant decided not to join up in 1939. However, he became war correspondent for a Parisian newspaper in May 1940 and stayed at the front until the Armistice; he was wounded again, but this time only very slightly.

12th September 1938, Paris

It must be admitted that events have forced the French to adopt a saner attitude to war than they did ten years ago. To believe that war is imminent, even though you don't want to prepare for it, is a saner attitude than believing—because you don't want to prepare for it—that it will never break out at all.

Whether they like it or not, the newspapers can talk of nothing else. Yet, only six days ago, when the first reservists were called up in France, I heard the news in London and rushed to buy a well-known daily paper. A headline in huge capitals covered half the first page: 'Garbo needs carrot juice.' It took me five minutes to find on the tenth or the thirteenth page the announcement that the French had begun to mobilize.

I am amazed that a responsible government should not ban for a certain length of time a newspaper which, because of a mere publicity contract, shamefully limelights the doings of some female film star, at a time when so many serious things are happening in the world. An honest government does not turn a blind eye when someone plays fast and loose with the intelligence of those committed to its care.

13th–14th September

I may go for weeks without writing a line. But during periods of crisis like the present one, *nulla dies* . . . And preferably about matters irrelevant to the crisis. It is clear that there will soon be a lot of wastage in our lives: we all know what mischief Bellona wreaks, and what 'action', in the broad sense, entails. It is vital that *everything* should not be lost.

What a blessing these crises can be from the point of view of work: letters and telephone calls become less frequent. Each of the French crises of the past few years—February '34, March '36, February '38—has allowed me to enjoy a peaceful interlude of work: people left me alone, because their attention was otherwise engaged. How wonderful, to have these hours free for work in the midst of the obscene din!

It is not through a 'sense of duty' that I am leaving for the front: my sense of duty no longer plays any part in my behaviour. I am leaving because, of the various courses open to me in what is now so charmingly termed a *trial of strength*, this is the one I prefer. I should hate to be killed but, all things considered, I prefer to take the risk.

15th September

Chamberlain is off to Berchtesgaden. Mohammed is going to the mountain. By plane too; since fear gives a man wings.

Since February 1936, when France, taking a vigorous stand, refused to leave Strasburg exposed to German artillery fire, my entire army kit has been laid out on a table reserved for this purpose. I have made sure that the buttons are properly sewn on, checked the laces, tested and greased the boots and got my feet used to them, and replaced the iodine pencil each time it deteriorated. I have gone carefully over everything I am taking with me: nothing is missing and nothing is superfluous: the maximum of usefulness and efficiency is compressed into the minimum of space and weight. Even my helmet strap has been adjusted to exactly the right length. For the past two and a half years, I have been ready to leave at ten minutes' notice.

How much simpler life is when everything is ready and waiting in this way! Not only is my military kit in order; everything else is too.

Only the mask is missing from my kit. Let us discuss masks for a moment, because there's a moral to the story.

I know how disorganized the French can be. I have no desire to arrive at the front without a mask. I want, as far as it is possible, to be killed by the Germans, and not by the French or French inefficiency.

So in February '36 I bought a mask. But almost at once I gave it away to a woman I 'loved', who wanted one. 'Take pity on women!'[1]

She tried it on and said she could never wear a thing like that, because it smudged her make-up and left a red mark on her forehead. 'Take pity on women!'

Moreover, she damaged it while she was trying it on. 'Take pity on women!'

Mea culpa: I never got another mask.

Now at last, after many unsuccessful attempts, I have found a manufacturer who is willing to let me have a mask, which was meant to be part of an official consignment. An obliging, comradely type, a wounded ex-service man, who has the *Médaille militaire*. We can recall our wartime memories, etc.

Some brief reflections on masks:

It is quite useless for one civilian out of a hundred to have a

[1] *Pitié pour les femmes,* the title of a series of novels by Montherlant.

mask, because, in the event of a gas attack, he will immediately be killed by the others, who will want to take his mask from him.

A sensible man has not one, but two gas-masks, just as he has two revolvers. Everybody seems to forget just how fragile a mask is: if one part is missing or defective, if the rubber splits or a celluloid eye-piece gets broken, you're done for. Everybody also seems to forget that at the first sign of panic masks will be the first things to be stolen. Finally, like revolvers, parachutes, preventatives and life-belts, masks are—there's no doubt about it—'unfaithful servants'.

I have written a novel (*L'Hôpital*) about people who die because they have no money to pay for treatment (this is especially true of consumptives). At present, a civilian can only get a mask by buying one: the cheapest costs a hundred and thirty-five francs. Imagine a family of four or five people, with no financial margin... You want to go on living? Stump up!

A subject for a short story: two lovers. A gas-attack. Only one mask.

A man has his mask, but his nearest and dearest haven't any. Is he going to take the trouble of buying one for each one of them? (In each case, it is a double nuisance; the mask has first to be bought and tried on, and then tested.) Yet if he doesn't do it, what is his affection worth?

16th September

Chamberlain has left Berchtesgaden earlier than was expected.

'I'll stay in Paris until the very last moment.'
'But what do you find to keep you busy here?'
'Love.'

I am busy both getting a new gas-mask and fitting up a new bachelor establishment—speculating on both war and peace—preparing for both death and life. 'Love and Death met on the road to Madrid' is the beginning of an old Castilian legend. Once again, love and death come together within me, and once again to the exclusion of everything else. They are the two threads that I weave one with the other; the two steeds that I ride and control and keep in step: the black horse of war and the white horse of violent living.

'*Hebe!*' cried the Athenians at some battle or other (and we know what youth meant to the Ancient Greeks). '*Venus Victrix*' was the cry of Caesar's Legions during the civil war. They had only one thought while they were butchering or being butchered.

I have brought the mask I bought yesterday to be tested in a laboratory. It is too big; not air-tight. 'Did you try it on?'—'Yes'—'And didn't you notice . . . ?'—'The only mask I know anything about is the 1917 model. I didn't realize there was anything wrong. The person who sold it to me said it fitted.'—'People like that are criminals. One whiff of gas and you were done for in that mask.'

The manufacturer had been trying to do me a good turn. He was cordial and friendly. And, as an ex-service man, *he should have known*. But being French, he was casual.

What I was leading up to with the story about the mask was this mixture of good and evil; a man was trying to save my life and at the same time doing exactly the sort of thing that would make me lose it. This is an everyday occurrence.—I would say that the days we are living through are full of instruction, had I not reached an age when it is not so much instruction that you receive as confirmation.

The paraphernalia of war, spread out on the table, quietly awaits its fate. The boots remind me of my football boots. The mask reminds me of the bull's head I wore at Binche carnival, six months ago. It is stamped with the initials ARS. What *ars* or art is this? No doubt, the art of dying. The mica coverings of the military maps are glistening like frost on a field. The dull helmet is earth-coloured, clay-coloured. I lay my palm on its round surface, which is smooth as the curve of a woman's breast. It feels as cool as damp clay. The pomegranate ornament on the front makes me think of the Athene

Nike on the Acropolis who held a helmet in one hand and a pomegranate in the other.

If I put it on, when I move my head I am conscious of the empty space between the steel shell and the leather head-piece—an echoing emptiness, as if my brains had turned to liquid, and were washing about.

As long as the human race exists the words 'eve of battle' will thrill with awe both youths and men. They are like the smell of the open sea when you step from the train on to the quayside. Or like the stallion neighing in the desert when he scents the far-off mare.

I'm a warmonger, aren't I? At least, that's what people say who don't know what to do with peace when they have it. 'Let's go to the pictures. That'll always fill in an hour or so.' These are the people who make a mess of peace. Whereas I love peace because I live it thoroughly, and try to make a decent job of it.

17th September

Yesterday and today, there has been paradisal sunshine: as wholesome as bread. And all the faces in the street look so pretty, as always happens in a town you are about to leave.

I shall have to aim at not taking the war too much to heart; to sort out the experiences it provides, and accept only those which will further my development; lastly, to learn how to assimilate it thoroughly. Above all, I shall have to see that it is not a waste of time: when the results are totted up, I don't want there to be any deficit.

18th September

One thing we like about animals is that we can kill them legally. In war, too, we are pleased to be able to kill legally. Of course, no man will ever admit this—any more than he will admit to being afraid.

19th September

My thoughts turn to those old men who know that they have

only a few more years to live, and can therefore hope to see in France nothing but internal decay and, possibly, externally provoked disaster. They know that *never again* will they live in an atmosphere of honour or peace.

20th September

Czechoslovakia has been sacrificed by the London Agreement.

'Sacrificed! Not at all! We are giving her an "international guarantee".' Think of that!

One of Barrès's early stories has the title: 'Superfluous Heroism.' There are, also, superfluous acts of cowardice, which serve no purpose. 'Port-Royal is afraid. Fear is a bad policy.' (Pascal.)

The Romans of the fifth century used constantly to buy back their freedom by giving the Barbarians gold, and yet still remained enslaved.

A French newspaper, of the Right Wing, which is the official guardian of honour, etc., after admitting that 'Some Czechoslovakians declare that war is better than a revision of frontiers', adds, 'Such excitability . . .' What is referred to, in every language in the world, as honour, courage, pride and dignity, is now called 'excitability' by some of our idealists when they refer to the Czechs, because it is an 'excitability' which might oblige us to honour our pledge.

Whether sensible or silly, decent or revolting, all the Press commentaries add up to more or less the same thing. However, Pierre Loewel, in *L'Ordre*, expresses an original idea. 'When a country has made up its mind to give in all along the line, surrender completely, repudiate its pledges etc. . . . it could at least refrain from making a show of sham anxiety before the event.' Loewel also quotes Faguet: 'I hope I die before seeing my stupid country succumb to the fate which it is bringing upon itself.'

When, in private life, people have persuaded you into doing something by putting forward either good reasons or bad, by trickery, charm, flattery or anything you like except threats, and you are on the point of saying 'yes'—you only need to sense the merest hint of a threat to switch violently to '*no*' and stick to it.

And just look at the behaviour of the leaders of the world—the so-called fathers of their peoples. . . .

It appears that the Americans are saying, 'We're sick of Europe.' Similarly, according to Epicurus, the Gods, weary of the stupidity and baseness of men, withdrew to Olympus. And we, who have work to do which is independent of countries and particular periods, should perhaps devote ourselves to something more important than getting ourselves killed. . . .

As a relaxation, and as a sort of challenge to fate, I have bought myself a small wooden Persian Plaque. It will soon be destroyed by a shell, or pinched by some connoisseur when my flat is left gaping to the heavens. But in the meantime I shall have got three or four days' enjoyment out of it: that will be enough to ensure its fame. I don't know its exact origin, nor what period it belonged to, nor what it was used for: it is probably a box-lid dating from the twelfth or thirteenth century. Of course, it may be fake. The King (he can only be a King) is sitting on a perfumed carpet (I insist on its being perfumed) in the shade of a slender flowering shrub: he looks like Matisse: everything indicates that he is contentedly preparing himself for an Anacreontine old age. He is handing an apple to a young girl with barley-sugar lips, pulpy breasts and a pink navel, who is sitting opposite. It is not the paradisal apple, that Gabriel offered to Yussuf, who smelt it and then gave up the ghost, being consumed with longing by the scent of the Garden: it is a love-apple, as delicate and exquisite as the white hand which is holding it. To the left, in the green distance, two armed knights are slaughtering each other; why, we don't know. Very probably, they themselves don't know either. But it must be admitted that the slaughtering fits very prettily into the picture.

Around the miniature is an inscription in Arabic writing. Is it, perhaps, a quotation from Hafiz: 'There is neither good nor evil. All our deeds, as recorded in the book of the universe, are indistinguishable'? Or perhaps from Saadi: 'The man who took pity on the serpent did not realize that in so doing he was wronging the children of Adam'? I fancy rather that it is an important maxim—

also by Saadi: 'In times of strife, the wise man will flee, because, on such occasions, wisdom is to be found at the frontier.'

This old man and dainty young lady cooing sweet nothings at each other against a background of derring-do, appeal to me very strongly. In such oriental imagery most people seek a starting-point for 'escapism'. What I find there is my own past experience and what could easily be my experience again tomorrow, if I so wished; it is only a question of pressing a button.

I think of the intellectual freedom and intelligence of Persian society, at a time when Christianity was smothering the Western Middle Ages under a lid of benightedness. May we enjoy the same freedom and intelligence.

I think of their poets, philosophers, historians and painters flourishing in the midst of the anarchy and civil war that were prevalent at the time on the Iranian plateau. Just as Greek thought flourished during the disturbances at Athens, and fifteenth-century art during the Florentine upheavals. May the same be true of us.

21st September

'The part played by our country during these anxious days of the late summer of 1938 will remain one of the wonders of contemporary history'—Colonel de la Roque in the *Petit Journal*.

Prayers for peace. Mrs Chamberlain. A newspaper item: 'The election of a successor to Joseph Bédier at the Academy. Mr X has a good chance. However, Mr Y is supported by Mr Z.' Europe is rocking on its foundations, yet these absurdities continue as if nothing whatever were the matter.

I can handle a rifle, grenades and—up to a point—an automatic rifle. But I can't handle a machine-gun. And in 1938 a man should be able to handle a machine-gun; just as he should be able to swim and drive a car. I gave C a ring to ask if I couldn't learn how to fire a machine-gun either, as a favour, with a group of soldiers (which is what I would have preferred) or in some military training organization. C laughed outright and said politely that he would inquire. I bet he did. C has plenty of money; a day may come when the communists rush upstairs to his flat and he finds himself with a machine-gun by him that he doesn't know how to use . . .

A woman correspondent, unknown to me, writes: 'Your "self-possession" is a farce. It's all very well being "philosophical" in peaceful times. But at a time like the present it is obvious that such a philosophy is nothing but words.' Speak for yourself, my dear. For many people, on the contrary, it is precisely in times like the present that it proves to be not mere words.

The papers say: 'All civilians who can leave Paris should do so.' Mlle V went to one of the stations to make inquiries about the evacuation. She, too, was laughed at for her pains.

A friend has reported this snatch of conversation to me; it is typically French in more ways than one. A tenant said to his *concierges*: 'Aren't you going to carry the sand up?'[1]
'We're not the real *concierges*: we're just reliefs.'
'When are the *concierges* coming back?'
'In three weeks' time.'

I would not dare publish all the notes I have made during the past seven or eight years about the attitude of the French to war and freedom—which are interdependent phenomena—an attitude that can be summarized thus: they don't in the least care if they are gassed or conquered in the near future, provided they get their 10 per cent increase here and now (or their holidays with pay that they don't know what to do with and long to escape from so that they can get back to their daily grind). In other words, they will cling to their petty pleasures, stuffing themselves sick until the first bomb drops, like flies so intent on dung that they will let themselves be caught rather than fly away. This attitude could have as its epigraph the following lines which come from Thucydides (second discourse of the Corinthians at Sparta, freely translated): 'He who

[1] For the putting out of incendiary bombs.

refuses to prepare for the future, because it would interfere with his pleasures, will soon find that those pleasures are taken away from him, precisely because he refused to prepare for the future.'

In March 1936, when the Germans reoccupied the Rhineland, and last March, when they took over Austria, I was struck by what seemed to me to be vulgar behaviour on the part of Parisians in public places, by their lack of dignity and seriousness. I would cast shamefaced looks to left and right, to see whether by chance there were any foreigners present—a stray German for instance. In the red-light districts of Algeria, you sometimes come across a house bearing the sign: 'Respectable dwelling'; in the same way, I should have liked to have a notice pinned to my back with the words: 'I'm not like all these people.' Now it is different, because we are faced with a direct threat—in fact, more than direct: imminent. As a result, the reason behind this light-heartedness seems to be not so much: 'I don't care a damn about my country's defeats,' as: 'I don't care a damn about the threat of war. I'm not afraid to be bumped off.' So there are moments when I can almost sympathize with an attitude which, in March, made me blush with shame. And I sometimes wonder if I'm not being unfair to my compatriots, and whether all nations are not just as crazy and as depressing. Struck by everybody's calmness and also by my own and having, as yet, seen no one give way to a fit of nerves, I begin to wonder: 'Should the apathy of the French not be called composure? Is their subconscious conviction that they can do what they like up to the last moment, and will always be able to save the situation *in extremis*, not a proof of vitality? (May it not be a partly conscious gamble, the gamble of the hare in its race with the tortoise?) Ought I not to admire their ability to live through tragedy—either actual tragedy as in 1914, or imminent tragedy—as if it were part of everyday life? I should like to be fair to the strange nation into which, through some divine prank, I was born.

22nd September

Caesar Borgia went off to die an obscure death as a mere captain, in some trench, in an anonymous town, in the wildest part of Spain.

23rd September

The Godesberg meeting has ended in failure.

The general in charge of the French Military Mission in Czechoslovakia has sent in his resignation to the French authorities and offered his services to the Czech government.

This afternoon, I feel rather upset. Other people, too, I notice, are showing some emotion. How I long to be in the train, free and purified! The last link will only be severed on the platform of the Gare de l'Est.

Instead of leaving at once, I am running the risk of getting involved in the confusion caused by the entraining of the various contingents, but it is because I want to stay with X, Y and Z. I cannot face losing one drop of these precious essences.

I saw, in the entrance hall of a newspaper office, a photograph of the French Ministers leaving a Cabinet Meeting. I am not influenced simply by the richness of the rhyme; I should like to find some word other than 'sinister' to apply to them, but it can't be helped, 'sinister' is the word. Fatigue, insomnia and panic have left their mark on their sinister faces. One of them has mad, staring eyes. They all look terrified—whether by the situation or themselves, it is impossible to say.

G came to see me, on her way from the hairdresser's where she had just had a perm. Is she unaware of what is going on? Plucky, resigned or dazed? The explanation is, I think, an unawareness which has the appearance of courage. But in that case I shall, perhaps, have to be more circumspect in my liking for courage. There can be no courage without lucidity, but as lucidity is extremely rare, courage worthy of the name must be extremely rare, too.

One more reason for rating people less highly, and loving them less.

Whatever the truth of the matter, and whatever name we give to the state that people are in, it is undoubtedly a form of composure. A good feature in human material which is to be worked on.

The equinox (24th September) always brings storms. Actually, the thermometer stands at 82° and the sun is shining more brilliantly than it has done during the last three weeks. I like such rather strange phenomena.

I have begun Curtius's book on Balzac. Curtius will be *my* perm. I've thought enough about war for today.

(No doubt, that's what those well-preserved, middle-aged men that I saw reading *L'Os à Moelle* and *Le Canard Enchaîné*[1], in the Métro on the 23rd September 1938, were saying to themselves.)

I am fond of my Corinthian vases with their long, pale wine-coloured lionesses against a light background, so light, indeed, that when I look at it, something melts inside me, as if the lionesses were walking over my heart with their soft, claw-armed paws (neither vases with a red background nor those with a black background arouse this mysterious emotion in me); these Corinthian vases that I have only to touch for my fingers to be covered with a dusting of pale powder, like the bloom from a butterfly's wing; vases which are more human on the inside because you can see there how the craftsman's thumb has shaped them, as faces are moulded by the soul within. If I weren't totally indifferent to what happens to my body after death, I would like them to be buried with me.

I am fond of my Corinthian vases, but I am even fonder of myself. And what this self asks is that I should be prepared to sacrifice my Corinthian vases as I am prepared to sacrifice everything else, except my conception of my destiny. My feeling for my Corinthian vases is made up of my tender affection for them, and my indifference to the fact that they must be sacrificed: these two emotions are as fused and as indistinguishable as the earth and the water which went to their making. May all earthly love be like my love for my Corinthian vases.

24th September

Czechoslovakia is mobilizing. The French government announces that it will honour its obligations if Czechoslovakia is attacked.

[1] Two humorous papers.

When I went out at eleven o'clock, people in the street told me that the first mobilization notices summoning certain classes of men had been posted up. And so they had. With their black print on a white background, sad and unlovely, they made me think of the posters in the Métro advertising 'A Visit to the Catacombs'.

Another Saturday. Yet another *sabado de gloria*. I have decided to leave.

I shall be gone then on the 24th September, the date of the September Equinox, when day and night are of equal length: it is the feast of the Sacred Mystery of the equivalence of the yea and the nay and of the unimportance of the victory of either. And it is true that for me the day of peace is equal to the night of war: one balances the other. One or the other, *no importa. Nada mas, nada menos,* neither more nor less, as is written on the Scales in Valdes Leal's famous picture. It is a mystery which occurs at the time of the grape-harvest and produces its own kind of wine.

The day is heavy and humid (according to the evening papers the temperature reached 83° or 84°). The officer I talked to at the War Office glanced every five seconds at the sweat that was pouring down my forehead, and that I couldn't wipe off, having forgotten my handkerchief. I was far less concerned for the moment about the 'situation' than about the sweat which was no doubt making me look peculiar and ridiculous.

Went to say good-bye to G. Already, among the passing faces, you can pick out the people you don't want to be killed, and those you *do*. Unfortunately such wishes go by contraries.

With G, complete chastity. My thoughts were elsewhere. And a good thing too.! When, in a little while, I cross Paris for the last time I shan't be eating my heart out at the sight of all the charming faces that have to be left behind: this is not the moment to think about such things.

For the same reason, there was no pathos in our parting, although she is very dear to me. We simply settled the material details. Nothing could have been cooler than our last kisses since we were both thinking about something else. I had still to learn that the 'soldier's farewell' can include absent-minded kisses.

My things were ready: all I had to do was turn the key in the lock, and I left at half past one. For Metz. Most authors, if they were describing a similar scene in a novel, would feel obliged to dwell on the soldier's last lingering gaze at his familiar setting. My last glance was one of indifference. I have so often set out from there to lead a life of danger; so often thought that I would never see my home again . . . Now I am setting off for my second war as if I were going on a fishing expedition. Courage? No, insensitivity. (But it seems logical that insensitivity should make courage easier. We shall see.)

The taxi went through the Square des Arts et Métiers where, only a few days ago, I had an amorous assignment. 'Now,' I said to myself with a certain satisfaction, 'we can save our phosphorous.'

At the Gare de l'Est. A mass of already solitary men. Until now, I have never regretted not having seen the soldiers leave in 1914, because at the time I would never have been a mere spectator, and I don't like being a spectator; either I take part or I go up into my ivory tower. But now I do regret that I wasn't there. I should have liked to make the comparison. Two facts strike me about the situation today: very few of the soldiers are being seen off, and all are cool and collected.

The thousands of helmeted soldiers look like a crowd at a Communist meeting; they are bound for the destination they most hate; they are setting out peacefully for war. Hardly any shouting at all. A few cries of 'Down with Daladier', a few bars of the *Internationale* rise up, from time to time, through the silence and then subside echoless, like the brief, circumscribed break made by a dolphin on the smooth surface of the Mediterranean. No anti-German slogans. Not a suspicion of the *Marseillaise*; no one has ever heard of the *Marseillaise*. And I must say, I almost prefer it that way. Enthusiasm is not an essential quality in a good soldier. Two days after this, a few miles from the Maginot Line, I was to hear a broadcast speech by Hitler unleash a great wave of German enthusiasm, but it did not make me change my mind; I *preferred* the *Marseillaise* to remain unsung.

A splendid wall map of Germany and Czechoslovakia, about

four yards by five, had been put up next to the barrier. How thoughtful and obliging France is towards her sons! She doesn't want us to be hazy about where we are fighting. 'I insist, I insist,' she seems to be saying, 'you must know exactly where Ash (Eger), Ratibor and Goerlitz are.' Working-class conscripts hob-nobbed with officers. Calm men were sitting in circles on their little bags, like so many football teams. A few priests were standing a little apart, on their own. The crowd seemed to be agreeably surprised that priests should be leaving for the front. I should have been shocked if they hadn't been. To believe in God surely doesn't give you the right to have a cushy job behind the lines. In the distance, in a siding where there was no train, men were sitting in a row along the edge of the platform, their feet dangling over the track.

The loud-speaker suddenly bellowed: 'Officers are requested to travel at the head of the train.' Why were they put there? Because an officer is bound to be at the head of whatever he is concerned with? (*Chef,* that is leader or officer, comes from *caput,* head.) Or so that officers rather than other ranks should pop off first in the event of a collision?

Crammed together in the stifling heat of the unlit compartments, the men took off their jackets and began to eat. At the entrance to the platforms reserved for soldiers, military police were stopping civilians, I could not see why, because already quite a number had got through. There was even a little woman in one of the luggage vans with her gigolo. She argued that she could travel to the next station and that no one would say anything. Quite right, too, I thought, remembering a passage in *Cyrano de Bergerac* where the guards allow an officer with a woman in his carriage to go through to the front line (the detail came, no doubt, from some contemporary memoirs), and another passage in Lauzun's memoirs, where the king tells the duke who is leaving to join his regiment in an American colony, that he will pay all his mistress's expenses if she wants to go with him. There was also an elderly couple on our platform. I heard the man say: 'I'm selling my cider at ten sous a glass.' A mother was helping her son to carry his mess-chest. A little boy, with his father's small suitcase on his head, looked just like a child carrying a basket in a Greek frieze. A few young women had tears in their eyes, and their hands pressed to their hearts. There was no lack of nose-blowing, but those of us who could remember the last war, knew that face powder is a great drier of tears and we said to ourselves: 'Mothers have a right to be here. But not the rest.'

But, I stress the point, very few of the men were being seen off. Could France have become a little more virile? I saw only one example of the vampire woman clinging to her man and preventing him carrying out his manly duties. Only one, among so many thousand males.

War means, first and foremost, waiting. I had to wait from two o'clock until dusk before I could leave (not that there was any great confusion, but I was a special case). By nightfall, a number of men had got tipsy over their picnic supper and threatened to spoil the general atmosphere of dignity that had characterized the day. Officers were accosted by the merry and unsteady who made either preposterous requests for information, or hearty protestations of friendship. It was amusing to watch the reactions; the older officers were patient and fatherly, the younger ones sometimes rather abrupt. The funniest thing was the look on the faces of the officers' wives. While some breezy mechanic clapped her captain-husband on the back, Mrs Stand-on-her-Dignity, with pursed lips, would keep her distance, even during those final moments. I may add that I was no more upset at seeing the men get tight than I had been at their failure to bellow the *Marseillaise*. Why should they not be allowed to sugar the pill? A harmless anaesthetic is permissible. (Already, in the station, cigarettes had assumed their wartime role: they were helping us all to bear up.) In any case the men were not going into action that night: they would be clear-headed by the next day. Seneca himself said that it was a good thing to take a drop too much. Lastly—and I say so without apology—it's not fair to be asked to fight without wine. An army of wine-drinkers has shown what it can do. I sometimes even dream of a political party based on intoxication.

Rain began to fall, summer rain, soft as the touch of a priest's hand. For me it heralded war; it was full of foreboding, 'the rain beloved of tombs' as Delteil called it. A civilian said to me: 'We must hope . . .' 'There's no room for hope,' I replied.—Hope will remain shut in the urn 'where none has ever put his hand'.

By now night had fallen and the station had its wartime lighting —a few dim bulbs, white, red and blue. My favourites are the blue. The light from one of these hooded bulbs fell straight to the ground in a magical shower of pale blue. If I were a painter I should do something with the blue of the bulbs and the brilliant starry blue of the *garde mobile* helmets, against the dirty blackness of the dark and the station setting and the dirty grey of the human herd.

In my compartment were officers or half-officers (that is, reservists), without number tabs on their uniform. One was wearing his puttees like someone who hasn't worn puttees in fifteen years; another had on an ordinary shirt and coloured tie underneath his uniform jacket. One of them went out to get an evening paper which he passed on to me. It solemnly reproduced a long-winded statement by some Women's League to the effect that they loved peace. What about us? Didn't we love peace, too? I could have defied anyone to show me a single soldier who did not love peace and who, at that moment, was not willing to sacrifice a great deal of what made his private life worth while, if by so doing, he could help to maintain peace with honour. It's no use protesting that you love peace: the problem is how to be strong enough to impose peace on those who desire war. And the strength of France has been sapped by woolly statements such as the one from the Women's League.

There is something I should like to say at this point. On the 24th September 1938, at the Gare de l'Est, I had a vision—a vision of a war being fought without bombast or rhetoric. I've said so before, and I say so again—as far as I am concerned, not only do I feel no emotion; I literally feel nothing whatsoever. In my 'professional' capacity I should like to feel some emotion—any emotion—anxiety, exaltation, melancholy, or horror. I have tried wringing myself out like a damp cloth, but not one drop of emotion appears. I feel neither fear nor pity, for others or for myself. Is it just the usual hardening that occurs at forty? Eight years ago, when I became sure that war was inevitable, for weeks on end I used to wake up with a wildly beating heart. I imagined myself being choked with poison gas, etc. Now, when it was quite possible that by the following evening we would be facing a gas attack, these visions ceased to make any impression on me: tragic possibilities no longer had any hold over me. I had had so many, varied reasons for emotion during the previous fourteen years that now I entirely failed to react. To leave without warning—knowing that it may well be for ever, to live for years on end out of a small suitcase, to part from my nearest and dearest, to feel that I would soon be engaged in killing or being killed, all this seemed so much part and parcel of my everyday life that the fact that war was the cause of this fresh journey was not enough to give me the feeling that I was doing something new. (It should be added that once the link is broken— by the railway barrier—once you are committed, everything becomes easier. Once beyond the barrier, you are like a boat entering the calm waters of the outer harbour after a rather rough crossing.)

Something similar seemed to be true of the other men. What struck me most about them was their calmness. And yet most of them were leaving behind them settled homes, wives, legitimate children, private lives whose pattern was less accommodating, more demanding, than mine: and for nine-tenths of them the financial problem must have been important. Yet they, too, gave the impression that they were setting off for a day's fishing. And I wondered whether the whole nation was not, as I was, worn out by an excess of experience; had it not given up worrying, was its imagination not exhausted, had its vital impulses not been dulled, and, after surmounting the social problems of recent years, was it not now ready to accept war as an almost hum-drum occurrence, refusing to pay any attention to it until the very last minute, and then, when it had finally broken out, accepting it quietly, as being all in the day's work? And we mustn't forget that for many of these men—and their attitude may have had some influence on their juniors—war is no new experience.

I don't know, of course, whether the lack of excitement at the Gare de l'Est is typical of France as a whole. I do know that it can be interpreted in various ways. You can admire it as a source of courage. You can also call it resignation, and say to yourself that if the most undisciplined nation in the world trots off so docilely to the slaughter—the 'reception area' into which the reservists were crammed before they entered the station reminded me of nothing so much as a pen full of sheep awaiting their fate—men will always accept war: but no sensible person has ever doubted the fact, and what we are witnessing at present is only a superfluous confirmation of it: French people have swallowed and absorbed twenty years of pacifist propaganda, without the slightest result, just as they have swallowed and absorbed great doses of synthetic class-hatred, also without result. Finally, we may ask ourselves if the calmness is peculiar to France, or if it is not, or might not be, common to all nations taking similar steps at this time.

Like many other people, I was saying to myself a little while ago: 'Even supposing that this time the crisis is averted, it will only blow up again three months hence. But if France has to submit to demi-mobilization every three months, the day will come when even the most ardent pacifists will want war in order to settle the matter once and for all.' Now I am not so sure. Force of habit is a well-known phenomenon, but we still don't know as much about it as we should. We can perhaps foresee a time when Europe will mobilize every three months, and come to accept this arrangement as naturally as circus folk accept the fact that they must fold up their tent and move on every three weeks.

The men were waiting, still waiting. They were waiting as patiently as they queue in front of a cinema for hours to see some really stupid film. And the stupider the firm, the longer the queue, and the more docilely they wait, which seemed to argue that what we were waiting for on this occasion must be something utterly idiotic. This was the opinion of an experienced lieutenant in my compartment (an army dentist as I later learned). 'There's only one difference from last time,' he said. 'Then we knew why we were going to war: now we don't.' But we do know, if we look at the situation from a certain point of view; we are going to war in order to prevent German dominance of Europe. But, from another point of view, the present situation is even more ridiculous than that which precipitated the slaughter of the 1914–18 war. The day may come when prestige rests on an even flimsier basis. The leader of nation A will say to the leader of nation B: 'If by midnight next Saturday, you have not cut off your quiff, I will invade your country.' And of course, in making a statement of this kind, he will have all his fellow-countrymen behind him. The leader of nation B will reply: 'I refuse to cut off my quiff. My country's honour is involved,' and his people will support him unanimously and with indescribable enthusiasm. Nation B will be invaded; another nation will become involved in the war, then two more, then three, thanks to the imitative tendency of our sheep-like breed. Still more army dentists will throw themselves into the abyss, without knowing why they are doing so but just vaguely assuming that this is the normal course of events and that human nature is made this way. And so it is.

The train moved off, very discreetly and smoothly. Another kindness on the part of the authorities! You would think they didn't want us to notice we were leaving. I expected to hear some shouts of 'Good-bye, Paris' or similar manifestations. But the men were as silent as the train. I kept my eyes fixed on the tiny shower of magical blue until it finally disappeared. There is someone I should have liked to see bathed in that blue shower. From now on, Paris, for me, was to mean that azure cone filled with a wild night-dance of insects. This was my last vision of Paris.

Yet I still felt no emotion. Yet only four years before, on setting off for North Africa, I had felt a pang and had wondered: 'Shall I ever come back?' Now I did not ask myself the question. It never even crossed my mind.

My companions, the reservist officers, echoed their newspapers, since they hadn't the wit to do more, and I retired into my shell so as not to hear them.

I got out the manuscript of *Les Lépreuses*[1] and began working

[1] The fourth and last volume in the series, *Les Jeunes Filles*.

on the style of a chapter, just as I had started *Le Songe* twenty years before under shellfire in the forest of Villers-Cotterets.

The suburbs drifted past in the night, deserted, and extraordinarily sinister. I remembered the name of a suburb that I have always found very evocative: *La Plaine* . . . The accursed cities, the cities of the Plain. The suburbs, as they drifted past, were like one of the cities of the plain, abandoned by men and awaiting the rain of fire out of heaven.

25th September

I spent the night in Metz station working on *Les Lépreuses* (at least the book didn't send me to sleep), because all the hotel rooms had been taken by officers.

A pleasant, unassuming young woman also spent the night on a seat in the station with her two little girls. She was an officer's wife, and her husband had been dispatched somewhere or other a fortnight before. But he 'hadn't foreseen' what was going to happen and as a result she had to leave without putting the family affairs in order, without being able to take her essential possessions with her (her husband had gone off with the key to the essential cupboards!) and without really knowing where she was going. It had never occurred to her imbecilic husband, either on the 11th September or later—although the post was still functioning—that his wife would have to be evacuated from Metz. Whereas I, who live in the clouds, and don't frequent well-informed circles, had had my wartime arrangements all settled for the past two and a half years: they went into operation without the slightest hitch, leaving my mind free and my heart unmoved. But here was an idiot, in charge of a family and in charge of his men, and it had never occurred to him to think what might happen. Imagine him living in Metz, twenty miles from the frontier, surrounded by his country's official defenders, and not bothering to think what might happen. And that's the sort of man who is responsible for a couple of hundred soldiers; his stupidity will send them to a death that might have been avoided, just as it has exposed his wife and children to danger and confusion. I cannot pity him; nor her either, since the social setting they were living in *ought* to have enlightened her, and *ought* to have forced her fool of a husband to look ahead. I can only pity the children, who are not in any way responsible. Why do I pity them? Because they have parents. It is a feeling that I have often had before. But they themselves will eventually be parents.

There are times when I wonder whether it is fair that those who had the foresight and courage to look ahead should take the rap, and not the others. But if you follow that line of thought to its logical conclusion, you would not set out for Metz but for Tulle or Bergerac. Or even New York. Fools should pay for their foolishness, and the others go on living.

On more than one occasion, recently, I had felt almost ashamed at enjoying such freedom of mind, as if it showed I was not sufficiently involved. After the night in Metz station, not a trace of shame remained.

There was another young woman there, a most remarkable one. Not really young—twenty-eight perhaps. But just the sort of woman you would like to hold in your arms. She was alone, although she had a husband somewhere or other, and was leaving Metz; from time to time, she exchanged a few words with a harmless old dodderer who was sitting next to her on the station seat. In that atmosphere of crisis, she exuded the joy of living with innocent shamelessness. Every time she uttered a sentence, whether it was innocuous or 'sad' ('I've left everything behind . . . I've lost my luggage . . . I don't know if my friends will be able to have me . . .'), her lips curved into a sharp, fawn-like smile as if under the pressure of some inner merriment that was beyond her control. She had no make-up, was beautifully built, as wholesome and healthy as a loaf of bread, and with nothing in the least coquettish about her: she was merely a happy woman who, incredibly, made no secret of the fact. I thought how easy it would be for the dear creature, by her mere presence, to quieten, comfort, cheer and revive men in pain—in hospital, for instance. But being so unconsciously alluring, she would eventually send all the men's temperatures up. Being a woman is no easy task, as has often been remarked; even the best of them puts poison into the cure.

The huge station was gloomy in the light of dawn. The men who, like myself, had been unable to reach their billets, were sleeping on the ground, or on the flights of steps. In a certain position, all I could see was prostrate bodies, looking as if they were already dead. They were bloodless dead, who seemed to have been killed by poison gas. And I wandered about, the only man awake, among all the sleeping bodies.

There was an old man lying with his fists tightly clenched as if he were afraid of letting something out of his grip. And there was a little chap who had his eyebrows raised as if something he was seeing in his sleep surprised him.

The children who had been asleep (and I'm reminded of D'Annunzio describing Dürer's *Melancholia*: 'On a branch the already unhappy child is asleep . . .') woke up. But they were not unhappy—they started to play straight away. Two little boys—not so little either (about thirteen)—sang a silly song together; it was not a bit patriotic but a peacetime, play song.

The wife of the imbecilic lieutenant said to her neighbour: 'Soldiers are risking their lives. Why shouldn't civilians risk theirs?' Very true, very true.

There were two currents flowing through the town: civilians were moving towards the station, and soldiers were going from the station to the barracks. As if to provide a little light relief, a daily paper appeared with the nice headline: 'King George is kept informed about the European situation.' You don't say!

At the —— office, there was a very varied assortment of officers belonging to the administrative services of the army to judge by their uniforms, but anti-administrators to judge by the pandemonium that reigned in the departments they controlled. (I omit the description of the pandemonium, in case it should be read by foreigners.)

. . . With my legs braced in puttees that I was wearing for the first time, I spent the whole afternoon taking the necessary steps to regularize my situation. The town was three-quarters empty: there were blocks of flats with windows shuttered from the top floor to ground level.

I feel at home only in the anonymous crowd—on the battlefield, on the sports' ground, or in the North African hinterland. My urge is to bury myself as deeply as possible in a teeming mass of unknown people—whole-heartedly sharing one or other of their passions. Their passion, here, is killing, without being killed.

26th September

Thionville was empty. Avenue Merlin. The wizard had cleared the town of people. A pair of sweethearts with arms intertwined crossed an empty square. The dimmed lighting was favourable to lovers.

Thionville was empty. I wondered how it was that a man totally devoid of the passion for ownership, whose whole life had in fact been based on its absence (except in the case of a few, very beautiful objects connected with his passions) and who had always been impatient to be rid of things he already possessed or which had been given to him, should suddenly feel a lust for pillage mounting within him to the point of obsession, once he had changed out of civilian clothes—I mean pillage of his fellow-countrymen's houses. How tempting they were in their emptiness! So much so that, in the heat of battle, they would have prompted 'admirable' acts of courage, if there had been any possibility of getting away with the loot. I think the reason lies in the following argument: 'I am protecting the lives of all you nit-wits, as well as nine-tenths of your possessions. I'm entitled to the other tenth as payment.'

Supposing Thionville were bombed. There are towns which acquire a personality only when they are in ruins, just as there are men who only acquire one when they become casualties.

Supposing Thionville were razed to the ground. Is it such a serious matter that towns like Thionville should be completely wiped out? Their inhabitants have gone. The few remaining human beings are either civilians who have chosen to hang on and whose death could therefore hardly be regretted since they could have left in time—or soldiers whose job it is to be killed.

The one thing I should mourn if Thionville disappeared would be the municipal theatre. With its massive iron-barred gates opening barbarically on to what look like time-scarred stone *oubliettes* (this is the main entrance), it looks like a cross between a prison and a public urinal. But above the lion-cage part, the façade is all elegance and rococo ornament. The general stylistic effect is remarkable.

A boy shouted to a little girl: 'France!'[1] I listened again carefully, thinking I must have misheard. 'France, bring the taxi back!' The 'taxi' was the bicycle the little girl was riding and she was definitely 'France'. 'Is "France" really the little girl's name!' I asked the boy. 'Yes.' 'But hasn't she got another name!' 'That's her name,' he snapped, looking suspicious and churlish.

How dull the officers' conversation was! They no more gave the impression of being technicians of war than the people who attend the official dinners of some important Parisian review give the impression of being intellectuals.

There were so many captains that there wasn't enough for them to do. Captain C—— had three stripes on his tunic and one of those blank faces that reveal nothing, even in moments of passion. He launched forth into a lot of spluttering nonsense about the services I could render. As I obviously looked rather dazed by the time he had finished, he concluded with: 'Do you understand!' 'No,' I replied, 'I don't understand a thing. But perhaps there is nothing to be understood.' This didn't seem to go down very well. Once again, I was confirmed in the belief that the main difficulty in a war is not the enemy, but the people in charge on one's own side. I came straight back to Metz among a lorry-load of zouaves.

Here, in the evening, there was a behind-the-lines atmosphere, typical of a town only a few miles from the front: it reminded me of Nancy in 1917–18. The female vampires were hard at work. You could see leaders of men, captains of war, males who might be dead on the morrow, slumped over a glass of Pernod and with a prostitute on either side. In Metz I saw the classical scenes I had already witnessed at Casablanca and elsewhere. I have written more

---

[1] 'France' exists as a French Christian name, but the little boy used the popular form with the article, 'la France', which sounds even more like the name of the country, and is untranslatable into English.

than enough on the subject,[1] so I shan't deal with it again. France is like that, and you must take her as you find her.

Besides, there were young girls (not prostitutes) who were really pretty. I came to the conclusion that desirable women are to be found everywhere, a fact which always astonishes me. And *brunettes* too! Brunettes at Metz! They were selling flowers outside the cafés and, infected by the excitement of the moment, were quite obviously ready to give their favours too. They put me into a merry, and remarkably inappropriate mood. I had come here to fight and was already thinking of chasing the girls. You can't always live up to the occasion!

There is no one who could not be found guilty of having, at some historic moment when everyone's attention 'ought' to have been concentrated on serious matters, written a letter which seems shocking because the writer is only concerned with some petty personal interest. My letter that evening to René Guastella, asking him for the exact wording of two passages from Thucydides, is a case in point.

After dinner, in one of the empty main streets, a shop resounded with a speech being delivered in German. It was Hitler making the broadcast during which, according to some people, he was going to declare war. Although I don't understand German, I stopped to listen to his fascinating voice. A very respectable man and a woman—the proprietor and his wife—came out on to the pavement. The three of us listened together, although they didn't understand German either.

How close the voice seemed. The lord of war was present, not more than a few feet away from me, in that room which would soon be destroyed by his artillery. And we were listening to him, although it was us that his voice was attacking.

Again and again, the 'sieg heils' came surging over the air like the mighty roar of the sea. And I should like to be able to say that they sent shivers down my spine—shivers of awe if not of fear. But I must admit that they had no effect on me either. Behind the voice was a vast body of men who ought to have made some

[1] In *La Rose de Sable*.

impression on me. But that body of men would find itself faced by another vast body. And also, I must confess that I'm not impressed by enthusiasm. After all, what was there on that side of the frontier except an infatuated mob? I was put off by the ritualistic, incantatory nature of the ceremony; the timing of the applause seemed to be governed by some barbaric tom-tom. I could see through the tricks too easily.

'They are like people possessed,' I said, since it was a kind of excitement that reminded me of scenes I had witnessed in North Africa.

'Vulgar hooligans,' corrected the shopkeeper. The term was surprising and surely unjustifiable. It was most unexpected to hear the solemn and righteous Germans referred to as vulgar hooligans, when I knew full well that my fellow-countrymen are universally considered as the vulgar hooligans of Europe.

At any rate, these decent folk were no more impressed than I was, and we bade each other good-bye very cheerfully.

Farther on, a crowd had gathered on the pavement in front of a café. They had just listened to the speech, too, and a few of them must have understood it. But I wasn't curious enough to ask them what 'he' had said. 'Let's go to bed,' I thought. 'If we're at war, I'll hear about it in the morning.'

'At last you've rid yourself of your poetic fervour,' Louis Gillet[1] wrote to me enthusiastically after reading *Les Célibataires*. Is poetic fervour so indecent a thing that you have to get rid of it? France as a whole must have been expressing herself through that agreeable Academician. Well, my dear Monsieur Gillet, you couldn't complain now of any excess of poetic fervour!

Historians should devote special attention to a period when people used the same *inner tone* in saying, 'We'll know by tomorrow whether or not we're at war' and 'We'll know by tomorrow the result of the France versus Italy match at Jean–Bouin Stadium.'

Common sense tells us that to live through tragic events as if you were on a fishing expedition requires considerable strength of mind. Philosophy has always preached that such composure and

[1] A member of the French Academy.

poise are essential for the achievement of the Sovereign Good. But the artist is frustrated, for what is left of the artist, when he ceases to feel? And when as a man, and not simply as an artist, you have made *living* synonymous with *feeling* . . . The Gods are jealous, and what they give with one hand, they take away with the other. 'Nothing in excess,' says the Oracle.

27th September

The train was moving towards Sierck. The stations, bathed in blue light, looked like blue-painted Tunisian houses. Horses poked their huge heads out of railway trucks. The gardens were full of roses tossed by the night wind. A cluster of engines looked like the elephants of Darius resting before battle. Beyond Köenigsmacker, came the first defence-works and barbed-wire entanglements. I hoped that our High Command didn't take its barbed-wire entanglements too seriously.

Somebody uttered a sentence of which I heard only the following snatch: 'When our kids see our graves . . .' Well, what will our kids do when they see our graves? They'll piss on them.

'Night belongs to the Gods,' as an ancient writer said. That's why troops travel by night. But in the cheerless dawn, I saw some who, like the lovers of Verona, hadn't been quick enough to avoid being surprised by daybreak. They climbed aboard, earth-coloured, the colour of their native soil, with here and there among their muddy mass the glint of gold braid, like the faint golden gleams that can be distinguished on the surface of some newly excavated archaeological find. I couldn't tear my gaze away! I looked at them with the same expression as I had worn twenty years before, an expression corresponding to one of my deepest states. If I had had to die, I should have liked the Wheel to stop when I was wearing that expression.

But could I be sure that it was quite the same expression? Julius Caesar, replying to an old soldier who had asked for permission to commit suicide, said, most unfeelingly: 'So you think you're alive, do you?' If I had seen these men killed the next day, would I have been able to check the thought: 'After all, were they really alive?'

I was no longer moved by the deep fraternal feeling I had experienced during the First World War. I had got to know mankind too well in the interval. I knew too much about 'ex-service men'. I now preferred to obey the voice which commands that one should 'not recite a prayer over the creature who has been nothing and done nothing.'[1]

We reached Sierck, and got out. There were soldiers sleeping on straw mattresses in the station waiting-room. It was a little pink town full of trees and blossom, and with a fortified castle of sorts. On a hoarding I saw the word: *Désarmement,* but it referred to the *désarmement* of petards.[2] I saw on a truck the notice 'Due for discharge,'[3] but it was the truck itself, and not its human contents, that was to be released from service.

About half a mile before Apach, a little frontier town at the junction of the road to Maudern, we came to the entrance of a fortification; I cannot, on pain of being court martialled, say whether or not it was part of the Maginot Line. More 'Gardes mobiles'. The structure protruded a little way out of the ground, its antennae resembling the conning-tower of a submarine. It looked as if it had surfaced for a breather and might dive again at any moment. More barbed-wire entranglements. At the entrance were two potted plants such as you might see in the entrance hall of a Villa at Arcueil-Cachan.

Here I met Lieutenant-colonel X of the ——th Artillery Regiment. (To conform with the usual practice I mustn't mention names and numbers. In any case, most of the uniforms I saw had had their identification signs removed; it was all very thrilling and secret service.) He was fifty years old, had a cropped, dark grey moustache, and a young face, although his hair had gone white at the temples. He was very tall, with a tremendous chest and broad

---

[1] Saadi: *Gulistan.*

[2] *Désarmement* means both disarmament, in the general sense, and the making harmless of explosive weapons by means of unloading or removal of fuse.

[3] *Proposé pour la réforme:* the commonest meaning of *réforme* is discharge from the army on medical grounds.

shoulders. He was the first officer I had seen in four days to make an impression on me. He had neither a shorn, Germanic vulture head, nor the pointed, clean-shaven face of the typical condottiere. He looked thoroughly French, a Frenchman of the finest type—there are still a few left. A real fighting animal, in repose. His face was sad, without any trace of evil gloating: his eyes, having become unused to daylight, were full of weariness. While talking to me, he occasionally patted his eyelids with his fingers: from time to time he cast a distant glance at the commercial travellers in soldierly disguise who were swarming dimly far below him—it was the jaded glance of a beast of prey. How lonely he looked! It was the loneliness and sadness of the creative artist, because his task was to destroy and destruction is creation reversed. In his long elegant fingers he was holding a letter, written in an affected hand on mauve writing paper. No doubt, the little woman was pestering him even here. What I found most moving about him was the rapid, rhythmic heaving of his powerful chest, a chest which seemed to have been created to swell with glory. Could he have been agitated, although he appeared so composed? Or could it be the letter that was torturing him? He was almost panting. But if you look carefully at lions, you'll see that they, too, are always panting.

When I saw the two empty red tabs on the upper part of his torso, they made me think of those pre-Islamic Arabs who used to smear the blood of their slaughtered prey on the breast of the horse which was the first to be in at the kill, so that its prowess should be obvious to all.

They said he was a 'swine'. I thought he was a strict disciplinarian, but not a swine. And the French High Command (like the French Government, and the whole of French life) is in sore need of discipline. During the 1914–18 war, it sometimes suffered from a failure of discipline.

From the top of the fortification, Germany was visible a mile away. To the west, on the far bank of the still, white Moselle, lay Luxemburg (handy, if you felt like deserting!). Clouds were passing, with the indifference of animals, from one country to another, but soon shells would be flying too . . . Once again, patriotic missiles would be hurtling through the upper regions of the air.

At a time when I hardly dared imagine the farmyard squawks and bad-tempered twitterings of the trainloads of civilians strugling for survival in the rush from Paris (and good riddance to the chicken-livered *bourgeois* who are always complaining of being 'martyred', always terrified at having to reap what they've sown; the future will belong to those individuals who have been able to adapt themselves), the men here seemed happy. In war, people who would be incapable of finding something to do of their own accord, are given a precise part to play. And whatever people may say, it is, and always will be, the sort of part that awakens in them a sense of their own dignity.

Also, there is something so monstrous about marriage and family life, that even when you are sending a man to his death, provided he begins by escaping from his home, he has a feeling of being on holiday. He may be solemn and anxious and fundamentally in rebellion, but he still has, *at the same time,* the holiday feeling. The men here were all on excellent terms with each other, not because of a sense of comradeship in danger, which had not yet had time to develop, but simply because they were all men together. Once you set men free from their homes and their womenfolk, they stop hating each other.

The current catch-phrase was: 'We're better off here than in Paris.' Perhaps: our preparations had been made, but nothing was ready in Paris. Yet it was obvious that if the Germans were to bomb anything it would be the Maginot Line.

There were some oldish men whose eyes were dulled by fatigue. It is true that some nations need to be given a shock from time to time, that is, need an occasional lesson in responsibility. But no nation should be required to fight a war more often than once every twenty-five years. It would thus have time to replenish its coffers and its cradles. It shouldn't always be the same people who get killed.

G was a twenty-three- or twenty-four-year-old farm-worker,

who owed his corporal's stripes to the call-up. They made him so proud that he had himself photographed wearing the badges of his rank. He ordered thirteen—*thirteen*!—prints of the photograph. However, when he had sent one off to the old folks, and kept one for himself, he didn't know what to do with the rest. No, after due reflection, he couldn't think of a single human being who would want a picture of him.

'Let me have one,' I said. 'It'll be a souvenir of the call-up.' But when, later, I tore up the photo, I had the feeling that I was performing a piece of sympathetic magic and that he, wherever he was, would have the sensation of being stabbed to the heart.

Although plastered with stripes, G had no vocation for soldiering. 'What! you dogs! do you want to live for ever?'[1] G reminded me of Mimile of the 360th Infantry Regiment in 1918: Mimile, a hefty greengrocer's assistant from Le Mans, I think, was a complete coward and made no bones about it. An excellent Spanish seventeenth-century maxim maintains that you mustn't say 'This man is brave' but 'This man was brave on such and such an occasion'. Mimile was never brave on any occasion. 'Come on, Mimile, let's go and get killed!' I would say to him kindly. As a matter of fact I used to like to have him near me in a tight corner. When the man next to you shows fear, he either passes it on to you, or on the contrary, helps to steady your nerves. My reaction was always the opposite of Mimile's. Just to vex him, I would treat with the greatest casualness situations which normally would have scared me, if Mimile's cowardice hadn't given me an exhilarating and dynamic conception of my own somewhat erratic bravery. When his fear got the better of him, I used to point the barrel of my rifle at him and say: 'Mimile, if you're afraid, I'll kill you.' I didn't kill him. And the fact that I didn't get him killed off as I dragged him through one unsavoury spot after another just shows that he had a lucky star. After all, it's not by taking cover that you

---

[1] Frederick II to his soldiers, who were attacking rather half-heartedly at the battle of Collin.

survive the worst bits: cowardice is the only saviour.[1] I have seen Mimile since; he has put on weight.

I suppose the rustic guns of the last war have gone for ever. One, I remember, was painted in various colours, camouflaged with branches and carried along on a truck with its gun crew seated round it, looking for all the world like part of some Dionysiac procession. Another I remember seeing on a road, being dragged along by its tail like a captive dragon and all bristling with the scraps of vegetation from its den that had clung to it during the final struggle. The turret of the present-day gun rises from below the ground. The concealed barrel darts from its shell, fires, and withdraws into its shell which sinks again into the ground. Everything about this gun makes you think of an animal—the lair, the tough protective covering, the initial slowness, the burst of agile movement, the venomous spitting, the withdrawal, the ferocity mixed with fear (or what seems to be fear), fear being a characteristic of ferocious beasts. A fortnight before, almost dazed by that Ali Baba's cave of treasures—the British Museum—I had thought: 'When you see life as a jumble, you can with reason deplore the human race. But how can you do so in a museum worthy of the name, when faced with a superb selection of man's most admirable achievements? Here you see how nature and man have combined to make this world a delightful place—delightful, that is, for intelligent people, since fools see it as a vale of tears.' By 'nature' I meant the forms which man borrows from nature in order to embellish his artistic creations. But man and man alone is responsible for creating the modern fortress gun: nature merely supplied the raw material. And man made it stronger, more accurate, more harmonious and more pitiless than himself—a veritable monster, in fact, if this word has any meaning at all. And he created it for the work of death, which is the furthest extreme of faith in life. I would have liked to see the following lines from the *Antigone* inscribed in a cartoon on a wall in the British Museum:

[1] *Il n'y a que les foies qui sauvent*: an untranslatable pun on *il n'y a que la foi qui sauve*: *foi* = faith; *foies* = the willies.

> Many are the marvels of this world
> But nothing is
> More marvellous than man.

But if words could be engraved on a modern gun, as ancient bronze cannon were cast with mottoes on them, I would suggest the following lines—which are an act of confidence on my part, that is more than just an expression of admiration:

> Many are the things of this world that can be
> > replaced,
> But nothing is
> More replaceable than man.

I know how a machine-gun throbs when it is being fired. I think of the throbbing of a steamer battling against the waves, of the mysterious, quivering throb of a horse, of an aeroplane throbbing when the engine has been started up before the take-off, of the quivering throb of our partner whom we cherish and yet terrify.

I had also said to myself: 'If these youngsters and men were not here, they would be buying tickets for the *Loterie Nationale,* or ticking off the names of horses in "The Lucky Punter" etc. It is better to be working a machine-gun than to be bothering about the *Loterie Nationale.*' But I cross out this sentence. There is an old Adam in me who believes, in a confused way, that courage justifies everything, and from time to time I struggle against him with varying success.

Have written to two Nazi friends (of military age). The gist of my letters was: 'It is *not even* salvation by the sword. It is something infinitely more simple.'

The end of the school holidays has been postponed for a week, and the children's delight is a delight for us in the midst of the great ordeal. Those who believe that children are the only members of the human race worthy of love, will go so far as to talk of 'compensation'.

* * *

An Englishman has gassed himself after listening to Hitler's speech. Farewell.[1] Bon voyage!

The political leaders of the great democratic countries, one after another, are rushing to climb Olympus and kiss the feet of Jupiter with-the-forelock, anxiously and openly watching for the slightest frown, gingerly patting him and at the same time wetting their pants with terror as they mutter, 'Your Excellency cannot wish to precipitate... Your Excellency will surely understand... We hope Your Excellency will condescend to accept...' begging for peace in a whining tone, as their predecessors did with the Kaiser in July 1914. Achilles had killed Priam's son, when Priam 'grovelled' at his feet; Hitler declares he will kill England's sons and France's sons, whereupon England and France grovel at his feet, bringing with them, as Priam did, 'an immense ransom' (with the difference that they are paying with what does not belong to them). This is such an astounding, disconcerting sight that when our sons ask us to instruct them in the rules of human conduct, we shall only have to point to the behaviour of national leaders for them to see at least what not to do.

The umbrella, the huge, stiff collar, the abbreviated trousers, the smirk which I refuse to describe—all these details are part of the consciously elaborated 'character' of Chamberlain, the Marx brother of peace: all these details, like Herriot's pipe, and some other politician's old-fashioned cravat, are intended to make us warm towards him. The other day, at Godesberg, Mr Chamberlain forgot his umbrella in the plane. Nothing will convince me that he didn't do it on purpose, to make all the ladies, young and old, sorry for him: 'Poor, dear old fellow!'[1] That's what politicians are like; they are able men, very able perhaps. But like clowns, they must please the public, if their contract is to be renewed.

Then there's all the business of the letters received by Mrs Chamberlain, and Mrs Chamberlain being photographed at prayer,

[1] In English in the original.

looking sublime, and all the 'she's behind it' nonsense. Whatever we may think of French politicians, let us at least give them credit for never using their families as a means to popularity.

28th September

(Written later.) In the morning I had some business to see to at the Custom's Office, and from there I went on to the frontier. It amused me to have seen German soldiers on the 28th September 1938. Beyond the Custom's house where *gardes mobiles* were standing by in readiness for an emergency, I came round a bend in the road, and saw a barrier which I took to be a level-crossing barrier. On the far side of it stood a little grey house with a piece of red material (no doubt a bed-cover) hanging from one of the windows. I walked on between apple trees in white waistcoats. Suddenly I saw another piece of red material hanging from a post. As it billowed out in a puff of wind, it revealed the swastika with which it was inscribed. I had completely forgotten the colours of the Nazi flag.

I moved forward until I was only a few steps from the barrier. I could have thrown a hand grenade into Germany. There was not a soul to be seen. France and Germany were sleeping side by side, like sisters.

Nothing is more a succession of crises and lulls than life on active service. One minute you don't know what to do next and the following minute you slump back into endless vacancy. After lunch, having nothing more to do, I went out again. It looked as if we were really in for it now. The 'half time' which had lasted twenty years was nearly over. Germany was to announce general mobilization at two o'clock if by then Czechoslovakia hadn't agreed to her terms. Fate was sealed and implacable—like those Mycenean masks with closed and tragic lips. I walked along the road from Sierck to Trier, holding the loose sheets of *Les Lépreuses* in my hand and working as I went along, as was my wont. At any moment now, I would have to summon up all my nervous energy. My best course, for the time being, was to hold it in reserve.

Now, all Europe was under arms; men and women were watching and waiting, or busily making ready, or taking refuge in flight or praying: never during the last quarter of a century had the world witnessed such a vast and universal upheaval of the human race. And beneath my feet, in front and behind, over a vast area, the ground was honeycombed with an army of killers, all ready for the irredeemable. Of all this I could see nothing and hear nothing. The noise of the world did not penetrate as far as that road, although it was one of the nerve centres of the globe, and at any moment would be transformed into something which, for horror, would equal one of the circles of Hell. I could hear neither the call of a bird nor the rustle of an insect. It was like the calm before the creation.

I was grappling with Costals and Mademoiselle Dandillot.[1] Suddenly from far away there came the ringing of a church bell. It went on ringing and ringing on the same note: or at least so it sounded to me. I looked at my watch (which was set in the same leather strap as during the First World War): ten to three. As I write this, I realize that ten to three is precisely the time for Vespers. But on the spur of the moment, I forgot this and said to myself that Evensong was not until five o'clock. I remembered having heard somewhere that to sound the alarm the church bells repeated the same note. It then dawned upon me that it must be our mobilization that was being announced. German mobilization must have been announced at two o'clock: ours had probably been decided immediately afterwards: the news would have arrived here at ten to three: all this seemed to fit in. And just then, as if to convince me still more, there came the wail of a siren.

The bell went on ringing. Soon another ringing sound blended with the first—it was the steady clink of a pick-axe. On the other side of the hedge bordering the road, a soldier was working. My first thought was: 'If that had really been the alarm, he would have stopped digging.' But having heard gramophones still playing after the sounding of a ship's alarm bell, and having so often witnessed the placid imperturbability with which people can behave,

[1] Characters in *Les Lépreuses*.

I was not at all convinced by this argument. Should I not say to the soldier: 'Is that the alarm bell?'—like Vigny's father who, when he was on his death-bed and in the last throes, had said to the doctor: 'Tell me, is this the death-rattle?' It seemed ridiculous for me not to know whether it was the alarm bell or not. I devoted my attention once more to Mademoiselle Dandillot and went on my way.

How many important—even vital—things do we fail to do in life because of possible embarrassment.[1] I have always thought that if I were set upon by a murderer, I would be incapable of calling for help. I can't 'see' myself shouting: 'Help! help!' Even in that situation, I would be ashamed to ask for assistance and unable to utter a sound.

The bell stopped ringing. The sky, through which invisible tons of explosives would soon hurtle along invisible tracks, was clear. In the distance, riders on plump little horses were galloping across the pink and green chessboard pattern of the fields. The hard, reddish road, spattered with blue where a passing car had spilt some of the paint used for darkening windows, rang beneath my feet: it was doubtless mined and would shortly be blown up. As I went past, a cloud of buzzing flies rose from a heap of horse-dung. Two non-commissioned officers went by on bicycles. Their faces expressed nothing out of the ordinary. I caught a scrap of their conversation: 'After the war . . .'

'After the war!' Until then I had thought only about what I would do during the war. Now I, too, began to wonder what I would do afterwards. And the France I imagined was neither an enslaved country nor a country torn by civil war: it was a victorious France, in which there would be another post-war period devoted to pleasure, licentiousness, and excesses of every kind: a France in which those of us, like myself, who had taken part in the fighting would be more than ever convinced that they had a right to behave exactly as they pleased. For at the time, it never occurred to me that I might perish in the fighting: death was not

[1] A woman I know has told me that if Paris were bombed, she could not take shelter in the cellar, because she was not on good terms with her landlord and might meet him there.

for me. I could see myself stepping over the disaster into a new world of bliss.

About seven o'clock, somebody said there was to be a Four-Power Conference but this rumour appeared to me to be all the more unlikely since we heard at the same time that the eighth group had been called up.

Although I had felt perfectly calm, I had not slept more than four hours a night for the past two weeks: we have to suppose that, deep down inside us, is another individual who lives a separate existence quite independent of our conscious life.

During the night of the 28th to the 29th of September, when in fact peace was decided, but when, to the layman, war seemed most inevitable, I slept seven hours without a break.

There may be women who whisper: 'How curious that you should sleep on the very night when peace was saved . . . Your subconscious may have received a mysterious warning, who knows?' I think the real explanation is quite different. If part of my subconscious had been uneasy for the past fortnight, it was probably because of the uncertainty. On the evening of 28th September, I was so convinced that war would break out that I felt I was no longer anticipating war but had actually embarked on it. And once more I found peace in the very heart of war. *Paz en guerra*.

29th September

Seven o'clock in morning. 'I would like there to be Gods so that we could have confidence not only in our military strength, but also in the justness of our cause': Cassius to Brutus, on the eve of the Battle of Philippi (Plutarch). How was it that this remark, one of the most moving in the whole of Caesar's tragic history, was not used by Shakespeare?

It compares in pathos with a still earlier lament (about the soundness of which I am, however, very doubtful): 'He who stays in camp and he who fights courageously play an equal part. It has availed me nothing to have endured innumerable ills, and exposed my soul in battle.' Who do you think uttered this lament, so modern in tone, the lament of the eternal PCDF?[1]—Achilles in the *Iliad*. There is no poignant cry that the non-Christian world did not utter as forcibly as the Christian.

Any man who, on the eve of battle, wonders as Cassius does whether or not his cause is a worthy one, is bound to be plunged into despair, if he is intelligent. Therefore, the situation should not be approached from this angle. The cause in itself matters little. What matters is knowing whether, in fighting under a particular banner, you can achieve fulfilment.

It seems to me that, in the Spanish Republican army (and without drawing a penny, of course), I would have been more at home among the mercenaries than among the idealists.

There is no getting away from it: the whole virtue of war is bound up with the risk of death. And yet you don't master war by getting yourself killed. However heroic he may have been, the dead soldier is a dupe. None of your martyrdom for me (particularly martyrdom for a *cause*!). The problem—a difficult one—is therefore to maintain a delicate balance between deliberately risking one's life and not sacrificing it. In actual practice, the consequences of an attitude like this can at times appear alarming.

The problem is how to reconcile two characters, who are in many ways incompatible, the hero and the intelligent man.

Heard a bit of one of Chamberlain's snivelling broadcasts. 'It breaks the heart to see how anxious mothers are, etc. How horrible, how fantastic, how unbelievable it is that we should have got to the point of digging trenches!' No, dear Mr Broken-heart, not unbelievable at all, when you consider the policy followed by your country (and ours) during the past twenty years. 'I am a man of peace, to the very depths of my soul.' Yes, of course, we know all about that. Don't go on and on!

Eight o'clock. A dramatic stroke. A Four-Power Meeting in Munich. 'If they're having a meeting, it means that an agreement has already been reached.' 'Peace has been saved.'

[1] An expression used in the 1914–18 war: *pauvhe con du front*—'silly b—— in the front line.'

(Thanks to Saint Thérèse of Lisieux, it goes without saying.)[1]

I feel nothing.

I feel no more exhilarated now than I felt distressed the day before yesterday when I learned that Germany had decided to mobilize. Peace? All right, then, let's have peace.

On the day of the September equinox, peace and war balanced each other on the scales.

Five o'clock. The Four Powers met at 3.30.

At five o'clock, one of the men said: 'The Government broadcast a request for one minute's silence at 3.30. Funny sort of war!'

Not daring to pray any longer, they've invented the minute's silence, and such-like inanities. When, for once, they achieve something worth while, they call it a miracle: the 'miracle' of the Marne. They always have to 'go looking behind the stars . . .'[2] They claim that they are making man look 'towards the light', and at the first signs of alarm, they drive him back into the mire. Today, just as they did six thousand years ago—but now in roundabout, hypocritical ways—they beseech the gods to grant them the victories which they are incapable of achieving by their own valour.

And to think that only the other day I was imagining a war 'devoid of rhetoric'!

(But I note the soldier's derisive laugh and his good sense: 'Funny sort of war!' He was shocked.)

What we need, Monsieur Daladier, is not a minute's silence, but aeroplanes.[3]

---

[1] I thought I was making a joke. But I have learned since that thanksgiving pilgrimages took place throughout France (and no doubt throughout England too). And in some cases, these pilgrimages were approved of by people who had objected to another thanksgiving pilgrimage—to the tomb of the Unknown Soldier. What is even funnier is that, according to several newspapers, Czechoslovakia was indebted for the beneficent conclusion of the Munich Agreement to her patron saint, St Wenceslas.

[2] 'I hate people who go looking for reasons behind the stars . . .' Nietzsche.

[3] It was not the Government which had the idea of the minute's silence but one of those news-sheets which make daily use of an elaborate technique of degradation to provide France with the soul and the morals of a *midinette*.

30th September

A young French couple have hanged themselves because they thought there was going to be a war. Good night! *Bon voyage!*

Now that the whole thing is over, the Pope is scattering holy water on all and sundry: everybody claims a drop—the good and the bad, the consenters and the dissenters. Now that peace has been achieved, the Pope 'offers his life' for the purpose of achieving it. (And if it hadn't been achieved, what risk was he running? No, a thousand times no, rhetoric is not dead!) Except in the Jewish papers, where the Catholic chord is dutifully sounded (I can hear the Prince of Darkness laughing). There, the homily of the head of the Christian Church is relegated to the back page, like a speech by the President of the Republic of San Domingo.

Why do I feel, more and more strongly, that the whole business has been a mockery? Because I have a sneaking suspicion that it was, and still is, deliberately engineered by the Hitler–Mussolini combination. Hitler knew all along that he was not going to embark on a war. Why, then did he . . . ? To get what he wanted, of course. But also to have a little game; to make the different kind of people he had opposite him dance like puppets; to play cat and mouse with them; or simply to amuse himself, in the manner of the demiurges and the rest of the gods. You only have to look at the way Mussolini is laughing on the Munich photos. I'll say nothing about the figure that certain famous democrats cut on the photos, because I don't want to appear unfair towards 'men of good will'.

Our groundless anxieties were also a mockery. I can imagine the cackling of the old women when we get back. 'So you really believed there was going to be a war? Well, I didn't, not for one moment.'

1st October

Thionville. Knights are holding their lances, which are billiard queues. Captains of killers are killing only time: billiards and drink: it's not as easy as all that to endure the shock of peace.

The situation here was bearable only as long as death was wheeling overhead. Today it is no longer bearable, at least in my opinion. Let me get away quickly! This is no place for me now! Let us not spoil the memory of the part of our experience here which might be considered as redounding to the honour of mankind.

2nd October

Thionville, Metz . . . The blue is being washed off the window-panes and the foliage which camouflaged the names of stations is being removed. The might-have-been heroes, with huge wild flowers stuck in the button-holes of their battle-dress or their tunics, are returning, singing *Sambre-et-Meuse* in a desultory fashion and walking with the help of the pilgrims' staffs they have cut for themselves from the trees in the woods. And like wood-lice, which scatter when you step on their nest and then come homing in again as soon as the danger is past, a swarm of women, young and old, of chicken-hearted dowagers and mineral-water-drinking elders, is coming back along the roads and into the towns where, only a little while ago, there was nothing but emptiness and fighting men. France can devote itself once more to its games of *belote* and to Tino Rossi.

'Peace with honour' is the cry of the evening papers. Of course, when a word has lost all meaning, you can dish it up in whatever guise you like. 'We have great hopes . . .' cry the grey-beards. I like childishness, but not when practised by grey-beards. Sentimental filth bubbles irrepressibly from the fountain-pens of dutiful journalists. On the semi-corpse of a betrayed nation, on the semi-corpses of their honour, their dignity and their security, millions of men are jigging in the St Vitus's dance of peace.

The childish demonstrations of the 'phlegmatic' gentlemen in the House of Commons do not prevent me being of the opinion— even supposing that England has got out of the jam very neatly, which I readily admit—that the reputation of the English has not been enhanced. As for the French, they hardly bear talking about. Rave to your hearts' content, you miserable helots, after letting yourselves be manœuvred, duped, weakened and insulted. Welcome defeat and humiliation with slavish transports of delight. Stamp on your gas-masks, you fools,[1] because tonight, like last night, it is true, you can have a good tuck-in and then toddle off to bye-byes. But tomorrow, you'll have a different tale to tell. Whether you like it or not, a day will come, you cowardly fools, when the stench from your quaking bowels will be obliterated by the acrid smell of your blood. Unless you preserve yourselves for ever from bloodshed by the acceptance of shame.

November 1938

[1] Three weeks after writing this sentence (i.e. about the 20th October) I was told by a maker of gas-masks that 50 per cent of the people who had ordered gas-masks a month earlier now refused to accept them on delivery.

THE 1940 ARMISTICE (IN MARSEILLES)

... I WANDERED amongst all this like a ghost, horrified and utterly exhausted. Fatigue causes sleepiness but over-fatigue makes sleep impossible: I had been unable to sleep when I was with the army. I could not sleep here, either, because a bitter sorrow also prevents sleep. You suffer more from a disaster that has overcome your country than you do from your own disasters. You can take the philosophic view when only you yourself are concerned; you would be ashamed to do so, when something other than the self is at stake. This may be wrong. The philosophic view should perhaps be indivisible. But this is the way things are, and it is just as well. As during my blackest period in former years—but a prey this time to a sorrow for which I was not myself responsible—I sought out distant zoological or botanical gardens in order to be alone with animals and plants who do not know what it means to have a mother-country. Or I went round and round the town on the 'circular line', putting my head out of the window to feel the wind on my face and closing my eyes so as not to see the people. And yet I said to myself that even that, some day, even that might perhaps seem to have been the last experience of Paradise.

I thought of crossing into Spain, and the day after the fall of Paris went to see the Prefect's assistant private secretary to ask for his help. (The interview was mentioned—with malicious intent, of course—in a number of the Montpellier *Journal des étudiants*, which came out during the occupation.) The assistant private secretary was rather short with me; whatever I do, think, say or write is always wrong, in whichever way it is interpreted. According to him, my place was in France. Confucius also was whispering in my ear a maxim of his which I have always been only too eager to heed, whether uttered by a Latin, Greek, Moslem, Japanese, Persian or Christian voice: 'Do nothing, and all will be done.' My private affections were a still weightier argument, so I stayed.

But let me finish with these strangers. The 1914–18 war, too, had its shirkers, its egotists, its brazen misbehavers and its ciphers. But there were others to redress the balance. Those short-legged gorillas with their *képis*, their floppy moustaches, their kit-bags, and their puttees, those ludicrous cave-men, provide the last worthwhile image of France. If, in 1940, I saw them again in films about the army or in old copies of *L'Illustration,* I know I should weep. It is not a question of growing sentimental about my lost youth. I don't care a damn for my lost youth; happiness came to me in maturity. I should be weeping for a time in French history when the country still had two twin virtues which now seem to have belonged to another world: true worth and disinterestedness. And perhaps I should be weeping at the bliss of having lived through such a time.

I bless my fate which threw me into that war; and which, better still, started me on my literary career with an account of the last event to redound to the glory of France, an event the memory of which I was trying to perpetuate. This event was Verdun. At Verdun, we faced the enemy alone, and we stopped him. At that moment, France was respected by the whole world. It was the last time. In 1917 came the military rebellions. Then, in 1918, victory, but France was by then supported, uplifted, materially and morally, by American aid: she was no longer alone. The year 1919 saw the beginning of a disgrace which has continued ever since. Verdun was the grave of four hundred thousand Frenchmen. Since they were the best Frenchmen, Verdun may have also been the grave of France.

Textes sous une occupation, 1953
(Written in the summer of 1940)

THE FAMILY, THE FATHERLAND, Etc.

IT IS A COMMONPLACE that the love of parents for their children is never returned. We put ourselves out for them and they are on their best behaviour with us, at any rate when they are in our company; all of which does a fat lot of good. They have not the slightest notion of the sacrifices we are making on their behalf, and if they had, they would only feel the additional embarrassment of having to be grateful to us. They make the same terrible remarks to us that we made to our fathers and mothers (for choice to our mothers) twenty or thirty years ago. The reader will be familiar with the lines of the nineteenth-century poet:

> Car il faut que les mamans pleurent
> Pour que les enfants soient heureux.
>   For mammas must weep
>   That children may be happy.

These lines are accurate in each particular, including the tears and the word happy, for it is the children's happiness, and not merely their existence, their health, or their ability to 'get on well', that depends on the mothers' tears. I shall not mention the tears shed by fathers because I am of the opinion that paternal love is a sentiment almost non-existent in nature. (The only felicitous expressions of paternal love I know of are the work of Catholic priests—Lacordaire, Lamennais, Freppel. . . .)

A useless service, then, as far as we are concerned. But for them, too. What will they retain of it? Life will have obliterated everything in time. In vain do childish winsomeness and the presence of great and unmistakable qualities delude us for a while; there come moments when we see the truth, which is that our children, although of such sterling stuff and so gifted, will one day, in their turn, be mediocrities. What man with the power to build for eternity, on considering the vast amount of energy he has diverted from his task to devote it to his children, and all in vain, has not cried within himself: 'Why did I create them?'

The same poignant melody is prompted by the love of the fatherland. *Patria* from *pater*; and we say 'France is our mother'; we are always looked upon as the children of our country. But when I think of her frivolity, her *naïveté*, her complacency, her constant backsliding, her love of the faked and her passion for the stupid, I am bound to say that our country is our child rather than our parent. In her ingratitude, too, she resembles our children. When we trounce our country, she thinks we wish her ill, just as our children do when we punish them. She is no more able than they are to recognize love. She is no more capable than they are of a proper scale of values. For every one of the servants she honours, how many others, more upright, are forgotten? Our unknown sacrifices, our needless acts of tenderness are lost beneath her surface and their black and golden gleam is extinguished in her depths.

Lost; yes, indeed, all we do for our country is as irrevocably lost as what we do for our children. For centuries our country has taken for granted the words and deeds of those who seek her well-being. She absorbs those words and deeds with indifference, assimilates them without a glimmer of understanding and remains unchanged. Just as, in the useless service we accomplish on behalf of our children, part of the effort goes to build up something which will one day be destroyed, while the other part creates nothing, does nothing (or next to nothing) to modify the character of the child whose inborn qualities and defects remain unaltered, so our country remains what she was on reaching the age of reason, having made no progress at all in some respects and in others having undone whatever progress she had achieved. 'We have been ploughing the sea,' said the patriot Bolivar on his death-bed. The phrase ought to be echoed by everyone like him who dares to face the truth.

Parental love knows all this, and carries on even so. Patriotism is aware of it, and also carries on. 'Hope is not essential to initiative' is a sound saying—sound like everything which discredits hope, and true as well, because the object of the undertaking is not important, only the initiative itself. Nietzsche's saying 'a married philosopher is a music-hall joke' is a superficial remark unworthy of his genius. Actually, the philosopher's wife and children are the instruments of his philosophy. Some fathers, when in their declining years they see that their children have absolutely no affection for them, are perhaps unworthy creatures, have become merely average, interchangeable, human specimens, will rest content with the thought that they have done their duty; others will feel that the experience of fatherhood has given them more weight, made them wiser, more conscious of reality, richer in those secrets that life deposits in us year by year—in a word, more human.

I imagine that those who have experienced the vanity of public service and know with what small thanks it is repaid, are just as little inclined to bitterness. They deflect their attention a moment from their country's destiny to consider their own, and see that it has suffered no loss in spite of the apparent waste of effort. If expended love is ever recaptured, it is within the giver himself. The secret of all service is that all the time we are, involuntarily, serving ourselves. You think you are working for the community, out of duty or love, and in the end it is the individual who triumphs. There is no need to be a mystic to believe that things move in mysterious ways: the mystery is present in the human heart. Saul went out to seek his father's asses, and found the kingdom of Israel.

Textes sous une occupation, 1953

(Written in 1940)

WORK

I AM STRUCK by the imaginative love that many French children—or should I say, Parisian children, since I have had the opportunity of noticing it only in Paris?—have for the trade or job they intend to take up. 'What do you want to do, when you are older?' 'I'm going to be a mechanic.' 'And you?' 'I'll be a carpenter.' (At the age of thirteen they all want to be carpenters because they have carpentry classes at school.) When they utter the words 'mechanic' or 'carpenter' their faces become literally radiant; the glow is as sudden as if an electric lamp had been switched on. If they were saying: 'We want to be lion-hunters,' they could not be more ecstatic. (They look straight in front of them with shining eyes, as if seeing a vision: 'I'll have a bench! All to myself!') Sometimes the mere idea of having a trade arouses the same enthusiasm. I have, for instance, expressed astonishment at the excitement caused by the prospect of going into some orphanage or other—a bleak outlook, it would seem to me. I say 'But tell me, why are you so excited about going there?' 'I'll learn a trade.'

The fourteenth birthday has always been a rather solemn date. At fourteen, the young Roman received his *toga praetexta*; the page became a squire, and now the French boy puts on workman's blue overalls. Or perhaps, although he is still so slender and child-like, he is given his father's or big brother's cast-offs and suddenly loses his shape, through changing from the skimpy and rather ridiculous garments of a schoolboy, who has been growing too fast, to the square, padded shoulders, voluminous jacket and baggy trousers of an adult twice his size (in winter, he may keep his schoolboy shorts on underneath): a gosling's head emerges from the body of a small elephant. It is also at this age that he adopts the elegant habit of putting water on his hair on Sundays, to make himself look grown-up; the teacher-who-doesn't-like-children will add:[1] water that might with advantage have been used for washing. Or perhaps the time has come to use brilliantine, which makes him look as if Mother Bear had lovingly licked his head. Brilliantine is the poor man's luxury in France, just as shoe-shine is in Spain.

Some people declare that from the moment he starts work, a sweet little boy will turn into an uncouth, resentful urchin, who is totally and irretrievably different. That certainly can happen, and nothing is more discreditable to the adult than the sudden deterioration of the child as soon as he is in frequent contact with his elders. But I notice other things too. After a few days he is pale and thin through unaccustomed fatigue, and has a perpetual black rim around his eyes—the factory dust darkens them like kohl. After a few weeks his hands are deformed—small, dry and wrinkled like a monkey's paws. You can find old men with deeply lined faces but whose bodies have remained as youthful as they were at thirty-five. When a child goes to work, what happenes is that his face and body remain child-like while his hands change into those of an old working man. Never again will he have a child's hands nor, for that matter, ordinary man's hands. Fifty years of manual labour lie in front of him; he will depend entirely on his hands and have no other resource to count on than them, and they are already permanently gnarled and roughened.

Jean ran away from the Youth Centre, after being there two years. He was fifteen, an only child, and his father was dead. His mother was not at home, having gone off with a lover, so he at once got himself a job (4,400 francs a month plus food and lodgings) labouring for the Germans who were fortifying Cherbourg.

'A fellow who has just come back says they have air-raids every day, but I would rather put up with that than go back to the Centre.'

[1] Some twenty-five years ago, a book entitled *Le Professeur n'aime pas les enfants* came out in Switzerland.

The French are like that; they would sooner be killed than bored. It is not living we are after, but happiness.

Jean had two small metal discs in his beret. I asked him what they stood for.

'Nothing at all,' he said.

This is the sort of answer I like. To want to find a meaning for everything is the sign of a small, pretentious mind. Besides, nowadays so many things are supposed to mean so many things that you get muddled. In point of fact, the two little discs had an aesthetic meaning. They had been put there because they 'looked nice'.

At the same time, I was glad to see that he had no badge on his jacket. In France, it is always a good sign when a child, an adolescent or a grown-up has nothing in his buttonhole. Just imagine finding a boy scout without a badge! It would be enough to make you think that he might have glimmerings of intelligence.

The only sign of enthusiasm I could find in Jean was for the comradeship that prevailed at the Youth Centre. 'Oh, yes, we were all pals there.'

In France, however great the gulf of indifference between parents and children, it is apt suddenly to be spanned by an unexpected and illogical thread of sentimentality. Over the belt provided by the Centre, Jean wore a second one which, it seemed, had belonged to his father during the 1914–18 war.

'I wouldn't part with it for 100,000 francs,' he said. One day he'll sell it for thirty.

At first, to be on the safe side, he had given his age as one year less than it was. Boys in their teens often do the opposite; they say they are older to appear more grown-up. And in their simplicity they believe that everyone else does the same. If you happen to say to one of them 'I'm thirty-five', he will answer, 'Yes, that's what you say, but I bet you're really thirty-three or thirty-four.' You have to be living in our day to hear boys of fifteen pretending to be younger or saying with a sigh, 'If I could only stay fifteen for ever!' They know what lies in store for them when they are a few years older.

When I asked Jean where he came from, meaning from what part of the country, he replied 'from *La Nation*' (the district in Paris called La Nation). So I christened him Jean de la Nation, which would have been a very good name for a little drummer-boy at the Battle of Valmy, but did not fit in very well with his wish to work for the Germans.

'Do you mind working for the Germans?'

'It's all one to me as long as I work.'

'But weren't you working at the Centre?'

'Huh! They made us do anything, just to keep us busy. One day we dug holes, and the next we filled them up again.'

'You want to do some real work, is that it?'

'When you're working, you're not miserable.'

(What a definition of happiness!)

He promised to come and see me during his first leave.

'If I don't turn up, I'll have been killed.' The remark, which was made in a very matter-of-fact way, is one that can be heard in any war. But to hear it coming from a child of fifteen . . . In 1943, everybody always seems to be going off somewhere. You have to count them as dead from the start. In 1943, woe to him who becomes attached.

But perhaps I shall meet Jean again one day and he will have the knitted brow, the indelible frown, characteristic of women and teenagers who have just come out of prison. He will no longer be talking about comradeship then. He will tell me that he got twenty-five francs every time he betrayed a friend.

'I've often done it,' he will say.

If bombs fall on Paris, a mother will send her thirteen-year-old child to some safe place in the country. But if he is fourteen and working, no mother would dream of making him leave Paris because of the bombs, since that would mean taking him away from his work and losing his earnings. And so the difference of a month (thirteen years and eleven months as opposed to fourteen) may save a boy's life. Or, to put it differently, for 800 francs a month some people die and others are prepared to condemn them to death.

Marcel, whose age is fourteen years and one month, has a job, so he stays in Paris. His mother is in a factory and his father, needless to say, is dead. In half the homes in present-day France there is no father. The boy works in a bakery, where he is the only employee. He starts at 6 am and finishes at 7 pm—often later—and has three-quarters of an hour off for the midday meal, which he is given at his employer's table. It is a good meal with meat every day. He has Fridays off but works all day on Sundays at the ordinary rate of pay. His wages are 780 francs a month.

He said to me with a laugh: 'Life's a funny thing. I work twelve hours a day. I see my mother for an hour every evening. It's like that day in and day out and will be all my life.' Then, after a pause, 'Friday's a grand day!'

He said it with a laugh, and yet his case is typical of the tragedy of the proletariat. He can laugh because he's only just beginning and because he has the sort of nature that puts up with things. I told him that he, or rather his mother, ought to ask for an increase in pay or a reduction in his working hours.

'I daren't,' he says, 'and she daren't either.'

'Aren't you tired?'

'Oh, no.'

But why, before replying, did he suddenly straighten his back and lift his head?

'And to think that there are chaps of your age who are page-boys in hotels, doing pretty well what they like all day and earning 3,000 francs a month.'

'Oh, I wouldn't be one of them. I'd sooner do real work, even if it's hard, than open doors for people.'

Like Jean who refused to go on digging holes and filling them up again.

Marcel's instincts are absolutely sound. He hands over his wages to his mother. If you make him a present of 100 francs, he won't have spent it in a fortnight. He has one hour a day, from eight to nine in the evening, to live—to LIVE—and during that hour he is always ready to run a message for you or to be helpful in some way or other. Once I said casually, without suggesting that he should do anything about it, that I found it difficult to get any thread. Whereupon he unwound the string of his kite and brought me the threads! An astonishing little fellow, so ordinary to look at and full of such rare courage, honesty, tact and decency. How can such characters continue to exist when (now especially) everything around them tends to corrupt? What produces the miracle? We have to believe—and I personally believe it more firmly every day—that some individuals are born with a given character so deeply ingrained in them that they grow up without being in the least affected by their environment. What they were at the age of ten, they will still be at fifty. Such individuals are unalterably honest or dishonest.

One day Marcel announced in joyful tones, 'I'm going to do night work. I'll start at three in the morning. I'll really learn the job now.'

But this is going too far I thought to myself. He is just fourteen, works twelve hours a day and is now going on night shift, and everybody knows that working in a bakery leads straight to TB! His young sister is undergoing preventive treatment in a home and his father died of tuberculous cancer of the lungs!

'And, you know, I'll get a rise for working at night.'

'How much?'

'Five francs a day.'

I explained the risk he was running. You might think he would deny it, but no.

'Yes, the boss said to me, "If the doctor knew what you were doing, he'd stop it".'

Then I hinted that I would go to see his mother or that I meant to consult a labour inspector. He immediately got into a panic. At the idea of losing a job in which he was being worked beyond his strength and exploited, fear came flooding in and I could see that he was ready to burst into tears. I felt that if I didn't leave him free to kill himself, I—and not the baker—should be *the enemy*.[1]

In one of the *Chansons de gestes* Guichardet, who is the fifteen-year-old brother of Vivien, has been forbidden to go to the wars

[1] Six months later, I had to get Marcel sent to a sanatorium.

because he is too young. Weeping with disappointment, he begs his aunt to dub him knight, so that he may be able to go. She does so, and off he goes, weeping now for joy.

Guichardet cried because he was not going to be allowed to fight, and Marcel because he thought he would not be allowed to work. Each of them, at a first glance, is obsessed with the idea of proving his manhood. But Marcel's tears, and the tears of all the other Marcels, big and little, make us sad, as Guichardet's do not. We are reminded of Tolstoy's words: 'Instead of those for whom they work being grateful to the workers, the workers are grateful to those who make them work.' What madness! And did not Unamuno say: 'Men behave like lambs to one another. It was not the tyrant who enslaved his fellow-man—just the reverse. There was a man who offered to carry his brother on his back. It was not the brother who forced him to do so.'

'When you're working, you aren't miserable.' How often have I seen working-class or middle-class children, working-class or middle-class adults, sighing for the holidays to end and school or work to begin again, or working overtime, or going to the office without being obliged to, or working after they have retired. Some do it to escape from home and others to escape from themselves. There is nothing more painfully obvious than the almost universal inability to be self-sufficient. But draw attention to it and you'll get your eyes scratched out. It is too serious a phenomenon, too pathetically serious, to be casually discussed. Let us not dwell on the catastrophic danger that would threaten mankind if, to suppose the impossible, there were no longer any work for men to do, for it is an established fact that prolonged leisure only leads to neurasthenia and evil-doing.

Once, and once only, have I had first-hand experience of work as a drug. It was in June and July 1940 in a town that shall be nameless, where the sinister and the grotesque, hand in hand, were doing a *danse macabre* over the body of France. I found then in the public rooms of my hotel, as I had found a few days before in the machine-gunned trenches of the Somme, that whatever I said was shocking to my hearers. Never have I felt more alone or more convinced that it was time for me to withdraw from a world so different from my inner world. It was work that saved me. I plunged into my play on Port Royal (so dazed that, as the manuscript shows, I was still unable to spell a fortnight after getting back from the front). The play itself seemed meaningless to me, and I could not imagine what society would be like when it appeared or what sort of a public would accept it or even if it ever would be acceptable at all. But the work itself had a meaning. It enabled me to forget the existence of other people and my own existence, too, and I might have said, like Jean de la Nation: 'When you're working, you're not miserable.'

But nature has invented other remedies for unhappiness; it would be too sad if work were the only one. A poor Marseilles prostitute once said to me: 'You forget your poverty under the bed-clothes.' Her remark is complementary to Jean's. Yes, work and bed-clothes, that's the answer—and you suddenly realize, not without emotion, that these obscure individuals are in agreement with Gobineau, who said (and I could take his words as my motto), 'There is work, then love, and after that, nothing...' You feel that for once, by some miracle, the *consensus omnium* covers a genuine truth.

Textes sous une occupation, 1953

(Written in 1943)

THE ASSUMPTION OF THE KING OF KINGS

THE *Châh Nâmeh* (The Book of Kings) was written in the eleventh century by the Persian, Firdusi. It is a poem of a hundred thousand lines, in which he relates the struggle between the Iranians and the Turanians; it is, in fact, the Persian *Iliad*. It tells of '*des armées innombrables qui tourbillonnent et s'effacent comme des rêves*') :[1] it was Gobineau, a remarkable brain but an untalented writer, who by some miracle wrote this impressive sentence. I have not taken the trouble to ascertain the cause of the war, because I am sure it was either trifling or sordid. In any case, in history the facts are less important than the way in which they are served up by posterity.

The poem contains one outstanding episode. Having had his fill of power and happiness, Khosrau, King of Persia, 'King of Kings', gives up his throne. He abdicates like Sylla, like Diocletian, like Charles V. He abdicates like a Hindoo king, a Merovingian chieftain or a Japanese shogun: the heroic peoples have always been sensitive to the glory and credit (delicacy prevents one from mentioning the advantages) that can be acquired by contrasting possession with dispossession, enjoyment with asceticism. I have already written about such cases of renunciation, and the fear of repeating myself will keep me short on this occasion, although it would have given me great pleasure to run on to my heart's content.

And so Khosrau has summoned his court in order to make solemn renunciation. I cannot imagine the scene, which took place in the seventh century BC—Rome was just about to come into being—

[1] 'Innumerable armies which whirl and fade away like dreams.'

without bringing it a little more up to date, by fifteen centuries or so, and giving it a Moorish setting, as the miniaturists of the Islamic period were to do. The king is sitting on a golden throne, and his right hand clasps a bull-headed mace. His age is an important point. We are told that he reigned for sixty years; let us suppose that he was twenty when he came to the throne. He is surrounded by his assembly of heroes: no women, only men, accompanied by military striplings, 'the darlings of the army'. Bearded heroes or heroes with Stalin-like moustaches, and then smooth-chinned youths, with long curls hanging in front of their ears; all of them with their bows and arrows, their sabres, circular shields, turbans or pointed Mongol helmets and lion- or bull-like cast of countenance; and their mounts with heads like sea-horses and plated with scales like fish, white-bearded mounts, whose beards are the tails of other horses attached to their chins; lastly, girdled with precious stones, a few white elephants. Men and animals are in diabolically brilliant colour. And looking down on them, as from another sphere, are two or three inmates of the seraglio at their windows; living young women with the sort of chin-straps worn by corpses, on a level with the oriflammes flapping in the wind.

Khosrau speaks in the royal tone (I can imagine an organ with a stop marked 'royal tone', as there are stops marked '*vox celestis*', etc.). He is saying great and simple things. How could I fail to be touched by these heroes, kings and princes, since they are all me? I am Minos, and Pasiphae, and Khosrau. They are not me in my day-dreams but me as I am in reality: their being is my being. I am also the fabulous beasts that I cause to bellow and die or thump the ground with their tails.

'Everywhere, in all inhabited countries, from India and China to Roum, from the west to the farthest limits of the east, on mountains and in deserts, on land and sea, everywhere I have destroyed my enemies, everywhere I am lord and master, and the world need fear the wicked no more. God has given me everything I desired, although my heart has been wholly devoted to vengeance. No one can win a greater name, nor better satisfy his desires nor acquire more power, happiness, repose and dignity than I have done. I

THE ASSUMPTION OF THE KING OF KINGS

have seen and heard everything connected with the world, with its happiness and unhappiness, both secret and revealed . . .'[1]

Thus saith Khosrau. I like men who admit they have had everything they could wish for. Their utterance is rich and full, exactly commensurate with their beings, which are completely satisfied too. I am well acquainted with this kind of utterance, having often been capable of it myself.

'But my mind is not safe against my passions; it thinks of evil and of the faith of Ahriman. I shall become wicked like Zohak and Djemchid . . . I belong to the race of Turan, which is full of magic. Like Kaus and like Afrasyab the magician, who even in his dreams saw nothing but blood and deceit, one day I shall be unfaithful to God and terror will destroy my serenity of mind, God's grace will desert me, and I shall abandon myself to injustice and madness; at last, I shall go so far into the shadows that my head and my crown will fall into the dust, I shall be of ill repute in the world and shall make a bad end in the sight of God.'

This is Shakespearian language: 'I come of a race full of magic...' and the evocation of the blood-obsessed magician. The king is afraid of himself. (He belongs to that people which, it is said, first distinguished between good and evil: a regrettable simplification.) In another book, the *Kush Nâmeh*, Khosrau is assimilated to a hero called Kush, of whom Gobineau says: 'His pride was always hysterical. He thought he was God and although he never openly favoured idolatry, in fact his only religion was himself.' Perhaps Khosrau is especially afraid of the re-emergence of this part of himself.

Also, he is weary. 'I am weary of my army, my throne and my crown; I have packed my bags and am impatient to be off. . . . It is my soul which is exhausted and my heart which is empty.' The men of antiquity showed an admirable lack of pretence. Never was the essential characteristic of old age confessed more simply or

---

[1] In the interests of logicality, I have brought in here two sentences (the last two) which occur later in the original. I have followed Jules Mohl's translation, except in a few sentences which I thought more expressively rendered in an improvised, unwritten version that Henri Massé was good enough to make for me.

better defined than by the monarch 'with the sun-like countenance'. Later, in a line of another poem, Firdusi himself confesses just as naturally: 'My heart is weary of Feridun' (one of the characters in his poem).

We males of the herd know the feeling. Khosrau can no longer see the brilliant display of his court; he has become blind to the external world, which is terribly boring after a certain age. There would remain the inner world of souls, if souls did not resemble each other too much: when you know one, you know the lot. And the individuals, the beliefs, enthusiasms and ambitions that once possessed us, after 'whirling' like armies 'have faded away like dreams'. We know what Khosrau said. But we can find within ourselves other things, very true for us, that he must have uttered silently. 'Earthly scenes, I have had my fill of you.' And again: 'I no more need to be admired than I need to be loved.' And again: 'That I should have done well what I had to do, that also has become a matter of indifference to me.'—'It is my soul which is exhausted and my heart which is empty.' Well, since it is, precisely, time to leave, has not nature arranged everything for the best?

In short, after a few commonplaces on the vanity of this world and some 'banal moralizing' (Darmsteter) which is no more important coming from a Head of State than it would be coming from a priest, Khosrau concludes: 'It is better that I should make haste to appear in the sight of God before my glory vanishes.'

The king wishes to finish in style. He exchanges his few remaining years—dangerous, onerous years—for the certainty of keeping his human and eternal glory intact. He strikes a bargain, but his personal manner enhances it with splendour.

He thereupon gives orders that anyone coming to the court should be turned away, and that the court itself should be closed. He puts on a new white robe and prays in his oratory. He remains thus seven days and seven nights. 'His body was there but his soul was elsewhere.'

We are a long way here from rose-petal syrup and arrangements of Omar Khayyam for American aesthetes. The prayer in the oratory, the white robe, the standing in vigil for seven days and seven nights, all hark back to Zoroastrianism, but are they not also reminiscent, even in their details, of Western chivalry?

However, the great nobles who find Khosrau's behaviour incomprehensible, begin anxiously muttering, as is the case with Jesus' disciples a little later. It is the usual reversal of values: while he is rising to the highest point of his being, they think he is trying to be in league with evil genii, *divs*. His reply is: 'When the time comes, I shall bring forth the clamour that is hidden within me.'

He prays: 'I have done much good and much evil. Yet grant me a place in Paradise.' If, after achieving all his desires, he had thought he was about to cease, absolutely, to exist, what pathos and grandeur there would have been in his renunciation! But when, into the bargain, he wants to be loaded with satisfactions for ever and ever, are we not slightly put off?

It is in the midst of these mystic effusions that Firdusi makes the admirable, the necessary statement: 'His soul, which was always escorted by intelligence.' If Khosrau is Cyrus, as some scholars maintain, this reflection links up with what Aeschylus makes one of his characters say in *The Persians*: 'He (Cyrus) was always loved by the Gods, because he was full of reason.' It is beyond my power to express the emotion these two remarks arouse in me.

In a vision, Khosrau gets a glimpse of his approaching end. And —again like Jesus—he weeps. The ancient heroes always behave naturally. Whether Greek or Roman, they weep. This is still truer of the characters in the French *chansons de gestes*, which are a real water-spout. The French heroes 'feel faint' like their Arab counterparts. Charles V wept during his abdication ceremony.

Khosrau shares out his treasures and his possessions and appoints his successor. Natural behaviour again: 'When the arrangements with the great nobles were completed, the King of Kings was ill with fatigue.' This is exactly right. Lofty tasks do not tire him; at the age of eighty, he can remain standing in prayer for seven days and seven nights, and Firdusi makes no mention of fatigue. But material complications exhaust him. Any dying man who makes a will hastens his end.

Khosrau says good-bye to his wives and his people. 'My days

are over.' Then, followed by eight heroes, 'great nobles, vanquishers of elephants, lion-faced men', he sets off to climb to a mountain peak, in spite of the lamentations of the crowd. He summons 'the most powerful among those who formed the crowd' and says to them: 'All is well here, and it is wrong to weep at that which is well.'

Some three thousand years after Khosrau, another old Asiatic of the same age, after writing his family a letter in which he used almost the same words as Khosrau: 'Like the Hindoos who, on approaching sixty, withdraw into the forests, it is natural that every old religious man should wish to devote the last years of his life to God', was to go off in the snow alone, or almost alone, to die, as Khosrau is about to do; and the *last* words written by Tolstoy in Astapovo station were to be identical with those of the King of Kings: 'And everything is well, for others and especially for myself.'

The mountain of the Assumption was the sacred Elbruz, 'an eminently pure land,' it seems. What was it like? In the Persian miniatures, the mountains show exquisite shades of colouring: mauve, salmon-pink, or port-wine; sometimes they are pale blue or pale green, with a slightly glazed effect. But the charming artists responsible for them avoid the harsh aspect of the Book of Kings: if the king himself is to be believed, the setting in which he lived his last hours was austere. After a week spent in 'resting and moistening their parched lips with lamentations', Khosrau tries to persuade the heroes to leave him. He speaks to them as Jesus was to speak to the disciples when he withdrew into the garden of olives: he knows how weak they are. And he wants to be alone. Three of them go away, but the others remain.

The desert and the lack of water exhaust the little group. One evening, they come to rest near a spring: 'Tonight we will go no farther. We will speak much of the past, for after tonight no one will see me more.' It is 'the night on the Bare Mountain': for a long time I had been haunted by this musical title, but here I have resisted the temptation to orchestrate my prose or to produce an oratorio. I have a great wish not to exaggerate. (Yet how resonant is the phrase: 'We shall speak much of the past'!) When the night is partly over, the King of Kings prostrates himself on the ground, washes his head and his body in the spring and says: 'I bid you an everlasting farewell. The sun is about to brandish his lance; after that, you will never see me again except in dreams. Do not remain in this sandy desert, for snow will fall so thick that you will be unable to find your way back to Iran.'

They sleep the sleep of the apostles. Have they taken the attitude that Buddha was to adopt when the time came for him to die: 'he stretched himself out as lions do, on his right side, with one foot over the other'? When they awake at dawn, the king has disappeared. While they are vainly looking for him, the sky 'takes on the appearance of a lion's eye' (still another reference to lions). A snow storm comes on. 'Hast thou entered into the treasures of the snow?' (*Job,* xxxviii.) They enter into it and are buried.

Khosrau vanishes like Romulus, during a storm; like Elijah in his fiery chariot. And on the spot where he has disappeared there descends a great myth, one of those great myths which come flying towards us from the depths of antiquity, and sometimes alight on a mountain.

Vigny wrote concerning Julian, who also died among the Persians, 'he resolved to die when he was sure he had gone beyond the point to which the coarse and stupid masses could follow him' (the masses who wanted to be Christian). Did Khosrau, before dying, go farther than the others could follow? His renunciation was very human and doesn't carry much weight. He rejected the world only when the world was about to reject him. Was it such an admirable achievement to know when to leave, particularly since he was so weary? After his disappearance, all is mystery. Did he change into a hermit and lead an ascetic life until his natural death? (If so, how are we to explain his prayers and the impression he gives of knowing his end to be at hand?) Did he die at once? (But, in this case, his renunciation would carry still less weight, since he would only have renounced what death was, anyway, about to take from him.) Has he gone on living in a secret hiding-place, as one tradition maintains, where he is awaiting the Messiah,

Shoshyans, who, on Judgement Day, will help him to revive the dead and redeem mankind?[1]

To tell the truth, I like none of these versions. Why, then, am I too transported in his train on to the mountain, and why is it that for years I have fluttered and raved around the frosty glow coming from its high summit?

I should need more books, many more books, in order to grasp the true meaning of the assumption of my King Khosrau. But I have enjoyed life too much to have been a great reader. And I have forgotten what I have read. Time obliterates the things I know before it obliterates me. Now when I should have a solid wad of learning to rest upon, I grope about and find nothing but emptiness. At least Khosrau fills my emptiness with a sublime atmosphere of sacred vagueness, in which both time and space cease to matter; no individual, no spot, can be identified; the yea and the nay revolve and intertwine; everything escapes into something else; everything proclaims: 'I am what I am' and 'I am what I am not'; all things always remain possible; everything comes to the same thing, Socrates and Augustus, Khosrau and Jesus,[2] heroes and demons, sages and warriors, hermits and sibyls, centaurs and saints; all of them belong to the same great family, don't they? This is the religion on the ceiling of the Sistine Chapel, the religion of the indeterminate that I was intended to embody in my person

---

[1] I disregard this hypothesis. It is not in keeping with the nature of either a hero or a god to love mankind. Hesiod was well aware of this because he says that Zeus, to punish some god or other (Apollo?), 'condemned him to be full of love for mankind'. The divine or heroic attitude towards mankind is one of indifference (hence those apparently incoherent interventions in human affairs, sometimes on one side, sometimes on the other).

[2] When I wrote these lines, I did not know that, according to the prophet, Cyrus is the anointed, the 'Christ' of Jehovah (*Isaiah*, xiv. 1 and 28), and so can be considered by Christians as an early prefiguring of Christ, who is *the* anointed. As we have seen, some scholars, including Gobineau, identify Khosrau with Cyrus. And so scholarship and my intuition lead to the same conclusion. And the parallels I have drawn here between certain aspects of Khosrau's behaviour and Christ's and which, on reflection, I found so farfetched that I thought of cutting them out, are given a justification which surprises nobody more than it does me.

and express in splendid words. But my life is running on and I have accomplished neither one thing nor the other, and I do not even know whether such a synthesis is the contemptible product of my ignorance and weak understanding, a monstrous phantasm building up elsewhere out of all the things that have escaped me or dropped away from me; or whether the opposite is true, whether the Mountain of Unity is the chunk of reality that I rescue in snatches from error and darkness, during those hours when part of me gives birth to things of light.

Textes sous une Occupation, 1953
(Written in January, 1942)

SAINT-SIMON

'Spinach and Saint-Simon have been my only stable tastes'
—Stendhal

THE DUC DE SAINT-SIMON was one of the cherished ghosts of my youth. No schoolboy ever read a smutty book in a greater flutter of excitement than I felt when, as an adolescent, I read passages of the *Memoirs* which revealed that certain close relatives of mine, the pride of the Faubourg Saint-Germain, were descended from a lady who, according to Saint-Simon at least, was a public laughing-stock at Versailles. From him, too, I learnt that others of my forebears, whom I had thought of as cutting a dash during the Crusades, were really the offspring of a financier and, seized with a noble urge, had bought their title during the reign of Louis XIV. Then, in 1928 or thereabouts, I read the Duke through from beginning to end, with delight. Now in this fine year of the Incarnation, 1943, I have taken up the *Memoirs* again and am nibbling at them, with some weariness and disappointment, in order to find material for this preface. A good preface-writer ought to conceal such feelings but I disclose them through my ingrained habit of not playing the game.

To think that he produced three thousand foolscap pages of closely written manuscript without putting in a single thought! Did he never reflect during the whole course of his life? The *Memoirs* themselves provide no answer. He has ideas about politics, but so has everyone in France, and political ideas have nothing to do with intelligence. One set of political ideas is never better than another: it may, or may not be, victorious on the practical level for a certain length of time, and that is all. The two memoir-writing dukes[1] shared out the task between them: one does nothing but generalize while the other confines himself to pure narrative. Saint-Simon's moralizings are short and flat. I regret his failure to enlarge on his themes or to produce any of those sublime and spacious musings which are the glory of some of his peers. One of the many qualities which give M de Chateaubriand a great and godlike superiority over Saint-Simon, is the way in which his narrative suddenly bursts asunder, revealing some vast and music-filled vista. Bossuet, Voltaire or Chateaubriand (to mention him again) each write history in their own way, but at least they write it, whereas the Saint-Simon of the *Memoirs* expresses no views. He is a mere chronicler, who has a very faulty sense of proportion, if he has any at all; he can be put down and taken up at any point and leaves no trace on the mind. He is neither profound nor sublime.

In his portraits he has an insipid, doll-like, sunny-lipped face and the sort of nose which is called witty when it belongs to a cabaret artist. As a matter of fact, he looks very like Mayol.[2] However, we can't altogether trust the portrait-painters. Perhaps they told Saint-Simon to smile, as photographers do. It appears that Saint-Simon was unusually small. He was a distinguished man, by which I mean an average man. A politician who went unheeded. A Catholic but unenlightened. When he gets on to the subject of the Holy Ghost, he becomes quite stupid. No lover, as far as I know. His work is painfully lacking in any sense of the feminine and does not contain a single movingly drawn portrait of a woman. There is no feminine note in his sensibility. He is a psychologist, but his psychology seems superficial according to the standards of the modern world, which is accustomed to instruments of greater precision. He was a man of wit, but his wit was not as keen as it ought to have been. He had a heart but a temperate one. When he describes suffering and expresses pity for it, he often does so merely to denounce the oppressor. It is the politician who is speaking, not a great humanitarian. Upright, for all that; occasionally, some virtuous character can be seen moving through his milling crowd of

[1] Saint-Simon and La Rochefoucauld.

[2] A cabaret artist of the beginning of the twentieth century.

show-offs and go-getters, and is saluted by Saint-Simon with an air of genuine respect. But neither his soul nor his intelligence was equal to the extraordinary gift with which nature had endowed him.

Yet I find it hard to believe that a man can be among the three or four most gifted writers of his nation and at the same time be lacking in all greatness of character. But how can one find greatness in Saint-Simon. Everything he saw, was involved in, achieved or planned was approached in a small-minded way; he was a duke in pettifoggery. There is something incredible in the depths to which he was prepared to abase himself in order to become a Spanish Grandee and to get the Order of the Golden Fleece for his son; his whole ambassadorship was undertaken for that sole purpose, and he admits as much, unblushingly; his modern counterparts would claim to be working for the good of the country, and frankly I don't know which is better or which is worse. In the end, he was made a Spanish Grandee; a manikin of Spain, I felt like calling him—but I am wrong! One of his acts is surely not lacking in greatness, the act of writing these three thousand pages of memoirs over a period of thirty years—three thousand pages which were written to be read and with a full realization of their rare quality; three thousand pages of a work which constituted his whole work, his only claim to fame, and which he wrote after deciding not to publish them in his lifetime. This wish for only posthumous glory, a glory devoid of the impurities that come from contact with those who bestow fame, surely points to a mixture of great-heartedness and disdain. Furthermore, there is no evidence that Saint-Simon made any plans for the publication of his thirty years' work on material provided by the previous twenty—that is, the product of a whole lifetime. This shows a second form of disdain, which enhances the first.

This doubly evident characteristic is not simply a sign of great-heartedness. It defines the type of man he was: the literary creator in his purest form. He is the kind of author who is only interested in what he creates and not at all, or only very slightly, in the relationship between his work and the public; the kind of author who says with Goethe, 'the only thing that matters is that it should be written'; the creator in all his purity and admirableness.

'He has nothing to say but he says it magnificently': who was it that I said that about? Saint-Simon has something to say, but the way he says it is more important than what he says. Here we find ourselves face to face with that monster, the master of language, who wins hands down every time not because he writes well but because he writes powerfully. Bossuet achieved immortality by saying nothing in a forceful style, and Saint-Simon by using a forceful style for his anecdotes. All these writers had to do, to make what they wrote seem true, was to express themselves in their own personal way. Don't you agree that such writers get rather more credit than they deserve? Why, it seems that if only they have this knack, they can get away with any nonsense or any untruth; they need have no conscience; they can be prejudiced, and ignorant; they can exalt or damn according to their mood or the amount they have drunk; and, as if the shameless impunity they enjoy weren't enough, they are the ones who are believed, who leave their mark, who survive, exist and are even granted a super-existence. Their gift enables them to eclipse everybody else; only they remain; St John of the Cross said, 'Good language and a good style can revive and restore that which is decayed and spoiled, just as a bad sentence can spoil and ruin that which is good.' This is a gentle expression of the roaring, ranting motto of every great writer—'Stronger than the truth', to which immoral fact may be added another, equally immoral, which is that all the worries, sorrows and disasters which befall great writers go into their infernal crucible and are transmuted into pure gold, so that, after being the most alive among the living, they live on when others are dead. Be that as it may, the monster, right or wrong, is here before me and, if he scandalizes me, I have no cause to complain; in fact I propose to go at once and make a thank-offering to the gods.

Léon Daudet wrote that for naturalness, ease of flow, strength, and the fashioning of a style 'which reads on paper as it sounds on the lips', you must go to Amyot, Montaigne, Pascal, Saint-Simon,

La Rochefoucauld and Sévigné. I have no quarrel with this list, but I would observe that you must first translate Amyot, that Montaigne and Sévigné are weak and prolix and that La Rochefoucauld is, after all, uninspired and deliberate. This leaves Pascal and Saint-Simon. As regards intelligence, there is no comparison. One is a writer of genius and the other a genius without qualification. But what is true is that both of them are masters of that incomparable, incandescent style which, like the Greek fire of old, forges ahead, consuming everything in its path.

When the *Memoirs* appeared everyone agreed with Madame du Deffand that 'they were abominably badly written'. Was this a misjudgement? Frankly no. No author has an untidier style than Saint-Simon. One might overlook his ellipses, his nagging mannerisms, his sudden careerings and caperings, were it not for his terrifying syntax, his endless strings of who's and whom's, his repetitions and re-repetitions of words, his sentences that have neither head nor tail, and his appalling blind alleys. For whole pages, especially in the early part of the work, the reader stumbles from one disaster to another. Saint-Simon drives his pen along hell for leather. But does he write 'badly'? If so, all we can say is that it is the badness of the writing and the possession of a mysterious something which gives him originality and force. That wonderful jargon of his belongs to one of the two most brilliant French prose artists (the other is Chateaubriand). Almost every other style seems by comparison thin or pedantic. Not without reason is Saint-Simon the teachers' bogey. But is it any less dangerous to let the young feed on the jargon of Boileau, the jargon of Corneille, the jargon of Molière (when he is writing in verse) or the jargon of Descartes, under the impression that this is good writing, than to allow them to read Saint-Simon, always providing that his impurities are pointed out and shown to be often the source of his beauty.

Saint-Simon never bothered to correct his style and Pascal left only notes. What would Pascal have been like if he had written an organized work? Or Saint-Simon if he had made corrections? Both would surely have been rather inferior to what they are in their present form. Their pre-eminence arises from their spontaneity which is so great that when you see it embalmed in some de luxe edition, you are at first bothered by the contradiction, as you would be by a frozen flame.

It would be interesting to know if Saint-Simon was conscious of this. He made notes from nineteen to forty, and then wrote them up during his last thirty years when he had withdrawn from public life into one of those immensely long periods of retirement, so common under the *ancien régime*; thirty years of obscurity, what a heaven-sent gift! Did he not correct his work during those thirty years because he literally had no time both for creation and correction and had to sacrifice the latter? Or could he have done both as he went along but preferred not to alter his first draft, because he was aware of its high quality?

To answer these questions we should have to know what his working capacity was, how he spent his time and what went on inside him. He himself, of course, makes a confession on this subject, or pretends to do so. At the end of the *Memoirs* he writes: 'I have been conscious of these faults (his faults of style which he enumerates clear-sightedly), but I have not been able to avoid them, since I have always been carried away by my subject-matter and have taken little care with my manner of writing, apart from seeing that the matter was clearly expressed. I have never had an academic turn of mind (the only academy he ever belonged to was a riding-school) and have never cured myself of the habit of writing rapidly. To render my style more correct and more agreeable, I should have to recast my work entirely and I cannot face the effort, which might in any case prove unrewarding. In order to improve my writing, I should know how to write well; it will be obvious from my work that I cannot pride myself on possessing this gift.' In short, he accounts for his style by saying how exhausting and boring it would be to make corrections and by pointing out that he doesn't know how 'to write well'. But we should distrust explanations given by authors: an author is always falsehood incarnate.

In any case, the most attractive and probably the most correct hypothesis is that Saint-Simon was well aware of what he was doing. He was 'carried away by his subject' and thought it 'unrewarding' to write more carefully. But he also knew how much he gained by his laziness—by his laziness and his independence. 'Above all, monsieur,' Louis XIV said to him, 'you must hold your tongue.' It was the King's will—and his will, it must be admitted, left its mark—that all his subjects should speak and act alike. Saint-Simon became Saint-Simon precisely because he did not 'hold his tongue' when he put pen to paper. Both in speaking of his contemporaries and in his general manner of expression he broke the rules of decorum. He refused to write in the current style though it would have been easy for him to do so, since he was capable of dull writing, even when he wasn't copying Torcy. He refused, because he knew his own value as a spontaneous writer and because, being an aristocrat with the most grotesque sense of caste, he would not lower himself. A touch of arrogance can be felt in the phrase: 'it will be obvious from my work that I cannot pride myself on possessing this gift.' He may even have systematically emphasized his mistakes, just as Brummel used to rub the nap off his dress coat. The conviction grows on the reader as he comes across one passage after another that Saint-Simon could easily have corrected by a mere stroke of the pen, during the most superficial re-reading. I seem to hear him say: 'You scribblers can labour over your sentences. Men of quality write with divine carelessness, haughty casualness and insolent weirdness. It suits me to write like this so you must put up with it.' He gets away with his sloppy style, just as the aristocrat gets away with his old-fashioned clothes and unshaven beard, knowing that whatever he does he will always be in the right. As for the contempt of the aristocracy or gentry for the profession of author, it is an old pose that was to occur again in Byron, Lamartine and others. It still persists, as we well know.

Saint-Simon, then, would appear to be the inventor of the natural literary style, by which I mean a conversational style, thoughtfully touched up from the literary point of view. He adopts the style which he hears spoken around him at the Court—a style full of the juiciness and brashness of the manners of the Court as he described them, together with a certain coarseness which was, and still is, an aristocratic trait (he tells a charming story about how a kitten strayed into the Regent's Council Chamber and was walking about on the table in the middle of a meeting, and the others wanted to shoo it out, but Saint-Simon told them to let it stay; this is symbolic of his unbuttoned style; he never shoos out the kitten). His style is both knotted and sprawling, sometimes highly involved, sometimes surging forward in a rush; at once concise and prolix, firm and untidy, and bristling with archaisms, vulgar expressions, technical terms, invented words and solecisms; no other French writer has gone further than Saint-Simon in forging a language of his own. But his naturalness is not, properly speaking, artificial; it is simply conscious, intentional and appreciated for its own sake. Compared to the language of the Court, his style is—how shall we say?—both similar and dissimilar. But he had the instinct, the antennae of a master-writer, and that is why his style has not dated, like that of authors who adopt a fake peasant or a fake popular speech. It is characterized by a staying-power, a verve, a venomousness, a hypersensitivity and a sheer pleasure in the writing which in themselves would be enough to give it life, that is to ensure its success. Will the authors and admirers of the lifeless style never realize that it is precisely these tonic features, that they affect to find vulgar, which do more than anything else to carry a work along until, with an irresistible impetus, it passes through the gates of immortality?

When you read Tacitus or Suetonius, you know what to expect and so are not surprised to close them with a feeling of depression. But Saint-Simon is not reckoned to be a gloomy writer, so that when you emerge, loaded with sadness and horror, from the vision he provides of an illustrious century, your reaction is all the stronger. Illustrious epoch, sombre epoch full of masterly intrigues, hypocritical pomp, impenetrable and unending lawsuits, and religious and ceremonial stupidities. Never was the art of trifling with the human person more stealthily enjoyed than under cover of those lace-edged breastplates, that soiled purple and blood-stained ermine. Force, tyranny and persecution reigned supreme. An omnipotent King, the Zeus of Europe, sets all the instruments of his authority in motion to torment and murder the innocent—and the result is Louis XIV's 'atrocities'. There was the general levelling down (a feature for which democracies have been so fiercely criticized) and the flunkeydom of the courtiers, all madly striving to please the sovereign; and word 'servitude' is one of those that occur most frequently in Saint-Simon's writing. Ruthlessness and trimming constantly win the day. We look in vain for an honest man; the stage is always crowded with scoundrels. And amidst the throng of persons struggling to obtain so much, what place was there for the man who asked for nothing? But we know that such a man is the most suspicious character of all; solitude can breed indignation.

No doubt Saint-Simon was always more or less opposed to this state of affairs. He was a natural opposer. When he is about to discuss Louis XIV, he admits that he does not feel sure enough of himself to be able to speak without hatred and merely says, 'I shall try to do so'—which is both endearing and ominous. Saint-Simon's *Memoirs* contain an indictment of Louis XIV just as the *Mémoires d'Outre-Tombe* contain one of Napoleon. From the former, we learn that the Man of Versailles was 'a King of very mean stature', and from the latter, that the Man of Austerlitz 'descended to sub-human levels' and 'put back the art of war into its infancy'. Charles X was quite right when he said that it was a bad thing to have 'a rascally journalist'[1] near one. Saint-Simon is against the King. He is against the Secretaries of State who had 'sprung from the gutter'. He is against the men of law whom he calls 'base *bourgeois*'. He is against Rome, never referring to it except in insulting tones and trouncing it bitterly in a score or more passages; astounding behaviour on the part of a man who was not only a Catholic but a good Catholic! He is, by implication, against upper-class French society, to judge by the colours in which he paints it. He is also against monastic life; he who used to make retreats in a Trappist monastery (in spite of his allusions to 'the filth of the seminaries' and 'the dirty beards of the clerics of Saint Sulpice' and other matters which I shall omit) proposed the closing of the monasteries and the dispersal of the religious orders. Not only did

[1] He made the remark with reference to Chateaubriand.

he say that the French were frivolous and unreliable, that they were mainly moved by vanity; and that they had a turn of mind which drove them 'to make war on one another, whenever they were not occupied in fighting with foreigners'; he also made grave accusations of baseness and scoundrelism. However, in spite of all that, Rome remains unshaken, the monasteries are in good shape, French society of the seventeenth century is considered as one of the glories of France, Louis XIV enjoys immortal fame . . . and try talking to a Frenchman of 1943 about the baseness and scoundrelism of the French and see what sort of a reception you'll get. Everything that Saint-Simon, the writer, attacked still survives, materially or morally, and the same is true of everything he attacked on the political level. He recognized this himself during his declining years, at the age when public men, even those who in the past have most needed the spur of contemporay life, turn against society which has discarded them and compose sonorous variations on the bitterness of life or plangent laments on the uselessness of effort. He says: 'This opportunity wrings from me a truth which I recognized when I was in the Council and which I would not have believed if I had not learnt it from sad experience, namely that no good is to be done. So few people honestly wish for it, and so many others have a personal interest in every kind of reform that may be suggested. Those that wish for better things fail to understand what shape they should take—and, without that understanding, nothing succeeds—and do not know how to counter the manœuvres or resist the credit of their opponents; these manœuvres, backed by all the credit of persons with a superior knowledge of business and holding positions of authority, are so complex and so obvious that all efforts to do good are inevitably doomed to failure. This lamentable truth, which will always subsist as long as we have a Government like the present one, brings infinite consolation to those who feel and think, but no longer have any active part to play.' This is clear enough, once it has been translated into intelligible language. Whatever one does, evil remains. Every age believes that it has plumbed the depths of ignominiousness and, frightened by the thought, turns to history, finds there a replica of itself in all its blackness, and goes on its way reassured, conscious that history will be no harder on it than on other ages, and that it can persist in infamy without fear of punishment. You read Thucydides and then Tacitus, and then Michelet on the Middle Ages, then Retz, then Saint-Simon and finally Taine on the French Revolution, and you find the same story everywhere, the same tissue of crime caked with blood. There is no need, then, to accept any restraints. Nero did not tremble on learning that 'Tacitus had already been born in the Empire',[1] and none of the world's great bandits worry about the verdict of the future. What does the future matter to them? It is enough for them that, here and now, they can satisfy their hatreds, their whims, their greed and their craziness. And that is what they do, knowing that they will have at least enjoyed their criminal intoxication. They can go to their deaths with an easy mind. History will be gentle to them. O gentle history, you will cradle your naughty children in your arms as softly as you rock your favourite ones! What was I saying just now about the great artist always winning the game in the long run? He wins and he loses. In accordance with the terms of Saint-Simon's will, which is usually reproduced in an appendix by editors of the *Memoirs,* his body was buried beside his wife's with the two coffins 'so closely riveted together that it would be impossible to separate one from the other without breaking both of them'. (I must have been mistaken in saying that Saint-Simon had no feeling for women; in this case he certainly had a feeling, and it was a strong one.) The Revolution came, the coffins were broken, the bodies torn apart and thrown into a common grave-pit. There is a symbol here. No more heed was paid to M de Saint-Simon's last wishes than is normally paid to the opinions or wishes expressed by any writer concerned with public affairs. The world admires the artist, but cares nothing about what he stood for, and so everything goes on as before. It is no bad thing that we should learn, when we have finished our reading, that the structure of the *Memoirs* has its foundation in a common grave. This not only reminds us how little remains of a man's dying wishes, but also how, in the long run,

[1] Chateaubriand.

good and evil are mixed indistinguishably together, just as bones and ashes are mingled together for all time by a random chance; and how true are the words of the Scriptures, which can be understood to apply to virtue no less than to wisdom, 'As it happeneth to the fool, so it happeneth even to me; and why was I then more wise?'

Textes sous une Occupation, 1953
(Written in 1943)

THE GODDESS CYPRIS

CHATEAUBRIAND, I think, put the question: how can a man who has been writing for fifty years have failed to contradict himself? But the most changeable of us has his fixed points. Twenty-five years ago, I wrote: 'Long live the senses. They, at least, never deceive' (*Songe*) and to represent physical pleasure, I used the symbol of a high peak lit by the setting sun while the rest of the world is plunged in vagueness and shadow. Then, ten years later, I wrote: 'Physical satisfaction is what I have always laid my hand on in times of turmoil, as I might rest it on a pile of papers in a rising wind. Let everything else blow away! This is an uncontrollable reflex.' (*Mors et Vita!*) And now, I write the following.

If it is the case that my work may have had a dubious influence in some respects, at least its constant affirmation of this truth will have been beneficial.

I sing the joys of physical love, which remain untouched while all else crumbles or fades away; I sing of Cypris, ingenious, crafty Cypris, who is never taken unawares. She, they say, is with the child in its cradle, with the old man who has one foot in the grave, with the invalid, whose sufferings she may momentarily dispel or whom she may even cure (a man with a temperature of 102° can take the plunge into wild sensuality and emerge feeling fitter than before), with the mystic: a monk stiffens during communion 'when the consecrated wafers are very big' (and the sage, St Theresa, consulted on this point, said that it was of no importance; St John of the Cross displayed the same wisdom in a similar case); with the pauper: 'You forget your poverty under the bed-clothes'; with the lame and the ugly, for desire is such that it can be aroused by pity or by exquisite disgust; with the prisoner, the lonely light in his darkness; with all those who labour; we may wonder if some tasks would be bearable without the hope of sensual pleasure to be enjoyed when they are over.

The idea that there is something reprehensible in carnal love could not occur in a healthy mind. Chastity and pride in chastity were considered by the Greeks as a twofold sacrilege, with regard to the divine, on the one hand, and the human, that is ordinary living, on the other.

I shall say about sexual pleasure what the Theresa I have already referred to used to say about mystical ecstasy: how could evil come of so great a good?—Evil? Holy pleasure, merely to dream about you does one good; you are like the fabulous Chinese tree that had the power to make sleepers in its shade think themselves in Paradise. The memory of past pleasure soothes and relaxes; it will, I think, bring ease in the hour of death. To think of purely imaginary pleasure, after some quite different, though agreeable, experience, is like seeing the sun come out from behind a cloud.

Respectable pleasure: the most genuine, clear-cut, all-square thing in the world. I have had satisfaction. So has my partner. We are agreed on the fact. The circle is complete; the point has been established once and for all; I mean, until oblivion intervenes.

Generous pleasure: our pleasure is our partner's pleasure. How wonderful to indulge oneself and have the sensation that one is accomplishing a good deed!

Drieu La Rochelle, I believe, has written somewhere that he found the peak of human experience in a bayonet charge. For my part, I have found it, and still find it, in sexual pleasure. If there had been nothing else in my life except the experience of accepted pleasure, it would be enough to justify my life, which is justified also by the pleasure it has dispensed. It is by the giving of pleasure that ordinary humanity redeems its stupidity and baseness; thousands of human beings have no reason for existing other than the fact that they are, or once were, desirable.

The ancient world, in its last phase, had come to worship only three divinities: the Sun, Chance and Cypris.

Potens diva Cypris.

*   *   *

Look at a French crowd, on its day off, from the fourteen-year-old youngsters of both sexes to those gentlemen who are mature enough to have to cut the hair sprouting from their ears. Apart from vanity and cupidity, the only driving force in such a crowd is the expectation of sensual pleasure and the need to manœuvre to obtain it. If you follow the movements of a man on a map, you see that his wild zig-zagging is determined by the pursuit of pleasure. Or take a man who is expecting a visit from the police: you would imagine him to be feverishly setting his house in order. Not a bit of it; he is lying on his divan, reflecting on the conduct of some sensual intrigue. Another man was running to save his life; a woman came past; he stopped and was caught. Only one thing prevents humanity despairing in periods of disaster: the creature seeks the creature; during bombing raids, among corpses and in spite of epidemics, this is their constant thought; this it is that keeps them going.

A single hour of blazing carnal sensuality makes up for a whole month during which one has asked oneself daily: 'In such circumstances, is life worth living?' When the sum total of miseries is so much in excess of the sum total of pleasures, it is natural to cry: 'Extinction rather than this!' But then we enjoy an hour of enchanting obscenity and our reason exclaims: 'No! No! Not extinction but life!'

'Wisdom and our passions support us in times of trial. Particularly our passions.' I made this note during the retreat, between Aisne and Oise. Not only among exploding bombs, but also through the more treacherous and tiring thickets of social chaos, such as occur in a town in a state of siege, I have seen passion progressing towards its object, sometimes by-passing obstacles, sometimes attacking and destroying them, with the strength and sureness, the invincible suppleness and obstinacy of a root reaching out towards water. 'I move according to my thirst' might be the motto of both.

Souls quail, minds are confused, the stoutest hearts are in dismay, everything hangs in suspense. Only the passionate man is unshakeable. Life retains all its meaning for him, since his passion survives and there are still circumstances in which he can satisfy it. In the midst of chaos, his passion perpetuates order; in the midst of collapse, it perpetuates the element of survival. With his eyes fixed on his target and seeing nothing but his target, he goes forward, insensitive to everything, mysteriously immunized as drunkards are. But woe to him if his passion deserts him! Woe to him if he is 'cured'! His collapse is immediate.

The attitudes of love are rather ridiculous, and virgins are right to insist that the lights should be out. This is an extreme case of the container being unworthy of the contents. It is a good thing to draw a veil over the proceedings, not through hypocrisy, nor even through decency, but to conceal the unpleasing appearance of something which is, in essence, so admirable.

Casanova retired at fifty-seven; Julius Caesar was fifty-seven when he died. But at sixty-seven, Tiberius was only beginning. Lift up your hearts!

Lift up your hearts! All the primitive peoples of the East, all the peoples of instinctive wisdom, believe that the body of an adult or an old man acquires strength through contact with a very young body. Abishag is a case in point, and there is also the legendary tale of a South Moroccan tribe, the Id bou Achra, which has been transcribed by Colonel Justinard.

During one of the tribe's migrations, a very decrepit old man had to be transported in a basket. After his daughter-in-law had carried it on her bare shoulders for a while, she put it down again and said, laughingly, to her husband: 'We must find your father a young wife.' They found him one, and he had ten children by her.

Night weighs down upon her from above, and she herself is night. Michel Angelo's *Night*. I see her with great, folded, eagle's wings, such as remote antiquity attributed to almost all the gods.

She . . . *sive deus, sive dea* . . . has the restfulness of the mountains from which spring the oldest rivers of the earth.

She could serve as an illustration for the following lines of *Mors et Vita*: 'Lying naked on the bed after making love, with a naked body across my outstretched left arm, a powerful body with a root-like smell, and of whose mass I was conscious as if it were a statue that had fallen from its plinth, I would conceive my thoughts and my dreams and they would go out from me like armies. For a while, I would retain command of them. But soon their spear-heads would begin to elude me and they would vanish into a region of shadow.'

I like great art, but why should that prevent me from liking prettiness? I like Scopas, but I also like Alexandrine sculpture (certain kinds of Alexandrine sculpture). I like Aeschylus, but I also like Martial. To choose is to be crude, to over-simplify.

In the end, the most that can be said for this little person who glows with a minor, and rather pathetic, grace, is what Mirabeau said to Barnave: 'No, you have no divine spark in you.'

All that there is in women, in addition to their bodies and the use they make of them . . . all of it unsuspected by men or so little liked by them.

Athene is a frigid blue-stocking; Diana a Lesbian in spite of her Endymion alibi; the Muses are deinspiring bores, the Parcae murderesses, Pythia a teller of fortunes from tea-leaves. Our contemporaries now admit that all these ladies are profoundly boring. But they cannot yet bring themselves to admit that beauty too (female beauty) intimidates, depresses and bores them. Beauty is still supposed to arouse desire. This is not the case. Beauty has nothing to do with the physical jerks under the coverlet. Ugliness, even when it does not amount to hideousness, is one of the most reliable stimulants. Bodily ugliness, at least, if not facial, but even facial ugliness sometimes. Partly, perhaps, because it arouses pity, which is a cause of desire. The searing sensation produced by a thin body, with its bloated stomach, bandy legs and long feet ... When you are absolutely disgusted by a woman, the only way you can further her return to grace is by taking her.

It is quite absurd to exclaim, in the customary way, at the sight of some ravishing female: 'Oh, to hold her in my arms!' We should reserve our raptures for the woman who 'wants it', even though she may be ugly. But I notice *in fine* that men are well aware of this.

You come out of the kingdom of Cypris, where sweetness and happiness reigns, and find yourself suddenly back in the other world, the totally different planet where people write poisonous articles about you, slander you, 'get the better' of you, do everything they can to hurt you and never realize for one moment that your vital, sensitive spots do not happen to be where they are trying to strike at them; they do not realize that they are bombarding abandoned literary territory ... Quite useless to try and make them understand that they are engaged on an absurdly wasted effort. I can just imagine their exultant cries: 'Don't believe him when he says he doesn't care! It's just another pose!'

The days and then the weeks gradually blur the traces of our *in flagrante delicto*'s. In this respect, *Il tempo e galantuomo* (Father Time behaves with great elegance).

Since the end of the war (1914-18), and since I gave up sport and bullfighting, that is, since the age of thirty, I have had only two things in my life: creative literary work and sensual pleasure. But as in the case of two horses that have been running side by side all during the race until, on nearing the post, one of them forges ahead and outclasses the other, so, as I enter my declining years, pleasure strengthens its hold and becomes the dominant interest. As I approach the void, I have only pleasure with me; all the rest has lost its meaning.

Here is a different image. As evening comes on, darkness climbs up the mountain-side like a rising flood. Soon the mountain is almost entirely engulfed in featureless night. Only its peak remains sunlit, then it fades in its turn. The mountain is my life; the darkness my death. The gradually climbing shadow is my growing indifference. The sunlit peak is the pleasure I enjoy with the daughters of men. I have used this image once before, in exactly the same form, in the opening pages of *Le Songe*. Then I was only twenty-three. This could be called sticking to the same idea, if it were an idea.

As one's remaining span of life decreases, it is logical to wish to devote it to what one likes best; this is only common sense. And so it is that you come to want it to be filled only with pleasure, which is so violently better than everything else. It is then that you realize that pleasure is your religion. I use the word advisedly: for a long time now, the only link that has bound me (*religare*) to society has been desire. So much the better, since man's whole dignity is in his body. All the feelings of affection, friendship, esteem, etc. that I happen to have had during the course of my life were always lacking in strength, if they were not accompanied by desire. My childhood affection for my parents, to begin with, and more particularly for my mother. And even at the time, I knew the reason for this lack of strength. In the case of my mother, I was perhaps fourteen years old when *I told her*.

It was in *Mors et Vita*, I think, that I related the story of the severely wounded soldier who tore off his military medal and his *Croix de Guerre* and shouted: 'I'm dying. I don't give a damn for all this. What I want is a woman.' (Did they give him one? Surely not; what would people have thought! Any form of charity except that.)

There is a sentence of Tasso's that I used as the epigraph for *Les Jeunes Filles*: 'Any time that is not spent on love is wasted.' Convinced as I am of this, and so much so that the conviction is an obsession, I am sometimes horrified at the total amount of time I spend, although only in snatches, on some matter or other which is likely to win me a hundred or so new readers. I have no literary vanity and I have no need of money, and yet I find myself doing something which would only make sense if I were motivated by literary vanity or needed money; or if the increased popularity of my work made pleasure or love easier to obtain (it was Chateaubriand who said: 'Fame in order to be loved'), which is not at all the case, since my love affairs, like those in mythological tales, are carried out under various disguises. I find myself doing something which doesn't make sense, and what's more, at a time when, because of the shortening of my life, I cannot afford such absurdities. It sometimes happens that the realization of this, like a sudden stab, cuts me short in the middle of making a phone call or writing a communication to the Press or dictating a letter. I am suddenly thrown off my balance, my arms drop to my side, I am halted in my tracks . . .

Tolstoy was unhappy because he hadn't the strength of character to make his life conform to the moral principles he believed to be true. I am unhappy because I haven't the strength of character to avoid certain types of illogical behaviour which cannot be justified. Tolstoy didn't always obey his conscience. I don't always obey my reason.

Whether it is the unjustified character of one of our actions which suddenly bewilders us or, as the end draws near, the vanity of all action, it is the same process of waking up from a dream and wondering why one is doing what one is doing.

Faure-Biguet, in his book *Enfances*, quotes a passage in which, at the age of seventeen, I described the feeling of pain aroused in me by the contemplation of human beauty. That was because, in those days, contemplation did not lead me to possession.

Now I feel no pain at the sight of beauty, because I possess any number of exemplars of it; almost too many, in fact. But the contemplation of beauty no longer even interests me, since it cannot end in possession (we are choc-a-bloc, as it is). You will never find me studying the body beautiful either on the beach or in the music-hall, so true is it that I cannot conceive of contemplation without possession and am incapable of being disinterested.

Is it not a very impressive thing that I should only be able to do without sleeping pills at night when I have made love in the day-time? Is this not a hint from Nature, who, on the other hand, also provides a warning when we go too far in this respect?

The journalists who ask me the classic question: 'If you could take only one book with you on to a desert island, etc.' are always surprised when I give as my answer not the *Iliad*, or Plutarch, or the Greek tragedies but the Old Testament. And if I had to make a choice within the Old Testament, in the last resort I would plump for Ecclesiastes.

No doubt Ecclesiastes is not the greatest book produced by mankind but more than any other—except the work of Nietzsche —it corresponds to my temperament. There is nothing new under the sun; everything has been said before—all is vanity apart from physical enjoyment—inaction is praiseworthy—reason and virtue are a source of pain—there is no punishment *post mortem* (the fool and the unrighteous man suffer the same fate as the wise and the just)—ends are preferable to beginnings: so much for the main outlines. As regards the details, there is the tragic story of the unworthy heir—contempt for women—and even the motto of my hero Malatesta... None of it (and I have missed a lot out) is lacking in incoherence and repetitiveness and over it all floats a weird God, whose name is mentioned here and there, but whom, I think it is quite easy to avoid, as I hasten to do. All very Montherlant, in fact, and exactly right for the desert island.

Just as, in a booth at a fair, electric lights switch on when you hit the bull's eye, there are physically nondescript women whose faces, at the precise moment when you give them money, glow with a pretty expression that you hadn't seen before.

A man doesn't desire a woman because he thinks her beautiful; he decides that she is beautiful to justify his desire.

A man doesn't dream about a woman because he thinks her

'mysterious'; he decides that she is 'mysterious' to justify his dreaming about her.

A pretty woman is a completion to life. A beautiful woman gives it stability.

Men are less interested in a woman's beauty than they are in possessing her, but they dream about her beauty more.

We give more of ourselves to a woman in sleeping with her after the carnal act than we did in the act itself.

How grateful, how deeply and eternally attached, must a finished woman feel to the man who was the last to desire her and cover her with kisses.

One of my woman friends has such a respect for sensual pleasure that nothing in the world would bring her to separate two copulating flies.

Moslem women do not go to Paradise. Nobody has ever known what happens to them after death. As for the houris they can change their sex according to the desires of the elect.
As proof of the absence of women from Paradise, a Moslem once quoted to me a verse from the Apocalypse: 'There was silence in heaven about the space of half an hour.'

One is appalled when one imagines the sort of life a man must lead if he despises women and yet desires them, and desires only them. The unavoidable obligation of having, under pressure of desire, to tolerate, or to be in danger of having to tolerate, a yoke that the reason condemns must unbalance the whole experience of love, which happens to need great stability, must corrupt it, must corrupt desire itself and bring its victim to a state of shame totally incompatible with human dignity. The ancient world—Greek, Latin and Oriental—which despised women, prevented such personal disasters by making legitimate, and even exalting, the love of young boys, in which the necessary difference was provided not by sex but by age; snobbish fashion propagated and glorified what was in itself an effect of nature. Frivolous men and coarse men with a liking for 'the vulgar Venus' turned to courtesans; Platonizing snobs, lovers of the sublime or those who were simply serious-minded or anxious to maintain the proper order of things, turned to boys. All of them moved at will from one Cypris to the other, thus satisfying alternately the noble and the baser parts of their natures. Most of them, into the bargain, were married and thus ensured the continuance of the home and the fatherland. All possibilities were catered for.

The need to respect the object of desire—a need antiquity was well aware of and provided for—is doubtless one of man's most noble needs. It is not a natural phenomenon. There is no natural connection between, on the one hand, desiring and possessing, and on the other bestowing, not love in the modern sense of romantic passion, but that fundamental approval, based on respect, which is worthy of the name of friendship.

This much established, we must remind ourselves that nothing is more important in love than to have one's partner *dans la peau*.[1] All flesh is dung, they say, but corruption and fertilization go hand in hand; no dung-heap, no flowers; and if the dung is dry, the flowers wither. And the tragedy of bed without friendship and respect is as nothing compared to the tragedy of bed too far removed from the dung-heap.

After the most brilliant erotic *faena* which, though I say it as shouldn't, deserved the ears and the tail, I awoke in the middle of the night and it seemed as if the vault of the heavens had shrunken to form the ceiling of my room and that I could put out my hand and touch the stars.

I thought of the team of human creatures, changing a little every year and completely renewed about once every five years, which

[1] *Avoir quelqu'un dans la peau*, literally 'to have someone under one's skin', a physical expression, for which there seems to be no equivalent in English, meaning to be incurably in love with.

for so long now has borne me on smoothly and calmly like a river and will, eventually, have carried me through all the varied landscapes of my life.

And I tried to understand why it is, exactly, that with people I meet or hear about, sensual experience is a source of worry, drama and upheavals, in short, the main source of the unhappiness in their lives, and in the lives of people connected with them, whereas in my life, on the contrary, it has been the regulating factor and a constant delight.

I am grateful for this, in the first place, to my Fortune, that indefinable combination of circumstances which ensures that things turn out to your advantage; and Fortune is particularly praiseworthy in favouring me since my pessimism should invite disaster.

I am grateful to my partners in love. I am quite flabbergasted when I think of the incredible amount of obligingness, niceness, fidelity, good-humouredness, honesty and punctuality that, drop by drop, has gone to make up the river I spoke of above. I find, in my *Notebook No. XXII*, the following, written in November 1932: 'How can I ever adequately express my tender gratitude towards those I have *never had cause to complain of,* and on whose faces I have never seen an unkind expression? If my books are worth anything . . .' That is the end of the page, and the next one goes on to deal with another subject, but I know exactly what I wrote or wanted to write: if my books are worth anything, it is thanks to the atmosphere of peace and freedom of mind that they have provided for me. And I may well ask: what would I have been, but for them? What would my life have been, without this experience?

Finally, I am thankful to myself for showing discernment and a sense of proportion first in the choice, and then in the handling of my partners; in finding, keeping, guiding and finally leaving them, or being left by them, with the maximum of pleasure and the minimum of inconvenience both for themselves and for me. Discernment is not the strong point of the society I see around me. Everything which should go without saying is always precisely what no one does; the things that stare you in the face pass unnoticed; experience bears no fruit; the royal virtue of good sense, whether or not it goes by the name of reason, is constantly flouted. Is it surprising, then, that in the conduct of their love lives the people forming this society should seem to me crazed and unhappy, a ready prey for charlatans great and small?

To discernment and a sense of proportion I may add genuine kindliness, with the generosity that is one of its natural consequences. It is a moot point whether by being kind and generous to someone you help to prevent that person doing you harm; some people will say no, or even, on the contrary. Whatever the truth of the matter, trusting my good sense or perhaps simply taking what was, for me, the line of least resistance, I have always assumed that friendliness, not diplomatic but genuine friendliness, is more likely to impress people in your favour than it is to turn them against you, and I have always thought, and still think, that people have been nice to me because I have been nice to them. (But I may be mistaken.)

The foregoing remarks may seem bitterly ironical some day—if I ever suffer a serious *cornada*. But even then, the proportion of *cornadas* will have been very small; the triumph of Cypris is already assured.

But there will still be people who say: 'What is the point of a love-life without commotion and suffering?' My answer is that both as a man and, what is more important, as an artist I have arranged things so as to experience the appropriate amount of upsets and pain, even in my love-life. ('Hold fast to all things, keeping each thing in its proper place,' as I wrote twenty years ago in *Les Olympiques*.) But a little was enough, since it is a feature of the artistic imagination that it should be able to reconstitute everything on the basis of very limited data. When Delacroix wanted to paint a tiger, he used his cat as a model.

I have often protested against the conventional belief that women are complicated, 'mysterious', etc. I have just come across the following remark in a book: 'Just as the scientist has fewer observations to make on female beauty, so the artist finds the study of female beauty easier and less complicated (than that of male beauty). Nature herself seems to operate with more facility in the making of women, if it is true that fewer male children are born than female.'

When, at the age of twelve, I used to go into the stable with my big collie and grip him with my arms and legs as we lay together in the straw, I with my face buried in his neck and he looking as happy as we both felt, I could not help realizing, although I was too young to have had experience of amorous embraces, that a big dog, who was the same size as I was when we were lying down, was really very like a human being. He had, at such moments, the human being's pleased and absent look and open mouth; he had four limbs, a drumming chest, a flat belly and a warm body in which furry areas alternated with others, at his groins, silky with a paradisal silkiness.

Lion-taming has always seemed to me to lead up to the classic moment when man and beast, lying in a clinch on the ground, and often breath to breath, imitate a lovers' embrace. The 'possession' achieved by the lion-tamer consists simply in having forced the animal to remain motionless and passive, relaxed and compliant. But might the lion-tamer not imagine a more lusty and exhaustive act of possession or, if you like, imagine putting a seal on his act of possession when, as happened to me long ago with my collie, he notices that dreamy look, those alternations of furriness and silkiness, the awkward, almost silly splaying out of the hind legs and the naïve drooping of the forepaws hanging in mid-air over the chest and so similar to the big, limp hands of the children of men?

I apply to beauty the remark that Cicero attributes to Cotta in connection with the Divinity: it is easier to say what it isn't than what it is. Beauty and ugliness are like health and illness: the second makes itself felt but not the first.

When X, after caressing her in a special and breathtaking way, asked if 'it was nice', she answered, with that beautiful simplicity typical of Racine's best lines: 'Everything you do to me is nice.'

When you see how much money it costs to be generous to people who don't matter to you, to go to law, to travel, to be burgled, to be arrested, to be ill and to die, you realize that the sharers of your bed, who provide you with far more pleasure than anyone else, cause you proportionately least expense. Happiness is far less costly than trouble. This is strange, but what isn't?

Sea-woman.—The light laughs around her dimples like the sun around the hollows between the waves.

Beach-woman.—A great mass, like the aerial view of a beach with its smooth expanses and its curving, sinuous outline.

Sponge-woman.—If you kneaded her body with your fists, you would squeeze sunlight out of it.

Metal-woman.—The little mark on her thigh is just like the hallmark stamped on a precious metal.

Earth-woman.—Naked and still, like a great, mild landscape, with its mountains, its dunes and its promontories, its valleys and its forests.

According to Plato, there is an immense cavity called Tartarus in the centre of earth, containing a vast, surging mass of water, mud and lava. The monstrous mixture is never at rest, but rises and falls unceasingly. When it rises, it spills out on to the surface of the globe. When it falls, its withdrawal creates terrific suction. The whole inner life of the globe is regulated by this great alternating movement, now ingoing now outgoing.

Earth-woman.—The goddess Ge.

Another parallel: just as the infernal rivers flowed partly on the surface of the earth but sprang from its inmost depths, does it not seem that the veins of the breasts have their roots in the heart?

The vicious resentment of the male against the male who has had great sensual enjoyment: Casanova is called a fool, Byron a cad, d'Annunzio a phoney, and Restif de la Bretonne a show-off.

According to the philosophers, universal beauty lies in the absolute appropriateness of the creature for its particular end, in a harmonious relationship of the parts among themselves and of the whole with the parts. But as this definition of beauty is synonymous with the definition of perfection, which is of too high an order to be properly grasped by the human mind, our conception of universal beauty remains indeterminate and forms within us through the combination of a number of individual perceptions. However, an element of comparison always enters into our perceptions, and beauty cannot be compared with anything higher than itself.

Beauty has its drawbacks. People afflicted with a physical imperfection should thank their lucky stars they have an excuse for their weaknesses of character.

The dominance of strong minds over weak. The story of Corbineau, one of Napoleon's generals during the Russian campaign, who was disarmed while on horseback and said to a Russian prisoner: 'Pick up my sabre for me.' The Russian handed him his sabre and he went on laying about him as before.

This is a very significant story, and of course, I discount any interpretation depending on 'unknown forces' (fluid, magnetism, etc.), which are not things I am much interested in: I have always disdained to use them.—'Lie down on the bed here.'—'Open your legs.'—'Don't make a fuss.' If these *commands* are uttered in a certain tone, the recalcitrant person *obeys*.

Contary to what may be thought, this experience, when it has become habitual, is not necessarily intoxicating. It inspires in the agent a rather sad feeling of gravity, a terrifying awareness of the power he possesses and does not wish, for various reason, to abuse. 'Never give any other man the power you have given me. He would make a worse use of it than I have done.' Such were the words that the dying condottiere, Colleone, addressed to the Venetians.

The age-old mass of prejudice—religious, superstitious, etc., in other words, the dregs of the mind—still influences people who do not think for themselves and leads them to consider as scandalous the act of love between men and animals. But neither reason nor conscience can find anything wrong with it. It is not 'the obscure part' of the soul which practises this act or which approves of it. It is the obscure part—which has been called, rather appropriately, 'obscurantism'—which is incensed by it (although, incidentally, it is practised on a large scale not only among the so-called Oriental peoples but in every European country known to me).

Some day, perhaps, when I have achieved that dismal boldness which immediately precedes the grave, I shall say what I have to say on this subject.

If, when a man who is sleeping with someone of a race or a civilization very foreign to him, or merely of a social class very different from his own, has the feeling that, because of shared pleasure and affection, barriers which are normally considered indestructible break down; if he is so constituted that the feeling fills him with awe, and if the awe enhances the sense he already has of the *sacredness* of such moments, how keen will be his awed sense of barriers removed and how greatly increased his feeling of sacredness, if the creature with whom he shares the pleasure and the affection is an animal?

It is in the exercise of sensuality that can best be gauged the great achievement of the man who 'puts himself in the other person's place' and constantly thinks of the other person's pleasure; it is here that he gives the measure of his delicacy of feeling and of his fundamental quality.

When we remain calm and our partner is excited, it takes an

effort to remember the (sometimes very recent) moments when we were excited and our partner remained calm. Other people's excitement, either physical or sentimental, seems strange to us, when we are its object; we are not far from thinking it pathetic or ridiculous; often it is displeasing to us or boring. Then it is that intelligence and kindness are needed if we are to let them drink their fill of us, as we would stand patiently with a horse at the drinking trough, willing him to enjoy himself and pleased with his enjoyment, even though it may seem rather long drawn out. It is probably easier to be patient with physical, than with sentimental excitement.

How many veils have to be removed before one can get to a woman! Even when she is finally naked, we do not know what she is like. Her nakedness must be presented in a certain way. I have no opinion about a body until I have seen it standing to attention, in which attitude the last trace of falseness disappears.

I remember how annoyed my female models used to be, in the days when I studied drawing, if I asked them to adopt this attitude. They felt that it showed them up completely. The final *terreno de verdad* or place of truth.

'Your tenderness fades because a liquid comes out of your body. Then it reforms because the liquid has reformed. It is high time the mechanism governing such tenderness was taken seriously; in the first place, it should be seen to be where it is—and it isn't in the stars.'

'Go on! You don't mean to say you call that tenderness!'

'I do. A minor form of it, but definitely tenderness.'

On the intellectual plane, nothing is easier than to judge a man at first glance: he is sub-human, crass, etc. So far, so good. But move on to the plane of action, even though it may be very limited action (for instance, connected with physical love-making), and you cannot disregard him: he is a father, a brother, a lover—a nuisance, a dangerous nuisance. The situation is quite different.

Another thing. As far as writing is concerned, I can do whatever I want to do. There are some books of mine that the public likes less than others, but they are, nevertheless, the exact and perfect expression of what was in my mind. In this respect, there has never been, for me, the slightest gap between conception and execution.

For the first, general, reason and the second, personal, reason, it is natural that I should come up against difficulties on the plane of action.

Yet this plane cannot be avoided by anyone resolved on complete self-development; still less so, by anyone desiring self-knowledge. This is one of the important points made by Goethe.

If we governed ourselves entirely according to our intelligence and character, we should have no contact with mankind; we should never move on to the plane of action, since it is our degree of intelligence and character which makes social relationships difficult and handicaps us with regard to them. But unfortunately, we also have passions.

People like myself who have never had any dealings with their fellow-men—I mean, fierce, pugnacious dealings—except in connection with physical love, have nevertheless had enough experience of action to look upon the life lived by pure intellectuals or contemplatives, even when it is noble and highly valuable, as being irremediably the line of least resistance.

Beauty in repose. Classical man had succeeded in making all terrestrial forces, including a whole enslaved mass of humans, contribute to the satisfaction of his sense of sovereignty as a free man. He enjoyed *otia dia* and, having few cares beyond his own self-improvement, sought it in the experience of non-activity; he wanted the final outcome of all the workings of nature to be his own serenity. In creating the fiction of the solitary individual, systematically limited to the minimum amount of internal commotion compatible with life, and a prudent spectator of the secret interplay and changing combinations of matter, classical humanism culminated in so purified a conception of man that it was valid for anyone dedicated to similar inertia and simplification, and led in the end to the notion that there was such a thing as an essential man with universal qualities.

'Young girls, priestesses of Aphrodite and purveyors of pleasure in the rich city of Corinth.' (Pindare.)

Textes sous une occupation, 1953
(Written in April 1944)

COMING BACK FROM THE BIBLIOTHÈQUE NATIONALE

I STARTED GOING to the reading-room of the Bibliothèque Nationale when I was seventeen, with my father's ticket. This piece of deception enabled me to put in several years of good work there, when I was still under age, just as another piece of deception—the writing of geometrical and algebraical formulae, dates and such-like on the inside of my starched cuffs and even on my nails—had helped me to pass my baccalaureat and so procured me some years of peace and quiet. Another advantage was that it made my father my accomplice, which was very good for our relationship and did not happen often enough.

At that time I lived in Neuilly, near the Seine. Our house was a long way from the BN and I had such an appetite for reading and for what might have been called culture, if the word had not been so bandied about as to become unusable that, to avoid wasting a precious half-hour, I used to take bread and chocolate with me and ate them openly at midday in the reading-room. Around me other readers, shame-faced and short of money, were also eating bread, but breaking off the pieces in their pockets. Twelve noon was the signal for a vast chorus of munching.

There were lots of madmen wearing capes in the style of Péguy's and socially-conscious beards and talking to themselves; all complete bachelors. Then there were tramps in canvas shoes (one of them used newspapers as socks) with crusts of dirt on their foreheads; neurotics, with rings under their vampire-like eyes, biting their thumbnails and trembling with nervous excitement; negroes, who were more reflective than anyone else; half-dead old men, already mottled with decay, reading palimpsests with the help of magnifying glasses—you would see them get up suddenly and walk about with the jerky gait of skeletons (you could tell when they were coming towards you by the smell of urine, because they were all hopelessly incontinent); and political fanatics, belonging to all sexes but mainly the fair, who picked me out at once as being the opposite of what they were and fixed me with such a look of hatred that I used to spend all my time staring back to show that I wasn't abashed. The stench given off by intelligence was so impressive that a uniformed employee used to appear at four o'clock to spray out the reading-room with some deliciously scented liquid. I used to wait for this moment with the impatience of a seal in the zoo, who gets his snack at four.

From half past three onwards, such was the crowd of thinkers inside that there would be a queue at the door. Anyone who came out freed a place for the next in turn. It was funny to think of oneself standing there, waiting for somebody to finish thinking.

At ten minutes to six the weight-lifting event began. There would be another queue at the counter, this time of people carrying piles of folios in their arms.

After a time I got tired of the midday munchings and used to have a meal in the canteen. Once I respectfully observed Bergson lunching there. Apart from him, I encountered no celebrities at the BN except Halévy and Bourges,[1] and Bourges was invariably asleep. Perhaps he had come to read his own works. The words '*Elémir endormi*'—'Elémir asleep'—have a very pretty sound.

I don't know why I mentioned intelligence just now. It played no great part there. The BN was, first and foremost, a temple of deceit, and it is typical of the place that I was only able to gain admission with a false ticket. The thinkers in the reading-room were, in fact, for the most part either busy copying obscure and forgotten texts which they meant to publish as their own, or writing works which were genuinely theirs but which they would sell to some Academician for him to publish under his name. Not to mention the bogus aristocrats, easily recognizable because of

[1] Daniel Halévy, Elémir Bourges, two French writers.

their heavy signet rings with huge crests like carbuncles, and who came there with folders full of documents under their arms to help other bogus aristocrats to claim titles. Finally there were a lot of people who came to steal the illustrations out of books. Sheltered by a barricade of folios, like a schoolboy hiding behind his books, the thief would wet a thread with spittle and stretch it underneath the adhesive edge of the print which would gradually come unstuck; all he had to do, then, was slip it quickly into his brief-case. Or he would rip it away with a pen-knife, or better still, just pull it loose, bit by bit. This was also the way readers provided themselves with lavatory paper, since there was none in the lavatory. But though all these methods are very simple, I never managed any of them successfully. I know why I have a weakness for backward individuals. The love-drama with which I shall make my come-back as a dramatist at the age of eighty-five will be called: *The Attractive Half-Wit*.

Just now, on my way back from the Bibliothèque Nationale, I walked through the garden of the Palais-Royal. I go there so seldom that it made me think back to the nineteen-year-old young man who, on leaving the Library at six o'clock, would sit there for a while before going back to Neuilly. No other image comes between that young man and my present self, because I have had no other experience connected with the Palais-Royal garden during the forty intervening years.

If, during these forty years, my face and figure have changed, nothing has changed in my mind or in some part of my body. But this cannot alter the obvious fact that I have only a few more years to live. I have often wondered about the mystery that surrounds old men; how do they reconcile themselves to their condition? Now, I am myself involved in the mystery. I wonder why it suddenly descended on me this afternoon in the garden of the Palais-Royal. For a minute or two, I was in a stupor, choking with an emotion that was at once reasonable and inept . . . This is what is called, I think, a moment of weakness.

As a child I used to sing a hymn containing these lines . . .

COMING BACK FROM THE BIBLIOTHÈQUE NATIONALE

Je suis le fils de Dieu le Père
Il me faut des biens infinis.

I am the son of God the Father
And can be content only with infinite gifts.

I am not the son of God the Father, no question of that, but it is true that I wanted infinite gifts, and that I have had them. But who feels the wrench most? The man who, never having had much, realizes that he has to go before he has been satisfied or the man who has had all he wanted and realizes that he is leaving all these infinite gifts behind him? I remember writing twenty years ago in *Un Voyageur solitaire est un diable*: 'When the Fortune that has watched over me falls at last into an eternal, a golden sleep, may I strike that delicate balance which will enable me to bid a serene farewell to life while still feeling for it as strong a love as I feel today.'

I know very well what I shall find waiting for me at home when I get back from the Palais-Royal; a mass of small chores thrust upon me by well-disposed persons, in some cases my friends, who never pause to consider that I have not long to live and that the first and perhaps the only duty of friends and well-wishers towards men of my age is to leave them free, during their short span of life, to do only those things which are a positive pleasure. A sacred duty and one that seems blatantly obvious . . . but how many people think of fulfilling it?

But, corresponding to this duty of indulgence to the old, is a duty incumbent on the old, and that is not to add unnecessarily to the sufferings or minor pains and annoyances which plague the majority of mankind. Throughout our lives we have not bothered unduly about sparing others pain, but now that we are old, that is something we should think about. I once wrote: 'Old age is a time to be open-handed.' (That does not seem to be the view of most of my literary colleagues who, as they grow older, grow more and more vain, avaricious and spiteful.) Open-handed, so as not to grab, but also so as not to claw.

When I got home I opened my diary in which, on 1st January, I transcribed three sentences which I want to keep continually before me; that is why I copied them into my pocket-book which is always on my work-table or in my pocket. All three sentences have the same meaning; one of them sums up all three. This sentence, which I came across a few years ago, is, I think, the one I shall concentrate on when death is in sight. It was not written by a great philosopher or a great genius. A much criticized novelist put it into the mouth of one of his characters in a much criticized novel. Petronius says to Vinicius in *Quo Vadis*: '*The man who has known how to live should know how to die.*'

A prayer for the hour of death composed during the night of January 24th–25th, 1955.

Divinity, if you exist, but assuredly you do not; Divinity, if you exist under whatever name you are worshipped, I thank you for granting me my reason, which has enabled me to avoid pain. I thank you for teaching me to enjoy the world, while protecting myself against it. I thank you for bestowing on me a body which up to now has known how to give pleasure. I ask you to enable me to face what is coming with an even mind. I ask you to grant that I may conduct myself decorously, for my own satisfaction rather than for the sake of others. I ask you to permit me to retain my reason so that it may help me to acquiesce unfailingly in what nature may do with me. There are other things I should thank you for, but I can think of nothing else to ask.

Le Fichier parisien, 1955
(Written in 1955)

EXTRACTS FROM THE NOTEBOOKS OF HENRY DE MONTHERLANT—1930-1944

NOTEBOOK XIX—*Algiers, 19th September 1930 to 21st May 1931.*

These extracts have been made from a volume of nearly 400 pages. For the Editor's choice, the author himself is in no way responsible.

We often read variations on the theme: 'No man can do anything for his fellow-men. Each of us is always alone.' This is a literary invention, and untrue. Men can do everything for one another. During my periods of inexplicable despair, when I was writing *Les Voyageurs traqués*, half an hour of physical pleasure provided by a fellow human being would change the colour of my spectacles: the world was no longer the suicidal place in which I had been immersed for days. And how can one speak of a 'solitude' filled with memories and expectations? If there are two of you, that is not solitude. I am prepared to invent a deity in order to express to him my gratitude for never leaving me unsustained by the human consolation of the flesh, a consolation which right up to the present has kept me from drowning in despair.

I kept repeating Gobineau's remark to myself . . . 'There's writing; then love; and beyond that, nothing.' (But I invert the order of the first two terms) Love and writing; they are passions, or rather, given their absolute necessity, I might call them drugs. If illness or social circumstances deprived me of both at the same time, what would become of me? Again the prospect of suicide.

If only man would exert himself as much for what exists as he does for what does not!

* * *

Throughout history the world has been laid waste to ensure the triumph of conceptions that are now as dead as the men who died for them.

Sometimes my good Fortune frightens me. Of all the solutions I foresee it is always the one I desire most that comes to pass. I construct a plan, and then something happens that seems to bring the whole structure down. After five minutes' depression, I am already roughing out a new plan. But next morning my original plan is rehabilitated. Not only that; but frequently the very occurrence that appeared to demolish it now gives it an added strength. This is the way things have gone now for years and years, with hardly a single exception; so much so that the possibility of disappointment has become unimaginable.

At times when Fortune seems to take pleasure in thwarting me, I say to myself: 'Naturally, to make remarks like this (about my good luck) is to tempt fate. What a fool I was ever to write such things! It is only fair that Fortune should give me the lie.' But no, next morning, Fortune puts me on my feet again, thus showing that I was justified in writing in this way.

What is the meaning of all this? Is it pure chance? Or is fortune really on my side? (To suppose this would be to indulge in mysticism.) Or can it be that, without being conscious of the fact, I possess certain deeply-rooted qualities, such as obstinacy, a physical inability to be discouraged, more than anything else perhaps, common sense, in other words, discernment, which prompts me now to take in sail and now to let it out, now to act quickly and now to let time do the work for me, now to keep a tight rein and now to relax—a whole technique of instinctive strategy that you either have or you haven't, and which cannot be governed by rules because, in certain circumstances, it would be right to disobey them.

In all this, I am guided by the narrowest form of egoism—the sort that has its seat in the vitals. Generally speaking, the sexual instinct is at the back of it all, and its infallible sureness of movement is, for me, proof of its greatness. If I were editing a newspaper, for instance, I should make the same blunders as I commit in matters I consider of secondary importance, such as the management of my property or the conduct of my 'career', because the newspaper would be even more alien to my real life than either my property or my career.

I have exerted myself to the full in living my private life. My less strenuous efforts have been given to my art.

For eight years I lived for nothing but pleasure, and the emancipation of all my instincts. During this eight years' Saturnalia, I hardly had time to experience desire. I sacrificed part of my work to pleasure, as well as my interests, my career and my social connections.

I cannot often enough repeat my firm conviction that, in the midst of so much that is called 'serious', only those pleasures which our senses convey to us directly, without the intermediary of our reason, are genuine and reasonable. They provide a coastline, a *terra firma,* which must never be lost sight of, when embarking with me on the perilous ocean of the sublime.

8th January. The first fire of the year. I lit it all by myself, and it is a flower, a wild beast, a flame madly in love with itself, a lovely, living fire. I'm very proud of having lit it all by myself, and without having to sprinkle spirit on it either! I keep gazing at it with a vague anxiety, as if it were some street-girl I had brought into my house in the middle of the night and I were afraid she might get up to some mischief. The fire, established in my room, is also rather disturbing. It has to be attended to the whole time, just like a woman. '*Qu'il est embêtant, cette créature!*' Ferdinand exclaims.[1] His exclamation has a two-fold beauty: it humanizes fire, as primitive peoples did (as a matter of fact, *cette créature* is just a Marseilles

[1] 'What a nuisance the creature is.' The servant mixes the masculine of *le feu* with the feminine of *la créature*, in a way which is not possible in correct French.

turn of speech) and gives it both sexes, as the ancient Romans would refer to certain divinities in both the masculine and the feminine in the same sentence. In a five-word utterance, my Marseille man-servant has recaptured two features of primitive poetry.

There is a point at which the beauty of human beings is such that you no longer hanker after possession. You are discouraged in advance, convinced that nothing you can do will equal their deserts and that you can only spoil their beauty. So you fall back on to the imperfect, which enables you to avoid humiliation.

What are, in my view, the three cardinal virtues?
They are, I think: intelligence, the capacity for sensual pleasure (called in French, *le tempérament*) and magnanimity.
I include culture in intelligence.
About sensual pleasure I have already said enough.
What of magnanimity or generosity? What name should be given to the act of going beyond the self into disinterested action or, still further, into self-sacrifice? It seems essential to me that this particular shade of behaviour should be represented.
None of these virtues can exist without the other two.

When X . . . failed to bring off a piece of business that would have made him 200,000 francs, because he couldn't be bothered to see it through, he was disapproved of, unanimously, and in the most vigorous terms. 'If he didn't know what to do with the 200,000 francs, he could have used them to relieve the poverty of others. Fancy turning them down! He must be devoid of feeling, as well as crazy, etc.' If they could have locked him up, they would have done so.

I am not in love with X . . . I am in love with the way I captured her.

The English like to be made fun of, because it gives them the opportunity of remembering, and of reminding others, that they are far above mockery.

If you want something to put you to sleep, take some collection of famous women's love-letters to bed with you. Maria Dorval's letters to Vigny for example—the stammering, whining plaints of a jealous, love-sick washerwoman.

Every woman who wants to have a child, 'to give some meaning to her life,' shows us that she is incapable of finding any meaning by herself. She also proves the existence of the vacuum when she seeks 'to give herself a personality'—another common female ambition.

We must fight hard against the unreasonable temptation to turn against our most cherished ideas, when we see them vulgarized and degraded by belated success. Lost causes are betrayed through cowardice, and victorious ones through fastidiousness.

Success redounds to my credit but I am pleased by failure.
Any apparent betrayal on the part of Fortune which sends you back 'to your books' is all to the good, because it restores you to your necessary function, that is, artistic creation. This has always been true of all writers. Exile is productive.

Bullfighters spend their lives hearing themselves being called cowards. It is time someone said that if they were cowards, they wouldn't have chosen to be bullfighters.

I did not unwrap the flowers the lady sent me and I gave them, just as they were, to another woman. I did not read the accompanying letter, which I left, unopened, in its envelope. But I went to bed with the little flower-girl who brought the offering. That will teach you, Madam, to send flowers to gentlemen.

* * *

I can only survive if I experience one keen pleasure every day; otherwise, I languish and wilt. I have sometimes thought it would be better to die than to pine in this way.

NOTEBOOK XXI—*Algiers, November 1951 to March 1932*
Paris, March 1932 to 26th April 1932

In order to avoid the danger of falling seriously in love, you should bring another woman into play to distract your attention, as a dancer in a ballet takes the first girl who comes to him, or a bullfighter uses his cape to draw off the bull which is threatening one of his comrades.

An Englishman does not hurry. A seventeenth-century Frenchman and a Japanese of the classical period incline to understatement. A Roman orator (I think Quintilian said this) never raises his hand above his head. The wise man has plenty of leisure, though, in order to disarm the envious, he always pretends to be overwhelmed with business.

Djâmi, *Beharistan,* p. 85

A man, hard-pressed by necessity, took refuge in the house of a person, whose father he had killed. This person, unaware of his identity, sheltered him. Eventually, he revealed his identity. 'His host's cheeks flushed red and his eyes became bloodshot. He remained for a while with bended head. Then he said, "It will not be long before you go to join my Father and he will take vengeance on you. But I have granted you asylum and I shall not betray you. Get up, now and go, for I am not sure of myself and may God guard me from doing you harm".' Then he made him a present of a thousand pieces of gold.

There is something extravagant about this tale and the part about the gift to the father's murderer seems inconceivable in a rational man. All the same, it is a kind of extravagance which is a part of human nature—at least in some men; such men need to act madly from time to time, and preferably against their own interests.

Madame V... fought against me, bothered me, slandered me and did her best to come between me and the object of my love. Years went by; she was reduced to poverty and asked me for help. I gave her more than could reasonably be expected, and why? *Because she had formerly done me harm.* Another of the deep mysteries of human nature.

(But, no doubt, my real motive was to surprise her and leave her with an extraordinary picture of my personality. Would I have given so much, if the gift had been anonymous?)

Stupidity does not consist in being without ideas. Such stupidity would be the sweet, blissful stupidity of animals, molluscs and the gods. Human Stupidity consists in having lots of ideas, but stupid ones. Stupid ideas, with banners, hymns, loud-speakers and even tanks and flame-throwers as their instruments of persuasion, constitute the refined and the only really terrifying form of Stupidity. For they are essentially dynamic, essentially rabble-rousing; they are eternally appropriate to organized Stupidity. Who will compose a great allegory showing how the present-day imbecile or charlatan opens a new Pandora's box to let loose over the world a flying plague of stupid ideas, which kill men as they adore them?

If I were twenty-five and wanted, as they say, to give a meaning to my life or, in other words, keep myself occupied, I would interest myself in the unification of religions. All of them correspond to the same human needs; all have a common denominator. What it is I dare not say.

Certain Greek statues show a widening of the eye-sockets, which we are conscious of in ourselves, when our gaze abandons external objects to retreat inwards. It is then indifferent to the things of the earth and their interplay.

It is a matter of small importance that our talents, our capacities and our characters should be limited, provided we know what the limits are.

* * *

Man strives, and makes it a point of honour, to go against nature and reason. The male human being is designed for short and numerous love-affairs: he is subject to marriage, which calls for fidelity to a single love. The child, if he follows his natural instincts, despises his parents and takes no interest in them, but he is required to respect, love and support them, as well as to sacrifice himself for them, if need be, for half a century. From the age of twelve the adolescent feels the call of the flesh, but he is allowed no means of responding before, say, the age of eighteen. At a certain age every girl ought to become a woman. If she sees to it herself without benefit of marriage lines, the finger of scorn is pointed at her. Homosexuality is part and parcel of nature, but it is treated as a vice or an illness, and may lead to prison or the stake. These are only a few instances. We can add religions, which are all founded on unnatural or unreasonable premises. We can also add political and social idealogies, which are, in two cases out of three, crazy, and always pregnant with catastrophe, since common sense gets its own back, when it has been outraged for too long. It is hardly surprising that in these conditions humanity should always be involved in suffering. We are born under a layer of superstition and false ideas; we grow up under it, go on living under it, and say to ourselves that we shall die under it, without ever, *for one single day in our lives*, having lived otherwise than in subjection to the ideas of idiots and the customs of savages, which we cannot infringe or even denounce without danger to ourselves. Into this environment we throw our children, who are defenceless or have defences as dangerous for them as the evils of the system. We say that life has always been like this and always will be, over the whole surface of the earth. We try to smile and bear things philosophically, but remain deeply impressed.

One can be sad without being downcast. One can be full of sadness and, at the same time, of courage and resolution.

At all times the surface of my life has been agitated by passions, while my inner self has been as calm as the depths of the sea during a storm. Both things should be experienced at once—attachment and detachment.

I have come across the following note on a loose leaf dated 5th March 1925:

'I am expecting to die from one moment to the next, but am not seriously disturbed by the prospect. It is really a matter of indifference to me. I have nothing new to look forward to, and even if the familiar experiences are good, they no longer arouse in me that ardent desire to go on living, which I felt when they were new. This apathy is the reward or punishment for having satisfied all desire.'

The ancient Greeks have been reproached for not having made a profound study of love and death. No doubt they felt that neither love nor death deserved so much attention. But casual treatment does not always imply superficiality. It may be the height of gravity.

The fact of living, and living healthily, and living happily as well, demands such a conjunction of circumstances and represents such a delicate balance and—if we don't mind using the word— is such a miracle, that when we have achieved it, we ought to swim in a stream of perpetual wonder, and the moment it ceases, should abstain from complaints or accusations and simply say to ourselves that miracles, too, require an occasional rest and that we have simply returned to our natural condition. If I enjoyed a moment of respite on my death-bed, I should greet that moment with delight and say to myself that the whole of my life might have been one long agony.

That is why the only lamentations I can endure are the great tragic lamentations (the Bible and the Greeks), for their literary quality, and deliberate complaints uttered with a view to obtaining something. As for miserable little *bourgeois* lamentations . . . !

I like to think of Michelangelo continuing to work at his statue of Night, although he was suffering through the misfortunes of his country. Who bothers today about the misfortunes of Italy in the fifteenth century, and what was their importance? Nevertheless, they had to be experienced as suffering.

Am I fated to be overcome by the misfortunes of the State when my private life, for more than three years now, has been stable and happy, and to suffer when no one else does? I am almost the only person in France to be distressed about France, just as I was the only person in North Africa to be distressed by the native problem.

To be a patriot and a Frenchman in 1932 is to live in a state of crucifixion.

France is falling apart.

No one talks to me about the condition of the country. When I broach the subject, the person I am talking to either looks completely nonplussed or else agrees with me, but always with a little laugh—a laugh of weak acceptance—and then hastily changes the subject: no point in dwelling on a painful theme. And so France drifts towards the abyss, between thoughtlessness on the one hand and cowardice on the other.

I can serve by creating disinterested works of art, informed with humanity; I can serve my country without thinking or speaking of France.

I am reproached for being an egoist. But how could I live except in blinkers? Everything evil wounds me, and if I were wounded too often, I should die.

It is the squalid little problems of food, clothing, money and getting about that cause so much ghastly worry and waste of time, while the two great essentials—love and artistic creation—give less trouble than anything else. Trifles cause difficulty and disgust, whereas the things which make life worth while are accomplished with an airy and god-like ease.

My attitude towards Catholicism has always been like that of the Mediterranean towards its beaches, now caressing and now retreating. Or, like a cat biting and licking at one and the same time.

I am convinced, in fact I know, that literary work is more important than action; I have never refrained from saying this and writing it. But should a disaster befall my country, then there's nothing to be done, my work collapses; to devote myself to it seems absurd and blameworthy ... If someone askes me 'What are you at work on now?' at a time when my country is in grave trouble, I can't help answering with ill humour, and also with embarrassment because, if I told him the real reason why his question had upset me, he would think I was striking an attitude.

Our most intimate feelings are, in any case, always unutterable. If, in Algeria, I had said that my pleasure in life was spoilt by the native problem, no one would have believed me. If I said that I care nothing for money and official distinctions, people would grin sardonically. They believe only in feelings of which they themselves are capable. They love money and distinctions and care nothing for either the Arabs or France.

My fate is to be hurt by things which cause no pain to others and to feel no pain at things which hurt them.

NOTEBOOK XXII—*Paris, 26th April 1932 to 21st June 1932*
Algiers, 21st June 1932 to 25th November 1932

R once said to me 'You are a survival from antiquity'. I replied 'That is true in one respect, which you certainly haven't thought of—my respect and affection for old people, which was a feature of life in classical times.' I listen to what they have to say; I believe they know more than I do: I sympathize with them because of their approaching death, and I pity them for their infirmities and weaknesses and because others despise them. Also, I think I can only feel at home with people who have no illusions left. Lastly, but most important perhaps, I pity myself in anticipation of the day when I shall be like them. I like old people, children and certain animals. I don't like adolescents or grown-ups. I like women to go to bed with, when they are very young, but I don't like feminity.

In evaluating a life, there is one essential element which is generally forgotten and that is the price paid for what was achieved. Not in money but in wearisome and humiliating acts. A life, admirable at first sight, may have cost so much in imposed liabilities, chores and self-abasement, that, brilliant though it appears, it cannot be considered as other than a failure. Another, which seems to have misfired, is in reality a triumphant success, because it has cost so little.

The precise, pure outline of face and neck against the dark cushion, the pure outline of the body too, and the open, tranquil face, offered so sweetly, and all that lies behind it: affection and security, four and a half years of affection and security and not a single occasion for reproach. . . .
You leave this world to enter the world of indifference, pesterings and spite. If this face did not create its own world, the other world would kill you. It is the first which justifies existence.

All those stories about Oedipus, Phaedra and Pasiphae which the world has got worked up over because of so-called crimes, which are, in fact, as innocent as the lighting of a cigarette, have an interest for the student of universal and eternal morality. It is undreamable that false crimes like these should ever disappear. The need to be wrongly shocked is fundamental to man.

The most abysmal depths are not where they are supposed to be. The worst are not connected with sex, passionate love or what have you. They are connected with egoism.

How dangerous is objectivity! Always suspect. Literally inconceivable for most people; what you are really getting at? The ruling passion of the man who is his own executioner is to judge objectively.

Every individual is like a company of infantry who leave their trenches and advance in certain places until they have occupied the enemy trench, while elsewhere they are held up or even forced to retreat. Every individual is similar to the line thus formed, with its spearheads and its recessions; admirable here, wobbly there, and both at once. That is the touching thing about human beings.

A man worthy of the name despises the influence which he exercises in whatever direction it may work, and he only *submits* to the necessity of exercising an influence, as the price to be paid for the itch of self-expression.

A woman makes herself into what the man wants. The trouble is that the man seldom knows what he wants. This is the cause of many dramas.
It also explains why, when I tell the truth about women, I find myself quarrelling, not with them, but with men, who feel they have been got at.

Keep passing your life through a sieve. Go on shaking and only keep what remains, which is your essential part. Go on shaking until it becomes second nature to do so.

Someone has written: 'Montherlant's tragedy is that he has never been able to choose between his propensities.' But what if this has been my good fortune—and also redounds to my honour?

An evening prayer:
O God, preserve me from my doctor: O God, preserve me from my lawyer: O God, preserve me from my man of business, from my secretary, from my servants, in a word from all those whose function it is to help me. Amen.

* * *

NOTEBOOK XXIV—*Algiers, 23rd August 1933 to 16th October 1933*
Paris, 18th October 1933 to 3rd January 1934
Algiers, 5th January 1934 to 15th February 1934

The main thing is to take a chance with life. It doesn't much matter what comes of it. Go off on a journey with a person you fear and have good reason to fear. And if there are fewer ups than downs, what matter? The essential thing was to take the mad decision to make the journey.

I get on well with children because we have so much in common. We both like amusing ourselves and living for the passing moment without prejudices and without duties, especially the duty of gratitude.

My first book, *La Relève du Matin*, which is being republished at the moment, was begun during the war at the Military School, where I found myself engarrisoned as part of the auxiliary forces, just after joining up. I still possess a snapshot of a soldier sitting on one of the dustbins with a fountain-pen in his hand and leaning over a bundle of papers. It represents the author of *La Relève* writing his book. As I didn't want to be taken for a literary man —I have always found the designation rather irritating—I used to tell people who asked me what I was up to that I was writing a *thesis* on 'children and music'. It was then, for the first time in my life, that I got some idea of the impression I might be making on my fellows, when I heard one of the men say to another, thinking me out of earshot: 'Have you seen the chap that's writing an essay on children and music? He looks a bloody fool.'

I had applied to join an infantry battalion at the front, but my application was hanging fire. The auxiliaries in the Military School were asked to choose between immediate posting to a staff and being detailed for a spell of work in the country, where there was a shortage of agricultural labour. As I infinitely preferred the prospect of being a farm hand to becoming a typist in an office, I was dispatched to the Marne where, after a few ups and downs and having claimed to have had experience with horned beasts, I was put in charge of the oxen on a farm. While looking after them, I went on writing *La Relève du matin, sub tegmine fagi*—a pretty motif for the cover of a box of sweets.

At last I managed to join an infantry regiment in the line and my manuscript, which had been started on the dustbins and had passed through the cowsheds ended up 'in the mud of the trenches'. For months, I kept the MS and the notes I used in composing it in an extra haversack, which I carried on my back. I can testify that papers can be very heavy.

I spent my leaves calling on publishers. Eleven publishers refused *La Relève*. All the publishers in Paris, in fact.

After the armistice, I made the acquaintance of a number of writers. My first published work was a ten-page extract from *La Relève*, which appeared in André Germain's review, *Les Ecrits Nouveaux*. This review occupies a special place in the literature of the immediate post-war period, as it printed the work of most of the now well-known writers, before their rise to fame (including Pierre Benoît, who was represented by some admirable poems). Before long *La Relève du Matin* came out in an edition limited to 700 copies, which was published at the author's expense and cost me Frs. 3,500. I also had to pay the stamp duty on the edition.

Binet-Valmer, a generous and much criticized man, devoted the whole of his regular article in *Commoedia* to an enthusiastic notice of *La Relève*. I suppose that is an experience common to all authors at the outset of their literary careers. Some critic who has never met the writer, nor heard about him from anyone else, and who knows him only through the volume that has come to hand, is carried away with enthusiasm and writes a paean of praise. In my case, the critic was Binet-Valmer. As he told me later, he knew so little about me, at the time of writing his article, that he thought I was a priest.

How infinitely more powerful and infinitely more helpless one is than people think or than one realizes oneself. Powerful at a quarter to twelve, helpless at noon. Powerful in the presence of X, defenceless in the presence of Y. Powerful in one place, helpless in another.

From the age of seventeen onwards when I started going to parties, I used to feel very strongly that: 'The bodies make up for it all.'[1]

After arriving at this conclusion, you can be as misanthropic as you like. But an odd sort of misanthrope whose sole reason for existing is to caress another being and then possess that being. Humanity may, at the same time, be the shame of the earth (or more accurately, the poisoner of the earth), what does this matter? The point is to protect oneself against it in that capacity while enjoying it, and giving it enjoyment in the other.

When you reflect that among all the bloody fools around you there is not one who was not desirable, for one fleeting moment in youth, who, in other words, did not have a reason for existing even if no one took advantage of it. . . .

The act of carnal possession gives me the strongest possible conception of what is called the Absolute. I am sure of my pleasure and sure of my partner's. I experience no misgivings, no questionings, uneasiness or remorse. The act is simple and whole, as definite and definitive as a circle in geometry.

You may ask: 'Why the sexual act in particular? A good meal also is something quite definite.'

Because of the human material: because of the respect you feel for your partner, and the friendship, tenderness, confidence and protectiveness, in short all the kind feelings one creature can experience with regard to another. And then there is pride in the pleasure you can arouse and sometimes pride in having taught your partner the pleasures of love, so that the gradual apprenticeship in sensual delight is as much your creation as your literary work.

And is it not a wonderful thing, when some new creature falls within your grasp, that your whole thought should be concen-

---

[1] A character in one of Malraux's books, looking at a crowd of people, says: 'Fortunately, there were the bodies.' Note written in 1953.

trated on the pleasure you are going to give, on the art of enjoyment you are going to teach, rather than on the satisfaction you yourself are going to enjoy?

(I have shaped my literary works and my love-partners with an eye to pleasure, theirs no less than mine. I have never achieved anything else—trained no minds, souls, or characters.)

I have often quoted Jean-Jacques Rousseau's remark: 'Sensations are merely what the heart makes them.' This is an exaggeration of course, but it is quite true that sensation is multiplied tenfold when it has behind it such human fellow-feeling. This is a feeling which is always ready to flow abundantly in me. Since I have little or no liking for creatures who arouse no desire in me, I am left with plenty of love for those who do—in fact, much more than the average man has to give.

In short, adapting the famous phrase,[1] I may say that I have never experienced any sorrow that half an hour's affectionate copulation has not enabled me, or could not have enabled me, to forget. And since I am quoting figures, I may add, adapting another famous phrase (Goethe's reference to his three weeks of happiness), that if I wished to work out the sum of all the happy hours I have enjoyed in my life, it would be quite enough to add up the hours of affectionate copulation, which would make a total of several years of happiness.

It follows that nothing is more important than the happy equilibrium which results from the regular practice of affectionate copulation. The foundation of life is tranquil sexual satisfaction. When the —— is all right, everything else is all right.[2] Everybody knows this, but the knowledge is not sufficiently applied in practice.

The splendid regular rhythm of sexual activity, in which the act of love, recurring like the regular reappearance of the sun, nourishes the individual, as sunlight does.

[1] This is a reference to Montesquieu's remark: 'I have never experienced any sorrow that an hour's reading was not enough to dispel.'

[1] This is a reference to another common saying: *Quand le bâtiment va, tout va*; 'When the building trade flourishes, so does everything else.'

* * *

A newspaper asked me which great men had had most influence on me. My answer was: 'Pyrrho, Anacreon and Regulus—the Sceptic, the Hedonist, and the Hero. I cannot think of one of them, without thinking of the other two.'

My answer was a repetition of the one I gave at the age of sixteen, when the same question was put to me at school in the form of an essay-subject.

The newspaper never printed my answer, no doubt thinking that it wasn't 'serious'.

NOTEBOOK XXV—*Paris, 17th February 1934 to 7th July 1934*

Unum necessarium. For me, this is to love and to create. Neither the pleasures of the heart, nor of the senses nor of the mind need much money. I have never had too much, and what I have had has always been more than I needed. I have satisfied all my desires, and let me add (which people always forget to do although it is so important) that I have done so without overexerting myself. I am thirty-eight years old and I have got all I wanted out of life.

I have always hated possessions and have never had any: neither an official family, nor a hearth and home, nor a group of friends, nor even a settled residence.

I have been famous at a time when fame is usurped by the most unworthy, but I obtained it without doing anything, or scarcely anything, to achieve it. Far from being bitter at not having more fame, or thinking I ought to have more, I have always regarded it as a miracle that I should have achieved so much, when I see who dispenses it and to whom. Even so, fame has brought me much more unpleasantness than satisfaction.

If any of my work is to survive, that part is already accomplished.

Supposing none of it survives, I have had the essential thing from life—enjoyment. Nothing and nobody can take that away from me.

A third supposition is that the soul may survive death and that I have to pay for some crimes or other that I may have committed here. I cannot seriously entertain this supposition; in fact, when I try to do so, I cannot keep a straight face.

1st June. With all the girls I like, my first instinct is always to marry them. Then I engage in a struggle with myself which leaves me trembling. I want them all. At the same time I love them genuinely and am grieved at the sadness of those whom I pass over, or who, quite simply, do not seem preferable to others.

If there is a deity (and neither my mind nor my heart desires that there should be) I call him to witness that I have never caused pain or harm to any woman for whom I had any feeling. (17th June.)

A golden rule: do little.
Don't write too much: don't read too much: don't undertake too much: don't know too many people: don't be familiar with too many questions; remain systematically ignorant of a good many.
Keep on saying 'no'.

Everything related to the heart is unrest and torment, and everything related to the senses is peace.

I have read twenty volumes about the great mystics. They have not convinced me that the mystic's condition is in any way superior to vertigo or sea-sickness.

One must love stupidity, as I do, and be stimulated by it, as I am, in order to run after young girls, who are infinitely the stupidest creatures in the world.

NOTEBOOK XXVII—*Algiers, 15th August 1934 to 2nd October 1934*
  South of France, 3rd October 1934 to 8th October 1934

Algiers, 15th August 1934. I can say that for more than nine years of my life, I have always been at leisure. That is why I have written good books, and why I have been happy. I hope I shall always be able to live in this way.

Spiteful like people who never take an hour off. I have always taken that hour off, even in the most agitated periods of my life, as the English do.

All the women who are weeping because of me. At the moment, I can think of four; it's a regular cascade. Meanwhile I am weeping for the only woman who isn't weeping. Where the business really becomes complicated is in the fact that her dry eyes are not an argument against the strength of her feeling, while my tears are not an argument in favour of the strength of mine.

It is unheard of that a father who has put his little son on the donkey which ambles round the square, should take him off because he bursts into tears. The father has paid and cannot waste his ten sous. The boy has to have his ten sous' worth of tears.

At the moment of writing this, the author sees the father take his boy off the donkey's back, but he does not cross out the remark in his notebook. It is a witticism; whether true or not doesn't matter. Much of the *profound psychology* to be found in books is manufactured in this way.

NOTEBOOK XXVIII—*Paris, 8th October 1934 to 21st November 1934*
Algiers, 22nd November 1934 to 17th February 1935

What an odd employer I should have made! If one of my workers had come to ask for a day off, because his wife was having a baby or because his child was ill, I should certainly and gladly have granted his request. But if he had said to me 'Let me have a day's leave because I've just had a worrying time and want to get tight and sleep off the effects tomorrow' or '. . . because this is the first sunny day we've had and I'm very keen to go to the Bois de Vincennes with my girl-friend', I think I should have granted his request even more gladly. The fact is that, respecting my own pleasures, I respect the pleasures of others.

* * *

EXTRACTS FROM THE NOTEBOOKS OF HENRY DE MONTHERLANT

It is hard to discern the moral value of most actions, and in many cases impossible. When a man marries his mistress, because she is longing to be married, would you call that good-heartedness or cowardice? A mixture, like everything else. Something it would be wrong to boast of and wrong to be ashamed of.

A man shoves a letter into a drawer without taking it out of the envelope because he thinks it will worry him, and leaves it there for months. An act of cowardice *in the first place,* because he has preferred to remain ignorant of the worry the letter might cause him. *In the second place,* a proof of force of character, because he has not yielded to the temptation to find out what it was.

I pity the young because I feel pity for my own youth, happy though it was. I think of the little fellow of seventeen I once was. Poor little fellow!

When I look back, I am sometimes dismayed by my rashness and sometimes by my lack of spirit. How right I was to dare, and how right to refrain! This eternal ebb and flow, like the sea on the beach, continues throughout life.

At the time of the 1914 mobilization, my mother, seized by one of those mad ideas that occur to right-thinking people in moments of crisis, became convinced that she could not go on keeping, in war-time, a fox-terrier bitch that we happened to have. So she gave it to the Duc de Rohan, who was going to the front and wanted to have a dog with him. I have just seen a little girl of two or three being driven off in a car, and as the car started, she turned round in the arms that held her for a last look at her parents with the identical expression of being torn away that the fox-terrier bitch had when she turned to look at her former owners as the duke carried her off in his arms. So deeply was I impressed by the humanness of the animal, that the impression is still fresh after twenty-one years.

NOTEBOOK XXIX—*Paris, 19th February to 31st March 1935*
Algiers, 2nd April to 20th May 1935
Paris, 22nd May to 1st August 1935

It is a good rule to act in such a way that the defeat of our hopes gives rise to some advantage.

Further: misfortune creates in us the strength of mind or the adaptability of mind with which we meet it, and which we should not have experienced but for it.

Occasionally, when very thirsty, I have succeeded in slaking my thirst with a cigarette. In the same way I can sense a strange and awful identity between the deepest manifestations of happiness and misfortune.

'He who hates the vices, hates mankind,' said Danton. People talk about 'the gift of tears'. I would rather hear about the gift of contempt—justified contempt, of course. Contempt is a virtue when it is aimed at stupidity, which is a sin against the mind, or at baseness, a sin against the soul, and at all the sins against morality. In such matters, it is contemptible not to feel contempt.

What saddens me is not so much evil itself as the indulgence, the connivance even, with which so many, men and women, who themselves lead decent lives, behave towards dishonesty. They laugh or smile at the exploits of utter scoundrels, shake them by the hand, invite them to their homes and are delighted to accept their invitations in return. Yet they take Holy Communion, bring their children up strictly and so on—in all sincerity. They are always, to some extent, society people. But there are others, lacking their up-bringing and social position, who are genuinely sickened by dishonesty. I don't know if their lives are absolutely blameless; perhaps not. I only know that certain things disgust them, which don't disgust the others I have mentioned, and the difference between the two categories is enormous.

The reason why I hardly ever read a newspaper except over somebody's shoulder in the Métro, is that I want to avoid feeling indignation and disgust. For instance, I could have gone to Deauville and written a vitriolic piece about the human fauna there, which would have done me honour as a man and as a writer. But I preferred not to go and to sacrifice my diatribe, because indignation upsets me too much.

No doubt, this is a weakness. All my life to the detriment of my work I have avoided and shall avoid places and people that revolt me. Those I can't avoid are quite enough for me.

The case of the girl you no longer love but whom you encourage to go on believing that you do, until her engagement to someone else delivers you from her (since, from then onwards, you will be forbidden to see her). In the space of four months I came back three times from Algeria to Paris, each time for ten days, in order to give J a proof of an affection I no longer felt. And I'm a bad sailor, too, and I hate travelling and at that moment I was rather short of money! Luckily she got engaged fairly soon, because I had kept up the pretence—of loving when I didn't love—for a whole year, and I was exhausted.

NOTEBOOK XXX—*Paris, 1st August 1935 to 7th February 1936*
Algiers, 7th to 23rd February 1936
Paris, 23rd February to 9th March 1936

I never walk up the Rue Pigalle without feeling a double emotion —first, at the touchingly ancient *Poste aux Chevaux* on the left-hand pavement, and then at the spot where I suddenly see, at the end of the street, the dome of the Sacré Coeur on the one hand and, on the other, a black horseman who, through an effect of perspective, appears to be poised above the roofs. (It is one of the two bronze statues representing I know not whom which stand in the square in front of the basilica.) And I think of the day when the Sacré Coeur, having been transformed into a museum of Irreligion, will tower over Paris with a brightly painted dome in the style of the Russian churches and when the two horsemen will be named Tamburlaine and Genghis Khan. (N.B. Aragon, at the age of thirteen, wrote, or thought of writing, an epic about Tamburlaine. An early sign of vocation.[1]

[1] Aragon is now a leading Communist writer. As a boy he was at school with Montherlant.

Communism will reign for a thousand years, and the *lendemains qui chantent*[1] will consist of the songs of certain bards, repeated in chorus by the masses. Eventually, there will be a second Renaissance, which will recreate the individual.

Against myself.—'Action and non-action will meet in eternity and intertwine there eternally.'[2] What will be, or will not be, after our death does not concern us, but we are concerned by the necessity to combine action and non-action in a full life. Although they may destroy each other in a logical vacuum, they are nevertheless the pivots of a daily conflict. *Aedificabo et destruam*: yes. But let us not deceive ourselves: at this game, it is the void which wins. I seem to be holding the balance even between life and death, between movement and immobility; but the equilibrium cannot be eternally maintained; the scales are bound to come down on one side or the other. I renounce completely the notion of worldly usefulness. But is service which is its own justification *useless* in the absolute? ('I have only my own conception of myself to sustain me on the seas of the void.') It is here that I see the true sense of *useless,* which abolishes service. I am not passionately keen to retrieve in some other world what has been lost here below; but I don't like to be taken in by words. Destruction, then reconstruction in the ephemeral, then redestruction. There is a danger that we may have illusions about the importance of this oscillation. I wonder if the Greek thinkers were not right to consider alternation as an equivalent of the void. The void is acceptable. Why give it a false appellation?

In my view, action covers more or less what the Church calls 'the world'. I accept its joys and some of its responsibilities, the rules of the game and the game without rules, and Heaven knows that, as far as the latter is concerned, I have not stinted myself! And then, high above and aloof, is 'that critical spirit which is intelligence'—the act of contemplation which makes all things

[1] *Les lendemains qui chantent* ('tomorrows alive with song') is a well-known Left-Wing phrase referring to the happy world of the future.

[2] *Service Inutile.*

equal, sees them from such a distance that all their differences, that is their identities, are smoothed out.

But can the critical spirit not play a less negative part with regard to action? It all depends on the point at which it is set in motion. To be freer in both act and thought, I throw myself into action with no other guide than the humour of the moment, having voluntarily discarded all preconceived ideas and intellectual limits. The moment for reflection and for going 'in search of lost time' comes later. But my experience of action, though so free and sincere, is limited, because it is no more than a translation of my likes and my instincts. It is enough for those who have no hope of receiving from the external world anything other than enlightenment about themselves. This is a great deal; it is something infinitely precious. Yet there are types of minds who, rightly or wrongly, will never abandon the attempt to get outside themselves. For them, if not for Goethe, *die Tat ist am Ende*; for them, action is neither useful nor useless, it is inevitable, it is a form of completion. They act, as a scientist does an experiment, by moving from one hypothesis to another; for them, action is a response, the judge of thought, a proof of truth. People of this kind will say to me that thought contemplating itself and playing at the creator destroying his creation, is nothing at all; but that their imperfect knowledge and the command of some province of nature is something. Greek philosophy tended to produce men of this kind, and there are still a great many of them today.

My struggles to seduce—to overcome resistance—to get rid of my catches—to escape from them—to renew relations with them after dropping them—to drop them again—have occupied the best part of my life and, by taking up a good deal of my time, have considerably curtailed my literary output, which I by no means regret.

It is to this that I have devoted all my will-power, force of character, cleverness, patience and audacity. Very little of these virtues has been left over for the rest of my life. Limpness in one department, tension in the other; the first created by the second.

* * *

P—A powerful tide of desire and conquest carried her up on to the beach, but has now ebbed, leaving her there, high and dry, like a dying fish.

The worse the situation becomes, the more 'decently' she behaves and, in fact, the prettier she looks. But there's nothing to be done about it. I know her too well. The effect is physiological.

NOTEBOOK XXXI—*Paris, 9th March 1936 to 25th December 1936*

Seeing what small allowances I make for France, I am tempted to believe that I love my country, since we are severe with those we love.

17th April—5.45 a.m. On my way to find J.B.

The night-watchmen are going home. On the deserted asphalt, the studs of the pedestrian crossings gleam with a pure brightness. After hunting at random, you get home at midnight completely done in, and then at 5.30 in the morning, you are out in the streets again.

As you hang about on the pavement, you are less noticeable from 6 to 7 than after 7.

This is the time when little girls go out to fetch the morning milk. After 9 o'clock no one leaves the house. You would think it had gone dead.

A battered felt hat, unbrushed shoes, a creased overcoat, yet I am coming back with my live prey. To think that I managed to bring the whole thing off with my shoes unpolished!

People who only live for literature. They write articles about books, conduct literary inquiries, start periodicals, come together to discuss literary matters, and rapturously bathe and wallow in this horrible juice. *I* live in the first place and then write my books; that's all. And even so, writing the books is more than enough for me.

In the preface to his very mediocre translation of *Some Odes of Hafiz,* Nicolas declares that the oriental reader gives these poems a mystical or sensual meaning according to the mood he happens to be in when reading them, and thus 'finds in the same page the poison and the antidote'. Similarly, should not everything an author writes have the double meaning, or the multiple meaning, possessed by all the manifestations of nature? The reader would thus be given not 'the poison and the antidote' but the different aspects of a single truth.

NOTEBOOK XXXII—*Nice, Peira-Cava, 25th December 1936 to 21st February 1937*
Paris 23rd February to 22nd June 1937

What have I been? An adventurer. Not a literary adventurer who gets himself photographed in a pullover or sitting on a camel, but a real adventurer who hides the fact that he is one.

I am looking for a word to express the feeling the adventurer experiences on certain days when faced by the unexpected. The one that occurs is 'ecstasy'. I turn it this way and that, and say to myself: 'Yes, it's exactly right to describe what happens when you provoke life and it responds with the unexpected.'

(16th May, after a hunt in a market at the Place d'Italie.)

To believe that Costals[1] is Montherlant shows the same feeble-mindedness as confusing a desire for good relations with Italy with support for Fascism, or anti-Bolshevism with a wish to cancel the Franco–Russian agreement. Our literary criticism, like our politics, is lagging behind internationally, because both our critics and our politicians have become crude and no longer make vital distinctions, a fact which will bring about the ruin of our culture.

I am only interested in my own private life, which consists of my relations with the creatures I desire, and my creative work in literature.

As regards my creative work, I am only interested in the work itself. Its relations with the public are almost completely indifferent to me. The thing is to get it written ... Hence my tendency not to

[1] The hero of the novel *Les Jeunes Filles*.

publish certain already completed works and even to contemplate their remaining unpublished during my lifetime (e.g. *Almuradiel*, which was finished in 1928: *Moustique* in 1929: *Un voyageur solitaire est un diable* in 1929: *La Rose de Sable* in 1932). I am not really interested in the incidentals connected with my literary works—their appearance in translations or their adaptation for the screen, or their performance, in the case of plays. I think of these incidentals only in terms of the waste of time they will cause.

I believe that very few contemporary French authors take less trouble than I do about the business and publicity aspects of their work, avoid the limelight more than I do, or are keener to remain in the background. I claim no credit for this; it is a matter of taste.

It is quite enough that we should depend on others as regards having to find out if they are prepared to go to bed with us or not, without being dependent on their good or bad opinion of our literary work. And so, while praise of my work gives me little pleasure, unfavourable criticism causes me little pain. I know that my eulogists and my detractors are all wide of the mark. I can easily imagine a Quattrocento picture representing Benevolence and Malevolence, each with a finger in one eye.[1]

NOTEBOOK XXXIII—*Paris, 22nd June 1937 to 12th January 1938*

People imagine that I am the fighting sort. I suppose that is because I have been an athlete, a soldier and a bullfighter. But in athletics, sport and bullfighting, the activity is considered as a game. Real fighting, of the kind we are forced by necessity to take part in, fills me with horror, as does the too simple verdict that 'Life is a struggle'. Anyone familiar with my way of life would realize that I manœuvre as much as possible to avoid fighting. Except in a few very, well-defined fields, I give up at the first obstacle (not to mention those cases in which I don't even tackle the obstacle at all). Perhaps this is because, in most instances, the prize does not seem worth the effort. A thing is not worth having, if the cost is too high. And some things are not worth paying for at all.

[1] In French, the gesture means to be mistaken. *Se mettre le doigt dans l'oeil.*

* * *

A cat finishing off a lizard. She gives it a smack with her paw—so!—and instantly starts back, like a gun recoiling immediately the shot has been fired. How I love the little movement of fear! (Fear of a counter-attack, of course.)

Cruel and cowardly. We know the combination.

Of all the prayers that writers have addressed to the deity, I know of none more touching than the one Tolstoy wrote in his diary as a young man: 'O God, grant me simplicity of style.'

NOTEBOOK XXXIV—*Nice, Peira-Cava, 13th January to 21st February 1938*
Paris, 22nd February to 5th June 1938

I once told the wife of an American publisher that I was collecting notes for a book about children, educational problems and so on, and her remark was: 'Wouldn't you do better to make films? That, at least, is life.'

Today, a Frenchwoman, after reading a newspaper article of mine which, for once, was more or less topical, said: 'I like to see you *really* playing a part in life.'

If you asked people what they meant precisely by *life,* you would be appalled by most of the replies.

1st June. In the summer night, I could see the lighted windows of the great buildings along the Seine and, above, the stars. And I said to myself that however wonderful the stars might be, I still preferred the lights made by man.

If our virtues are neither recognized nor appreciated by anyone, what is the point of having them since, humanly speaking, they only do us harm? Why cultivate strength of character, or delicacy of feeling or disinterestedness? Why be always giving up something, always making bad bargains?—'So as not to be ashamed of oneself'; the answer is a very simple one but at times it seems quite senseless.

NOTEBOOK XXXV—*Paris, 5th June to 3rd September 1938*
London, 4th to 8th September 1938
Lorraine, 24th September to 3rd October 1938
Paris, 4th October 1938 to 19th January 1939

What uses up a life is not so much its great tragedies as its small annoyances and the recurrent waste of time. It is not our enemies who wear us down, but rather our friends, or those half-friends who keep on wanting to meet us, although we have no corresponding desire to meet them.

23rd December 1938. For years I have been keeping the Spanish Civil War at bay—as I know how to keep things at bay. The reason is that I would become too involved. I need only get my little finger caught in it to be swept away entirely. Last April, Aragon told me that the Spanish Government would like me to lecture in Barcelona. I had flu at the time, but even if I had been well, I should have refused, knowing that once they got me there, they would have shown me round the trenches and then I should have grabbed a rifle and stayed in the line. It is more important that I should finish *Les Garçons*.

This evening in a restaurant in Rue Tronchet I heard an Andalusian song on the radio. It was something totally incomprehensible to a Frenchman, a song from a land of strength and gravity. Here we have 'the little woman' and there they have 'woman'. I remember that only this morning L.V. said to me: 'Do you want to go to Spain? I can offer you a marvellous opportunity.' I replied: 'In the spirit in which Lyautey said "I don't want to hear any more about Morocco", I say to you "I don't want to hear any more about Spain".'

I have on my table a little round scented sandal-wood box, the lid of which was painted towards the end of the eighteenth century. The picture shows a handsome tree, a stream, a hog-backed bridge, a fisherman, and a mill. In spite of the delicacy of the painting and the wonderful golden light in which the whole landscape is steeped, the miniature would have little appeal for me were it not that a young man and a young woman are just stepping on to the bridge. Tiny though they are—not more than a centimetre high—they transform the whole scene. They represent Adam and Eve, love, and setting sail for Cythera! During these dreary December days, I gaze at my little box, gleaming on the table and sometimes—believe it or not—I press it against my heart. I still have faith, I still have hope—O God, everything is still possible . . . And I smile at my future and my past.

NOTEBOOK XLII—*Paris, 1st January to 5th May 1942*
Grasse, 6th May to 14th June 1942
Paris, 15th June to 31st December 1942

In a period like the present, a writer has to ask himself, after every sentence he writes, 'Is this going to look silly in ten years' time?' He does so, is convinced that he is safe—and a year later he finds himself looking ridiculous.

Oh, to be able to re-read what one wrote yesterday, without blushing. . . .

The true man of letters is saddened by the thought of death, but less by the prospect of dying than by his inability to invent even one original thought on the subject of death.

5th March. I watch those great heavyweights—Germany, England, Japan, and Russia—exchanging terrible blows, and I know that, whatever the final result may be, for me my salvation is within myself and can only come from within.

You have to choose between a quiet life and telling the whole truth. My choice is made; I shall only tell part of the truth (and that will cause me trouble enough). As regards metaphysics, politics and society, on the subject of ideas and morals, the truths I should have to expound and which are self-evident to any rational being —however, the type is extremely rare—run so directly counter to popular and I might say universal, opinion, and in short are so explosive that my private life would be endangered by the blast. I will not sacrifice my private life. I am more attached to it than I am to my work.

Is this a sign of cowardice? No, because I am more than sure that society would not only not welcome the truth, but would be made indignant by it. Do not let us try to enlighten a world that does not want to be enlightened. A Persian proverb says: 'If your mouth contains a truth, keep it shut.' We should think rationally only for our satisfaction. I am even afraid that we should run too great a risk if we insisted on trying to enlighten those we love.

The bitter thing is to think of the few hundred free spirits in the country who will reflect: 'What! Is that all he has to say?' You have to put up with the thought.

I spoke very cruelly to a sensitive woman, who happens to love me. To my great surprise, she did not burst into tears, remained quite calm and did not seem unduly worried. I admired her for this and felt mollified. She almost regained my affection by showing me that she was not as attached to me as all that.

The sun shines round her dimples as it does round the hollows of shadow in a calm sea.

I have said and have written that one of the keys to the understanding of the French of today is their desire for happiness; I have since had the pleasure of finding the same thought, which I consider important, expressed by Benda.[1] This desire for happiness, whether it is a virtue or a vice, enables the French people of today to 'lead their normal *bourgeois* lives in the midst of the greatest tragedies' (as I said in *Service Inutile* or *L'Equinoxe de Septembre*).

The desire for happiness in present-day France explains our unpreparedness for war. Perhaps it explains, too, why the revolution of 1936 was a failure. It explains our 'wait and see' attitude,

[1] Julien Benda, best known for his book *La Trahison des Clercs*.

which eight times out of ten is a sort of euphoric inertia. It explains the optimistic forecasts regarding the fate of Paris and France, which were intended to reassure us and enable us to go on being happy. It is likely to wreck the revolution which will follow the present 'national' one.[1] That future revolution hasn't a chance if the post-war return to prosperity comes too quickly.

In classifying human beings I make two distinctions: (1) between those who are intelligent and those who are not; (2) between those who are capable of noble behaviour and those who are not.

We easily recognize among the people around us those who are capable of noble behaviour. They are mostly women. Many people are intelligent, honest, likeable and so on, but we may have been in their society for ten years without ever having detected in them a trace of what might be called nobility.

Others may have accomplished only a single noble action during those same ten years but it is enough to put them in the category of the redeemed, since a second noble action is always possible. You feel like saying to them: 'Be noble, and do what you like'; only it seems more becoming to say 'Be capable of nobleness, and do what you like'.

(It would be interesting to find out why almost all noble actions can be summed up as the refusal of an advantage or as a sacrificing of the self.)

NOTEBOOK XLIII—*Paris, 1st January to 22nd February 1943*
Grasse, 23rd February to 13th April 1943
Paris, 14th April to 31st December 1943

18th January. It is France's misfortune that in her unheard-of humiliation, when she needed to be reminded of greatness of soul, only the stupid or the hypocritical spoke out, with the result that the virtue they claimed to be proposing for her admiration, and which is indeed worthy of admiration, has been made to look ridiculous.

[1] Pétain's *Révolution nationale*.

* * *

I have never written anything without, at some time or other, feeling the urge to write the opposite.

Sticking to one's own opinion without letting oneself be influenced; holding imperturbably to conclusions one has reached after mature consideration, whether they coincide with the popular view or not; I think there is no rarer nor more admirable achievement in the world.

A scene for a play about Don Juan—one of the characters starts a conversation with an unknown person (unknown to him and to the audience), and questions him about women. The stranger at once begins to complain: 'To think that I couldn't persuade so-and-so! When I remember all the women who have escaped me or turned me down or did not turn up when they promised . . . a chorus of missed opportunities . . .' The conversation continues on this note until the time comes to part, and then the stranger reveals that he is called Don Juan.

All he remembers of his life is the women he has not possessed, like an author who, after reading a eulogistic article on his work, forgets everything except the critic's single reservation.

When a man in his last moments seeks the support of some faith, he reminds me of the fighting bull who, on feeling that death is near, props himself against the *barrera*.

How fine to see someone, under threat of death and weakened by the prospect, suddenly acquire strength because he has begun to believe in something, through an act of will, and to give himself support. Stayed up by a vapour, he is strong and valiant. (A good subject for a play—Title: 'Courage through Faith'). Thus duty, altruism, charity and religious faith no longer work against man and therefore cease to be in any way scandalous; they take their place in the respectable and sober category of the things a man does because they are useful or give him pleasure.

He who is rich in humanity finds in himself the germs or the flowering of all the feelings. His imagination enables him to put himself, constantly and with the greatest ease, inside other people's beings and thus to realize that, from their point of view, their actions are logical, even when directed against himself. Whenever a discussion arises, he supports each side against the other. He even goes so far as to put himself in the place of his own opponents and to argue on their behalf against himself. This, of course, is detrimental to his own interests, since individuals, being always blindly partial towards themselves, have not the slightest notion of objectivity. This way of behaving, or rather, this profound natural bent, is a great hindrance to action, since it practically eliminates all passion against individuals, and everyone knows how difficult it is to conceive of action without passion against individuals. In private life, this natural bent has the advantage of enabling you to understand more fully the workings of others, and the disadvantage of any peculiarity, which is to isolate you from others, that is, to make you appear suspect to them.

It is possible to conceive of man as being composed of three parts: the Apollonian or creative part, which produces his work; the Dionysian, which consists of the passions, the soul and the bowels; and the Ulyssean, which governs conduct and social manœuvring.

Undated Notes written between 1930 and 1944.

For the artist the act of creation is a physiological relief of the same nature as copulation. The precept *nulla dies sine linea* is intended to create organic equilibrium through a daily process of unburdening.

What 'saved' me in 1930 was starting to write *La Rose de sable*. I was saved from the crisis expressed in *Les Voyageurs traqués* and which was partly caused by the fact that in 1927, 1928 and 1929 I had done no serious work.

But when vitality begins to decline, the relief also comes from the fact that the artist, in the act of creation, forgets the many failures he has experienced in actual living: only when working does he cease to suffer. This explains Baudelaire's remark 'I work through despair', and also what Matisse said to me, after undergoing a serious operation when over seventy—'As long as I can continue working . . .' Work is a form of escape.

It seems to me that for an elderly artist the important thing is to know which will perish first, his vitality or his creative faculty. If it is his creative faculty, all he can do is devote his remaining days to enjoying life, as best as he can. If it is his vitality, and he has only his creative power to sustain him, when that dries up, he will be really dead, dead in all respects; a living corpse.

One of the stock phrases used by fools in writing and speaking is: 'An author should never explain his work'. An author has every reason to explain his work, because otherwise the public and the critics would not understand it, or only half understand it. I myself in my infinite stupidity—which I am at least ready to admit—do not usually understand, or at best inadequately understand, a work that has not been clarified for me by explanations given by different people, and I prefer one of those people to be the author himself (this applies particularly to plays that are swallowed in haste at the theatre and have not been read).

The difference between me and my fellows is that they live solely for the satisfaction of their vanity and to make money, while I live solely for the pleasures of the senses and for creative writing.

Reality is the enemy!—A professor tells us that one of his girl students 'an excellent pupil, while studying the fortified castles of France, refused to visit the celebrated castle of C, in case her ideas on the subject should be confused.' The implications are enormous!

Hurrah for troubled waters and gamey societies!—This is all very well, but when society has reached a certain stage of rottenness, so abundant are the opportunities of taking advantage of this corruption, that we can't 'do justice' to them all: the supply is greater than the demand; our desires cannot cope. Annoyed by

the discovery of my limitations, I become indignant and demand a return to some degree of virtue.

As the planks of the ship keep us afloat at sea, so the secrets about us that other people refrain from revealing support us on the brink of another kind of abyss. We live at the mercy of others' silence.

The 'devilish itch to do good'.—Good actions do not bring peace and joy to the conscience, but a bitter, despairing feeling such as is never produced by our evil actions and is quite *sui generis*. We sense then that nature is protesting, that nature is evil, and that generous impulses are similar in kind to vices.

He who pities others, pities himself.

The art of disengagement is infinitely more difficult than the art of arousing love.

The profusion and accessibility of beautiful creatures in Mediterranean countries is, I think, one of the reasons why I always feel sad there. On the Mediterranean sea-board, you can't 'go in pursuit', and the great number of creatures you would like to possess and could possess, but have to forego because nature has limits, if only those of satiety, fills you with bitterness. The situation is quite different in countries where beauty is rare; there you can 'go in pursuit'; the possibilities are within human scope. Paris, for instance, does not produce the same feeling of misery as Rome, Barcelona or even Marseilles.

Rehabilitating the chameleon. I admire a man who can immediately adapt himself, sometimes at very short notice, to whatever he meets with; who can return honour for honour, fraud for fraud, violence for violence, and even possess the mysterious power of returning love for love, like a taut string which is said to vibrate in harmony with its fellow.

* * *

There is nothing more reliable in a man than his passions, nothing that others, and he himself can depend upon with greater assurance. Take away his pettinesses but let him keep his vices.

In me, sensuality mingled with tenderness does not amount to love. One of my great strengths is to be able to avoid love, while enjoying a blend of tenderness and sensuality.

It is not sufficiently realized how sweet and lovable young people of either sex can be when they are really young—say up to seventeen inclusive. An immense amount of interest, respect, sympathy and love runs to waste because the human race does not grasp the fact that it reaches perfection at that age. The same is true of animals, which are also miracles of beauty when very young.